About the Authors

JAMES F. KRILE is the director of the Blandin Community Leadership Program (BCLP). Since 1985, over four thousand people from rural Minnesota have taken part in this program, which includes a five-day residential retreat and two follow-up workshops. In an independent evaluation of the program, John F. Jones, PhD, of the University of Denver Graduate School of Social Work described BCLP "as a model for training anywhere in the world."

Jim's academic background is in sociology with an emphasis on organizational and community development. Before joining the Blandin Foundation in 1986, Jim was a member of the Department of Rural Sociology, University of Minnesota; the Center for the Study of Local Government, St. John's University, Collegeville, MN; and the Center for Community Organization and Area Development, Augustana College, Sioux Falls, SD.

GORDY CURPHY is the president of Curphy Consulting Corporation (C^3), a leadership and organizational change consulting firm with a clientele of major corporations. His work with C^3 includes consulting to develop an organizational vision, align strategies in support of the vision, and identify and develop the talent and teams needed to realize the vision. Prior to starting his own company, Gordy was the vice president of Institutional Leadership for the Blandin Foundation where he was responsible for the design, delivery, and evaluation of comprehensive leadership and organizational development programs; a vice president and general manager for Personnel Decisions International (PDI); and on active duty in the U.S. Air Force. As a tenured associate professor at the U.S. Air Force Academy, Gordy coauthored the number one selling leadership textbook, *Leadership: Enhancing the Lessons of Experience.*

A native of Two Harbors, MN, and a graduate of the U.S. Air Force Academy, Gordy also received an MA from St. Mary's University in San Antonio, TX, and a PhD in industrial and organizational psychology from the University of Minnesota.

DUANE R. LUND is senior consultant to the Blandin Foundation and was a part of the original design and implementation team for the Blandin Community Leadership Program. He has a long background in education and public service, including twenty-five years as superintendent of schools in Staples, MN, and several years as staff member and chief of staff for the late U.S. Senator Edward J. Thye. He is the author of thirty-nine books, including *Lessons in Leadership: Mostly Learned the Hard Way* and *Our Historic Upper Mississippi*. He is the first-named honoree in the Dr. Duane R. Lund Staples Community Service Award. He holds a doctorate from the University of Minnesota.

About Blandin Foundation

Blandin Foundation, a private foundation based in Grand Rapids, MN, has a mission to strengthen communities in rural Minnesota, especially the Grand Rapids area. The foundation's vision is based on healthy rural communities grounded in strong economies where the burdens and benefits are widely shared. The foundation's core strategy is to develop leaders and focus communities to identify, align, and mobilize their assets and opportunities.

To these ends, Blandin Foundation offers

- Leadership development programs that help communities capitalize on their assets
- Public policy programs to inform and engage the public on issues affecting rural economic viability
- Grantmaking to support community-generated economic strategies and—in the Grand Rapids area—economic advantage and responsive grants

Learn more about Blandin Foundation at its web site: www.BlandinFoundation.org.

The Community Leadership Handbook

Framing Ideas, Building Relationships, and Mobilizing Resources

By James F. Krile
with Gordon Curphy and Duane R. Lund

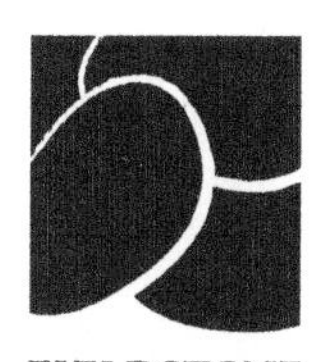

FIELDSTONE
ALLIANCE

SAINT PAUL
MINNESOTA

We thank The David and Lucile Packard Foundation
for support of this publication.

Fieldstone Alliance
An imprint of Turner Publishing Company

445 Park Avenue, 9th Floor
New York, NY 10022
Phone: (212)710-4338 Fax: (212)710-4339

200 4th Avenue North, Suite 950
Nashville, TN 37219
Phone: (615)255-2665 Fax: (615)255-5081

www.turnerpublishing.com
www.fieldstonealliance.com

800-274-6024
www.FieldstoneAlliance.org

Edited by Doug Toft and Vincent Hyman
Text designed by Kirsten Nielsen
Cover designed by Rebecca Andrews

Manufactured in the United States of America
Third printing, October 2010

Library of Congress Cataloging-in-Publication Data

Krile, James F., 1944-
The community leadership handbook : framing ideas, building relationships, and mobilizing resources / by James F. Krile ; with Gordon Curphy and Duane R. Lund.-- 1st printing, February 2006.
p. cm.
ISBN-13: 978-0-940069-54-1 (pbk.)
ISBN-10: 0-940069-54-7
1. Community leadership. I. Curphy, Gordon J. II. Lund, Duane R. (Duane Richard), 1926- III. Title.
HM781.K75 2006
303.3'4--dc22

2005034664

Dedications

To my family and friends, whose lives of leadership guide my journey:
My best to one and all.

— Jim

To the place where I learned my first lessons of community leadership:
Two Harbors, Minnesota.

— Gordy

To the legions of volunteers who give unselfishly of their time and energy:
You make your communities better places in which to live, work, and raise children.

— Duane

Acknowledgments

This book is an outgrowth of the dedication and leadership of many people. First and foremost, it is inspired by and grounded in the experience and wisdom of the more than 4,000 leaders who have participated in the Blandin Community Leadership Program (BCLP). However, BCLP would not have been initiated in 1985 and sustained to the present were it not for the courage and commitment of the Blandin Foundation Trustees and administration. And of course, the content of BCLP—from which most of this book is taken—is the product of an ever-evolving, highly talented team who make excellence seem almost commonplace.

Special thanks go to Cindy Wilcox, who contributed the tool, "Building Social Capital Across Cultures"; Geralyn Sheehan, who produced the "Identifying Community Assets" tool; and Randy Gagne, who provided "Accessing Community Data."

Many people read drafts of this book during its development: Doni Blumenstock, Jane Garthson, Vaughn Grisham, Michael Kinsley, Carol Lukas, Jeffrey Nelson, Dick Senese, Janice Walker, Diane Wanner, and Richard Woo. Much gratitude is owed to these people, who took the time to thoroughly read the manuscript, raise provocative questions, and offer practical suggestions that greatly improved this book.

Thanks as well to the people who helped prepare this book. Karen Heikkila and Terri Dufner tirelessly typed numerous versions of this manuscript. Being able to edit the words of others while maintaining the integrity of their thought is a rare gift. Those who wrote and those who will read this book are beneficiaries of that gift, which was so skillfully displayed by Vince Hyman, Doug Toft, and Terri Hudoba. Finally, thanks to Kirsten Nielsen, whose design skills give life to the printed page.

Contents

Worksheets

INTRODUCTION

Getting the Most from This Book

At the end of his long career as a leadership scholar and advisor to four U.S. presidents, John W. Gardner issued a challenge and a plea for community leadership:

> I keep running into highly capable people all over this country who literally never give a thought to the well-being of their community. And I keep wondering who gave them permission to stand aside! I'm asking you to issue a wake-up call to those people—a bugle call right in their ear. And I want you to tell them that this nation could die of comfortable indifference to the problems that only citizens can solve. Tell them that.[1]

This book was written because there are people like you who have heard the "bugle call." You are not willing to let our neighborhoods, communities, or nation "die of comfortable indifference." You attend those early morning and late night meetings to determine what needs to be in the community. You give up your time and energy to make things happen, and you struggle to get others involved.

This book will support you in those important tasks.

[1] John Gardner, unpublished speech presented to the San Jose Rotary Club, September 2001, quoted in Sanford Cloud, "Dealing with the Unfinished Business of America: Fighting Bias, Bigotry, and Racism in the Twenty-first Century," University of Arkansas at Little Rock, 2004. Retrieved October 12, 2005, from http://www.ualr.edu/cpsdept/bridgingthedivide/cloud_whitepaper.html.

Insights from the Blandin Community Leadership Program

The Community Leadership Handbook responds to requests from community leaders and community development programs to share ideas and tools from the Blandin Community Leadership Program (BCLP).This residential training program includes a five-day retreat and two follow-up sessions over a six- to eight-month period.

BCLP was developed by a team of people with backgrounds in sociology, psychology, communications, adult education, business community development, government, and economic development. They've conducted BCLP since 1985 for over four thousand participants, testing and refining the content along the way. One result of this program is in your hands right now.

The heart of our approach to community leadership is the adage (paraphrased): You can give people some fish and feed them for a day. Or you can teach them to fish and they will feed themselves for a lifetime. Therefore, our program aims to build capacity—that is, to develop people's skills in working with each other so that they can address a community's opportunities and problems.

BCLP challenges the "myth of the facilitator." This myth holds that to get anything done, you need a facilitator from outside your community—an expert with a bag of tricks who can get people working together in productive ways. Instead, we assume that community members can tackle the job themselves. Using your own skills and employing the right tools, you and your neighbors can move your community forward. *The Community Leadership Handbook* highlights many of these tools.

Community leadership comes with a job description

There are many definitions of leadership. We define a **community leader** as a person who works with others to develop and sustain the health of the community. This definition seems simple and straightforward. But experienced community leaders know that in practice it is quite complex.

The job description of community leaders—to work with others to develop and sustain the health of the community—includes two elements.

The first comes from the question, Leadership for what? We answer that *the purpose of community leadership is to develop and sustain a healthy community.* A **healthy community** is a place where all people can meet their economic, social, physical, cultural, and spiritual needs; work together for the common good; and participate in creating their future.

Note that this definition refers to community in geographic terms, as an area that you could locate on a map. This could be anything from a single city block, to a small town, to an unincorporated rural region, to an entire city. People sometimes speak about other kinds of communities—such as an online community or a community of scientists. However, our use of the word **community** describes people who share a particular place and all the resources located there.

Also note that leadership is not an end in itself but a means to something else. In general, leadership is a way to produce a result—not a unique set of traits or a specialized job. *Community leadership occurs when anyone, regardless of their official position or lack of it, works to develop and sustain the health of their community.* Think of leadership as a job that's defined by what people *do* rather than by their personality or position. You may never apply for a paid or volunteer position that's titled "community leader." Yet you become one whenever you take on the functions that a community leader fulfills.

The second element of the job description is captured by the saying, "Leadership: You have to do it yourself, but you can't do it alone." The "you have to do it yourself" part says that leadership means recognizing an issue or opportunity—one that is so critical to a community's health that you must be involved. It is so important that you feel compelled to take some type of action. And the "you can't do it alone" part says that leadership is about working with and through others.

To understand this point, consider a simple case. Picking up the litter along your street by yourself may be good citizenship, but it is not community leadership. Yet if picking up litter along the street leads others to do the same, or if you organize others to help pick up litter, then you are exercising community leadership.

Some definitions and premises

Community leader: a person who works with others to develop and sustain the health of the community. This definition rests on several key ideas:

- In general, leadership is not an end in itself, but a means to something else. It is not a set of traits or a special position.
- Community leadership occurs when *anyone* works to develop and sustain a healthy community.
- Community leaders are identified by what they *do* rather than by their personality or official position.
- Communities usually don't need outside leaders or facilitators to make things happen. Community members, using their own skills and employing certain tools, can bring people together and move the community forward.

Healthy community: a place where all people can meet their economic, social, physical, cultural, and spiritual needs; work together for the common good; and participate in creating their future.

Community: people who share a particular place and all the resources located there.

Community leadership is *not* rocket science!

Communities are changing. They are more racially and ethnically diverse, more urbanized, and more integrated into the global economy. The meaning of the word "family" is being transformed because of the new ways that we form households. And an increasing proportion of our population is now age sixty-five or older.

These changes make community life more complicated. As our population becomes more diverse, our communities must deal with a variety of traditions, values, and viewpoints that can seem merely different from each other at best—and directly opposed at worst.

Commentators on the nightly news (and neighbors in the next office) remind us of deepening divisions in religious beliefs, political philosophy, and economic status. The changing makeup of households creates different patterns of consumption, different expectations for public services, and different types of participation in community life.

Not only is our population changing: The ways we get things done to provide needed services and regulate community activities is also being transformed. As far back as 1978, sociologist Roland Warren described what he called the "great change" in American communities.[2] This change is still under way, and it has several dimensions.

- Greater division of labor: more types of specialized jobs and occupations
- Greater differences in interests and association: for example, more special interest or special purpose community and civic groups
- Increasing systems that relate to the larger society: more ties to state and national governments, and more links to economic conditions across the nation and throughout the world
- Increased bureaucracy: more government agencies to provide more services and regulate a growing number of activities
- Changing values: greater emphasis on individualism, financial success, and consuming material goods

In short, what's driving this change is specialized activity and fragmented relationships. To get something done—even if it seems simple—community leaders have to deal with more individuals and more groups, each with their own "take" on things.

Diversity can be a source of creativity and strength. It can also be a community leadership challenge. All of us want to have happy and healthy children, to have our elders well cared for, and to have safety and security for ourselves. Yet we may discover great differences in what all this means to other people and who is responsible to provide it. We may all value families, for instance, but disagree sharply about what or who makes up a family.

[2] R. L. Warren, *The Community in America* (Chicago: Rand McNally, 1978).

The challenge is finding a way to manage these differences so that individuals and groups work together on building a healthy community. If community leadership were always a paid position, this challenge might qualify leaders for hazardous duty pay!

Community Example: Skateboard Park[3]

A local boy had been critically injured when a car struck him as he was skateboarding on a city street. It was time to build a skateboard park. Shirley and Leticia thought the idea was a good one, and the task seemed relatively simple. As parents of skateboarders and friends of the mother of the injured youth, they agreed to lead the effort to make the park a reality and to do so before another tragedy took place.

Within a few days, they talked to the mayor who said that a city-owned lot was available. They got two of the largest businesses in the area to agree to cover the cost of design and materials and organized a cadre of volunteers to do the actual construction.

At that point, the complexity of community life caught up with them. A series of events slowed the process down to a snail's pace:

- The city attorney advised them that the city's liability insurance would not be adequate for a skateboard park on city property. The chief of police sent a memo to the mayor and city council stating that an increased youth presence and activity in that neighborhood could be problematic and require more attention from her officers
- The local economic development group and Chamber of Commerce pointed out that several years earlier the City Planning Department had designated that lot as a business development site
- The City Park and Recreation Department was not sure if they had the staff to run the park

In addition, the "Y" raised the concern that the park's location was across town from them. This could have a negative impact on the "Y's" youth programming, which was a major interest of the private foundation that provided a considerable part of the "Y's" funding.

Shirley and Leticia took a step back and formed a steering committee composed of key stakeholders—parents, the city, the chamber, and the "Y." Eventually, all the major issues were successfully addressed. The park was built and opened two years after the original proposed completion date.

---

[3] The Community Examples found throughout this book are based on the experiences of Blandin Community Leadership Program participants. In some of the examples, details from more than one community have been combined.

The example above describes a situation that leaders often face. It reminds us that community leaders must deal with growing specialization, complexity, and interdependence. Making the skateboard park a reality required

- Legal advice from the city attorney's office
- Police officers to ensure safety and security
- Help from the City Park and Recreation Department to operate the park over time
- Support from the "Y," a source of future volunteers and funding

The involvement and support of these groups could not be taken for granted. Community leaders had to gain that support by dealing directly with each group.

Community leadership is about taking action in a changing, complex, interconnected world. In this world, no one has all the answers. No one has all the authority. Almost everyone has a different agenda. And at any given moment, everyone has a dozen different things to do other than what you would like them to do.

That's why we say community leadership isn't rocket science—it's a lot more difficult than that!

What You'll Find in This Book

The Community Leadership Handbook distills the essence of many theories into tools and techniques that you can use. The emphasis is on taking action, not on becoming an expert in politics, psychology, or sociology. The material is divided into four major parts.

PART ONE: Three Core Competencies for Community Leadership

Here you will find an overview of the three main competencies, or skills, needed to fulfill your job description as a community leader:

- Framing ideas
- Building social capital
- Mobilizing resources

Developing any one of these competencies will enhance your effectiveness as a community leader. However, your community project will truly ignite real change as you learn to combine all three. In community leadership, the sum of the core competencies truly yields more impact than any one of the parts.

PART TWO: Tools for Framing Ideas

Part Two presents ways to define opportunities, challenges, and strategies. Look here for techniques to help your community groups develop compelling vision statements, settle on clear priorities, and set challenging but achievable goals. Tools include

1. **Identifying Community Assets.** This is a process for pulling diverse parts of the community together to discover its opportunities and strengths—and how they can be enhanced.

2. **Analyzing Community Problems.** Reaching an agreement on what the "problem" is can be one of the biggest barriers to getting something done in the community. This tool gives a step-by-step group process for defining problems.

3. **Accessing Community Data.** This tool provides a list of resources and procedures to help you find relevant facts and figures about your community—economic, demographic, and more.

4. **Doing Appreciative Inquiry.** Here is a way to focus on *what* is working in your community and *why.* Planning for the future can maintain these strengths. Appreciative Inquiry breaks the cycle of frustrating and discouraging conversations about how bad things are in a community.

5. **Visioning.** Visioning means answering key questions: What do we want the future to be like? and Why do we want the future to be that way? This tool gives the basic steps for producing a clear, compelling direction for a neighborhood's or community's future.

6. **Translating Vision into Action.** Using the processes explained in this tool, groups can advance their vision for a healthy community through priorities and goals that focus their effort and energy.

PART THREE: Tools for Building and Using Social Capital

Effective community leadership pays attention to not only *what* gets done but also *how* it gets done. Part Three explains individual skills and group processes that produce results in ways that build positive, productive relationships over the long term. Those kinds of relationships represent social capital, which is just as important as money in the bank. Tools include

7. **Building Social Capital through Effective Communication.** If you can't communicate successfully with others, then you won't be able to work with them successfully. This tool provides a model for improving communication and a checklist to help you implement that model.

8. **Managing Interpersonal Conflict.** Community leaders must assess conflict and manage it in ways that do not deplete relationships. This tool will help you better understand and control your responses to conflict.

9. **Building Social Capital Across Cultures.** In multicultural environments, building social capital can be particularly challenging. Here you'll find practical techniques for situations where cultural differences make trust, reciprocity, and durability more difficult to establish.

10. **Mapping Your Social Capital.** This tool will help you assess your community relationships and networks, along with the resources that they make available to maintain community health.

PART FOUR: Tools for Mobilizing Resources

In Part Four, you'll discover ways to gather community resources—ideas, people, money—and move them into action to achieve a specific outcome. The tools in this section allow you to identify key stakeholders, discover potential partners, and align diverse groups around a common purpose. These include

11. **Analyzing Stakeholders.** Use this tool to create a map of the stakeholders in your project and determine their attitudes and degree of power.

12. **Building Coalitions.** Effective collaboration does not happen by accident. This tool presents ways to organize diverse groups around mutual self-interest in a community project.

13. **Building Effective Community Teams.** Use the model explained in this tool to build effective action teams and continually improve their performance.

14. **Recruiting and Sustaining Volunteers.** Volunteers are a precious community resource. An effective community leader approaches them as such. This tool provides techniques for attracting the right volunteers to the right roles and helping them to succeed.

Appendixes

Look in the back of this book for ideas that expand on the core competencies and tools presented in Parts One through Four:

- **Appendix 1: Getting the Most from Your Meetings—A Primer for Facilitating Community Groups.** Most of the tools presented in *The Community Leadership Handbook* are designed for people to use in groups. This calls for meetings. One way to immediately increase the value of any tool is to make your meetings more effective. See this appendix for tips.
- **Appendix 2: Additional Resources.** Volumes could be written on each one of the topics included in this book. We do not claim that *The Community Leadership Handbook* is complete or exhaustive on any of those topics. Included here are references to other resources where you can probe deeper and learn more.

Worksheets

Included throughout this book are worksheets that guide you through the action steps presented in each tool. You can duplicate and distribute them to members of your community.

The worksheets in this book are also available in electronic form exclusively at the publisher's web site. Buyers of this book may download them at no cost. To access these tools, go to the following URL and use the code below to download the material.

http://www.FieldstoneAlliance.org/worksheets

Code: **W547cLH06** (this code is case sensitive)

These electronic materials are intended for use in the same way as photocopies, but they are in a form that allows you to type in responses and reformat the material. Please do not download the material unless you or your organization has purchased the book. When using the worksheet in electronic or photocopied form, cite the source of the publication.

Who Can Benefit from Using This Book

This book is for anyone who wants to be effective at developing and sustaining the health of a community. We start by assuming that you are

- Wanting to be involved in community life
- Open-minded
- Willing to take risks
- Interested in creating and sustaining social change
- Willing to work collaboratively
- Willing to work at mobilizing people in your community

We also assume that you

- Will most likely use this book in your capacity as a community volunteer
- Are employed full- or part-time in, or are retired from, another field
- Have a high school education
- Are action-oriented
- Are pressed for time

We do *not* assume that you are a member of any particular profession, that you have a college degree, or even that you have a background in community organizing. You might be planning your twentieth community project—or contemplating your very first one.

Alumni of BCLP include educators, businesspeople, elected officials, health-care professionals, and members of the clergy. As a user of this book, however, you might well be a teacher, homemaker, truck driver, factory worker, computer programmer, farmer, or student. You might want to address issues created by cultural diversity or create opportunities for economic development. You might want to reduce violence in your neighborhood, revitalize a small town business district, create affordable housing, or meet the needs of seniors in your community.

If you are interested in any issue that calls for a community-wide response—one that excites your passion and commitment—then this book is for you.

How to Use This Book

Browse this book and you might feel overwhelmed by the amount of material it contains. You might wonder how you will ever make time to read all this.

Relax. Though we've packed *The Community Leadership Handbook* with content, you do not have to read it all. In fact, much of this book is designed to be used primarily as a reference work, like an encyclopedia. You do not have to read it from cover to cover. Instead, turn to it for the specific ideas and information you want, *when* you want them, by using the following suggestions.

Preview this book

To find content that's relevant to your current needs, first get a sense of the whole. Do a book "reconnaissance"—that is, a preliminary inspection. Preview this book by flipping through the pages, spending a few seconds on each one. Skim the text, looking for boldface headings and anything else that catches your eye. You can pick up many key points simply by doing this.

Pay special attention to the This Tool at a Glance sidebars located at the beginning of each tool. They offer a summary of each tool and some suggestions about when and how to use it.

Read Part One in detail

Part One explains the core competencies in detail and provides the groundwork for all the content that follows. Many of the key messages in this book are found here. Remember that each tool in this book is simply one way for you to practice a core competency described in Part One.

Approach this book as a toolkit

Parts Two, Three, and Four of this book are like a set of bins or compartments in a huge toolkit. In each of these "bins" you will find related tools. Because they're structured this way, you don't have to read the tools completely and in order.

Instead, set priorities. Ask yourself: What tool would make the greatest positive difference in my role as a community leader right now? Answer this question by choosing one to three tools. Then learn about those in detail.

Master carpenters don't use all their tools at once. Instead, they just reach for the one that serves them best at the moment. In the same way, just focus on the community leadership tool that best suits your current project.

If you're just beginning that project, for example, then pay special attention to the planning tools described in Part Two. If your project is already well planned, then turn to parts Three and Four for ways to gain community support and mobilize action.

Note: Because this book is structured as a toolkit, the authors do not assume that you will read all of it. Therefore, you may find that certain key concepts appear in several places. For example, the distinction between *product* and *process* is explained in the introduction to Part One (see page 1) and mentioned again in several of the tools presented in Part Two. This repetition is deliberate. It's done to make sure that you'll get the core content you need even if you only read a small section of the book.

Read the whole book

This suggestion might appear to contradict the previous one. In fact, reading the whole book is just another option for obtaining the most value from it. It's true that you don't *have* to read this entire book. However, you certainly *may* if you want to.

You may find that reading through all the tools in sequence deepens your understanding of each one and reveals connections between ideas. A complete reading might also help you diagnose why certain community projects are currently struggling or why past community efforts failed.

The tools in this book offer many opportunities to assess your own leadership, as well as the effectiveness of your community's group efforts. Use this book to answer questions such as, How well have you taken into account the three core competencies in your efforts? and Which competencies need more attention?

Put ideas into action

Some books are just meant to be read. This book is meant to be *used.* That means reading the book and then taking ideas off the page and into the world. As you read, constantly ask yourself, How can I apply this to my community project right now? The suggestions that you put into action will truly become your own.

You'll find many worksheets in this book, and each one offers an opportunity for you to move from theory to practice. Use them as checklists for planning new projects. The worksheets will take you through steps to define problems, create solutions, gain community "buy-in" for your projects, strengthen working relationships, and move people to action. Many of the worksheets also suggest ways to evaluate your projects, including questions that you can ask to get feedback on your results. Blank copies of all the worksheets are available from the publisher's web site at

www.FieldstoneAlliance.org/worksheets (use code W547cLH06)

Refer to this book often

The Community Leadership Handbook is not like a novel, a book that you might read through once, put on the shelf, and then forget. Instead, plan to return to this book often. Reread the parts that interest you. Highlight key passages and make notes in the margins about ideas that worked particularly well and points that raise questions. Make this book your own—a chronicle of your community achievements and a plan for acquiring new leadership skills.

Begin from where you stand today

As you explore the ideas in this book, remember that community leaders do not have to start their work with a mastery of all the tools described in the following pages. Instead, good community leaders are those who bring some key skills to a community project, understand their personal limitations, and collaborate with other people who have complementary skills. Start working with the skills you already possess, and then be willing to acquire new ones. There is no end to this process of learning—all it takes is a willingness to begin.

This book may not save you time or energy as a community leader. However, it can help you fulfill your leadership job description. Each tool you use promotes a better return on all the effort and time you're about to invest in creating your community's future.

Facilitating Groups: One Tool That Enhances All the Others

Community projects get planned and implemented by people who meet to combine their efforts. For this reason, your success as a community leader can hinge on your effectiveness in facilitating groups.

Perhaps you already have extensive experience in group projects and feel confident in your facilitation skills. But if you're new to working in groups or want to review this topic, then turn to Appendix 1: Getting the Most from Your Meetings—A Primer for Facilitating Community Groups, on page 185.

There you'll find ways to prepare for meetings, conduct them, and follow up on the decisions that meetings produce. These skills are not specific to framing ideas, building social capital, or mobilizing resources. Yet they will help you create more value from every tool presented in this book.

PART ONE

Three Core Competencies for Community Leadership

Job descriptions usually list required skills, or competencies. As explained in the Introduction, the job description for community leaders is to work with others to develop and maintain a healthy community in a changing, complex world. So what are the competencies needed to do this job successfully? There are three:

- Framing ideas
- Building social capital
- Mobilizing resources

These competencies and the way they relate to community leadership can be compared to what happens when you light a fire. What does it take to get that fire going? Your first answer might be fuel, oxygen, and an igniter. If so, your answer would be partially right. Fuel, oxygen, and a spark are necessary. But by themselves, they are not sufficient to start a fire. It is when these three *interact* that you get combustion.

So it is with the three core competencies. Each is essential for effective leadership. Yet desired results happen only when the competencies are combined.

As you explore the three core competencies, remember the distinction between product and process. **Products** are *what* gets done—specific outcomes, programs, or changes in the community. When used in combination, the competencies make it possible for community leaders to create better products in the community. **Process** refers to *how* things get done in the community—who gets included, how decisions are made, the way people work together, and related factors. Skilled community leaders use processes that build a sense of community *and* get things done.

The relationship among these three competencies is illustrated in Figure 1: Three Core Competencies of Community Leadership.

Figure 1. Three Core Competencies of Community Leadership

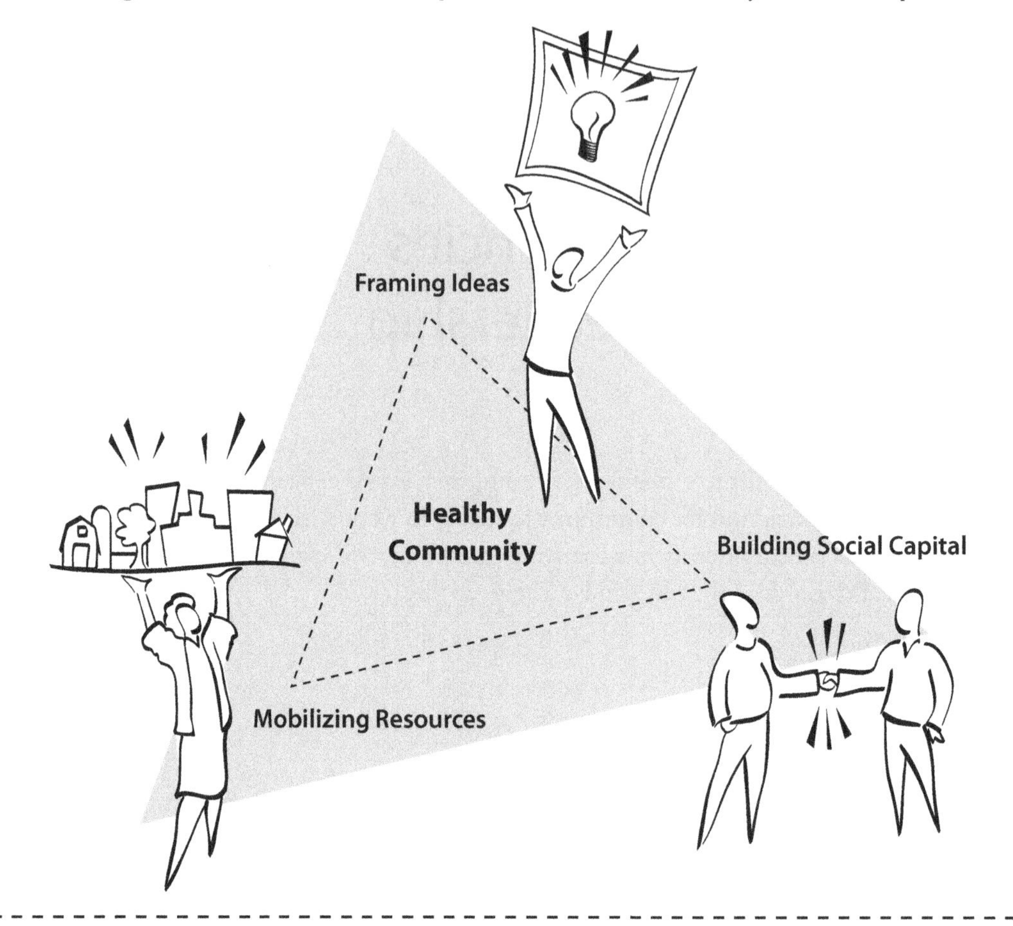

The Three Core Competencies at a Glance

Successful community leaders are able to

- **Frame ideas.** A community can define opportunities and issues in ways that lead to effective action. Through framing, a group understands and decides *what* needs to be done, *how* it is to be done, and *why* it is important to do.
- **Build social capital.** This means developing and maintaining relationships that allow people to work together. In the process, they share resources to address community opportunities and issues. Having social capital means we can call on and depend on each other to get things done.
- **Mobilize resources.** This involves organizing and engaging a critical mass to take action to achieve specific outcomes. Gaining a *critical mass* means getting enough people, financial resources, votes, and organizations to make the project a reality.

To understand how these competencies work when combined in action, consider the following community example.

Community Example: Pro-Bond Committee

The school board had just voted "aye," and for a moment the only sound in the room was the hum of the fluorescent lights and murmur of the ventilating system. After all, it had been ten years since a school bond issue had been approved, and that was for an elementary school. The proposed bond issue this time was for a new high school and for a lot more money.

However, the local and national economies were now sputtering and wheezing. The charismatic school superintendent who championed the elementary school had retired and moved out of the community shortly after voters approved the bond issue. Although she voted for the new proposal, the chair of the school board summed up the attitude of many in the community when she said, "Odds are at least 2 to 1 that this thing will never get passed."

Shortly after the school board authorized the bond referendum, a small group of parents decided to form a pro-bond committee. This committee quickly expanded to include members who represented diverse neighborhoods, groups, and organizations in the community.

One of the committee's first tasks was to develop the case as to why approving the bond issue and building a new high school was the right thing to do *now*. The committee met with school administrators and faculty to gather their input. They obtained data from the State Department of Education, the State Demographer's Office, and City Hall. They held community meetings and open forums to hear about what people wanted and did not want in a high school, and the pros and cons of the timing and total amount of the bond issue.

The committee took what it learned and developed the following key messages:

- The number of high school students will increase for at least the next ten years
- The current high school facility is too small to accommodate the expected number of students
- The present facility is old and deteriorating and maintenance costs are rising
- The present building is not designed for the type of learning technology necessary to prepare students for present and future jobs or higher education
- Local physician recruitment teams, human resource directors, realtors, and employers all report the negative impact the current high school has on people thinking of moving to the community
- Given the low interest rates, building the school now rather than later will result in cost savings
- The community cares about its kids and providing good educational facilities demonstrates that care

The pro-bond committee intentionally included people who had diverse contacts and networks in the community and who were adept at putting these connections to good use. One member of the committee, for example, was on the city council and was highly regarded by the other council members, the local news media, and union representatives. Another committee member was the high school soccer coach who had a broad and deep network in the Hispanic community. Still another committee member was a retired businessman who not only maintained his ties within the business community, but also had developed a reputation as "Mr. Senior Citizen" because of his involvement with local senior groups and issues.

The committee developed an action plan in which members were individually responsible for directly communicating with their key contacts about the benefits of approving the bond issue. These key contacts were then asked to talk about the bond issue with people in their own networks. In addition, committee members engaged their networks to organize block parties in every neighborhood in the school district and to set up a pool of volunteers who did a "get out the vote" phone blitz the week before the election.

Voters approved the bond issue by a two-to-one margin.

Whether the members of the pro-bond committee were aware of it or not, they used the three core competencies of community leadership. And they combined those competencies in ways that reinforced each other to get something done in spite of the odds against them:

- First, they *framed* the benefits of approving the bond issue and building a new high school in a variety of ways that made sense and appealed to diverse sectors of the community. In addition, they framed the needs and opportunities around the bond referendum in ways that gave the issue a sense of urgency.
- The committee members used the good relationships they had with others in the community as *social capital.* This gave credibility to their ideas and moved others to actively support the issue. In framing the bond issue and developing action strategies to get it approved, they also involved people in productive, respectful ways. This helped to build new relationships and strengthen old ones, adding to the supply of social capital.
- The committee's well-thought-out action plan took into account the diversity of the population and the complexity of community life. This plan drew on the clear and compelling way the issue was framed and on the available social capital. As a result, the committee *mobilized resources* to get the bond approved.

Every community change effort, whether it succeeds or fails, can be viewed through this three-part model: framing—social capital—mobilization. Initiatives that succeed do so because

- The issue or opportunity is framed in such a way that people are motivated to act
- There are enough people involved who are linked to others through direct relationships or networks, creating a critical mass of resources
- Action plans are developed and implemented in such a way that activities are focused and coordinated

In contrast, initiatives that fail often do so because

- The opportunity or issue was ill-defined, making it almost impossible to take action
- There were not enough people involved who had networks that gave them access to additional resources
- There were no clear plans, or people were not motivated to act on existing plans

What follows is a deeper look at each of the three core competencies. Understanding this material can help you select from all the tools, techniques, and tips found in the other parts of the book and use them for maximum benefit.

Framing Ideas

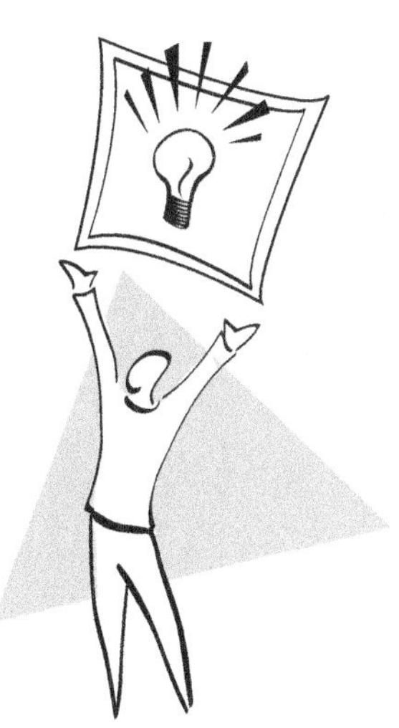

Framing means helping a group or community recognize and define its opportunities and issues in ways that result in effective action. Framing helps the group or community decide *what* needs to be done, *why* it is important that it be done, and *how* it is to be done—and to communicate that in clear and compelling ways.

Framing is a key competency for community leadership. It is also something we do in our daily lives. We are constantly framing opportunities or issues so we can do something about them.

For example, say that your television stops working. You take it to the store and discover that the cost of repairing it is more than buying a new one. You believe that a television is an important source of news and entertainment for you and your household. So you set aside some time and, using the Internet, research the quality of different models and then visit several stores to compare prices. After all this, you make a purchase.

What did you do? In short

- You defined reality: the television is not working
- You decided *what* needed to be done: buy a new one rather than repair the old one
- You determined *why* it was important to have a television: television provides entertainment and information

- You figured out how you would find a new one: through Internet research and comparison shopping

All these are examples of framing.

Framing might become more complex and require you to work with a greater number of people. But framing in any form still means determining the *what, why,* and *how* that directs action and produces results.

Community Example: A Welcoming Community

When you drive into this town your first reaction is, *This must be that mythical, quiet small-town America community I read about somewhere. It looks like a Norman Rockwell painting.* Within five minutes, however, you realize it can't be that place. Everyone may be "handsome" and "good-looking" (borrowing Garrison Keillor's description of people in the mythical small town of Lake Wobegon, MN). At the same time, you see faces of every hue and color. You hear children speaking to each other in English and to their grandparents in Spanish, Cambodian, or Somali. You sense a vibrancy in the community as a local radio station runs ads for the upcoming multicultural festival.

The transformation of this community started fifteen years ago. That's when the labor needs of its major industries, which focus on food production, outgrew the local workforce. Soon jobs were being filled by waves of newcomers from Latin America, Southeast Asia, and Africa.

As this trend accelerated, the mayor convened a diverse group—people from communities of color, members of the city staff, representatives from the schools, and spokespersons from the area's major employers. She asked these people to become a task force to document the population changes that had already taken place. She also wanted them to anticipate what changes were coming next and predict their implications.

The task force's report was rich in detail. Yet it could be summarized in two key points:

- The population trends are likely to continue, with the community becoming more diverse in the foreseeable future
- The way that current residents, units of government, local groups, and local organizations respond to this change will significantly affect how unified or fragmented the community becomes in the future

The report was shared with and discussed by the various community groups represented on the task force. Next, the members of the task force challenged themselves with a question, What values should guide our community's responses to newcomers?

The conversation was not easy. But the group was able, with the help of the mayor, to agree that

- Every resident is a potential asset to the community
- No matter where they come from, new residents are more apt to see themselves as an asset—and to be seen by others as an asset—if their transition into the community is a positive experience

As this discussion drew to a close, one of the task force members captured the essence of the group's agreement: "I was taught that community is the gift or legacy we give the next generation. Tonight we've decided that the legacy we want to leave is to be a welcoming community for everyone."

When the task force completed its work, the mayor appointed a committee of thirty people from throughout the community to create a comprehensive approach for helping new residents address their issues and opportunities. Before their first meeting, each committee member was asked to list the three most urgent issues or opportunities for the community's newcomers. Based on these lists, the committee divided itself into six working groups: housing, transportation, childcare, health and public safety, welcoming, and education.

Each working group used the values identified by the original task force to develop a vision statement and set of action plans. The effort involved struggle, frustration, and conflict. Yet over the next four years, the working groups involved hundreds of people in their activities. And they managed to raise a total of $10 million for projects, including a multicultural welcome center, a twenty-four-hour childcare center, affordable housing units, and low-cost public transportation.

The story of how this piece of small-town America dealt with significant population changes illustrates three important things about framing and community leadership:

- *How* an issue is framed influences *what* gets done
- Framing is complex
- Framing creates focus

How influences *what*

What gets done about a community issue is based on how that issue is framed. Suppose, in this case, that the influx of people from other cultures had been framed as a liability rather than an asset. It's doubtful that many of the projects done by the working groups with broad-based community support would have been attempted at all.

Framing is complex

The second point is that framing has at least four connected aspects: analysis, values and motivation, vision, and strategy.

Analysis means answering questions such as, *What is happening?* and *What is the current reality?* In the above community example, the task force analyzed a wide variety of information to help them determine the following:

- The size of the population shift, including how many residents had moved in since the last census and where they came from
- Projections for the future and the basis for those projections
- What the new and old residents were experiencing—expectations, fears, frustrations, successes, failures
- The experience of other communities in dealing with similar situations

Note that the task force based their analysis on actual population figures, people's real-life experiences, and past experiences of other communities. These were alternatives to *opinions* about what people thought *might* be happening.

Regarding **values and motivation,** the relevant questions are, *Why should we do something about this reality?* and *What should guide our action?* The task force provided a sense of urgency by issuing a report that emphasized two key points: First, that the population would continue to become more diverse. Second, what was done (or not done) *now* would have significant long-term consequences for everyone in the community.

The task force also made value statements about leaving a legacy of being a welcoming community and about all residents being potential assets. These statements not only reflected the task force members' values—they also channeled the community's energy into positive actions. People were attracted to the task force's efforts because they recognized and agreed with the values underlying those efforts.

Creating a **vision** means asking, *If we do something to change or respond to the current reality, what do we want the new reality to look like?* In the above example, community members started with the task force vision statement: "Our legacy is to be a welcoming community." Each working group developed a vision, or picture, of success in its area of interest. Furthermore, each group used a vision statement to guide its efforts and measure its success. The bottom line: If the desired outcome of a community initiative is not clear, the initiative will probably fail.

Strategy means asking, *How do we achieve the new reality we have envisioned?* It begins when community leaders articulate a vision, set priorities, and develop processes and structures to make the vision a reality. In this example, the overall strategy was to address the real-time, practical issues experienced by newcomers to community. The structure for doing that started with a planning committee of thirty people. This later became the coordinating committee and expanded into six working groups that involved many people from diverse sectors of the community in activities that were meaningful for them.

Framing creates focus

The third point this story illustrates is that framing creates focus. Through framing, we choose what we pay attention to and what we do not, what is important and what is not, what we give energy to and what we do not.

Framing is like taking a photograph. When we frame an image, we focus the viewer's attention on what we think is important and away from what is less important or distracting. As you look through the viewfinder, you decide what will be in the photograph and what will not. You might do a close-up of a child's face and let the kitten on her lap disappear. Or, if you take a picture of a room, you might angle the camera one way and see a lamp and your mother's favorite vase resting on a table. Angle the camera another way, and you see the big chair in which your uncle is fast asleep. The point is that as you press the button down on the camera, you are choosing what story your photo will tell—and what it will not tell.

When the task force in the above example analyzed what was happening in the community, they focused on population data, the actual experiences of new and old residents, and the experiences of other communities. Task force members decided that this information would tell the story they wanted told. In their vision statement, they chose to appeal to some values rather than others. Working groups also created strategies designed to emphasize certain outcomes more than others. Moreover, the strategies included processes that were framed to involve diverse populations instead of only a few select people. In each case, framing provided a focus that made effective action possible.

Building and Using Social Capital

Building social capital is the leadership competency of developing and maintaining relationships that allow us to work together and share resources in spite of our differences. These relationships can be between

- Individuals
- An individual and a group
- Groups

Relationships that yield social capital are marked by

- Trust: the belief in and reliance on the honesty, integrity, and reliability of the other party
- Reciprocity: a mutual, fair benefit from the relationship over time
- Durability: lasting over time through stress and changing circumstances

Community Example: Industrial Park

Her face was deeply wrinkled. But her voice was steady and her memories clear as Anna described the region that has been her home for the last 87 years.

"We've always been about differences, contrasts, and conflicts. Our landscape alternates between pristine forests and open-pit mines and slag piles the size of mountains. We've been divided between labor and management. We clustered in our towns and neighborhoods as Finns, Italians, Serbs, and Croatians. Our economy swings back and forth between boom and bust. But it's made us tough. We will fight anything or anybody we don't like—especially each other."

Then she threw back her head, laughed, and said, "That's why I don't understand some of the things going on now. I didn't think it was possible. But I'm so glad to finally see them happen."

One of the "things going on now" that Anna appreciated but could not explain was the new industrial park located between her community of Zirconia and the neighboring community of Fawn Lake three miles away. The park was set up to serve both communities through a joint-powers agreement.

Equally amazing to her was the new coalition of business leaders and local elected officials from the two communities. These people came together as a lobbying group, pressuring the state legislature for funding to upgrade the airport in Fawn Lake and turn it into a regional hub.

In her description of the area, Anna neglected to mention that the mining industry, which drove the region's economy for so many years, had shifted from boom-and-bust to a steady downward spiral. A small team of leaders from Zirconia and Fawn Lake recognized this fact early on. They also saw that old, fragmented approaches to economic development would not address current realities.

These community leaders discussed the need to develop a broad-based, comprehensive, multicommunity economic development strategy during a weeklong retreat. Like Anna, they knew that gaining support for any type of cooperation between the two communities would be difficult at best. They also recognized that a multicommunity approach to economic development would require formal agreements between local units of government and their various agencies. Such agreements would happen only with sufficient public support.

This leadership team decided that its first step was to create better relationships and links between their communities. Their primary task was to break down barriers, develop trust, and lay the groundwork for an intercommunity strategy for economic development.

Team members recognized that they represented strong ties to important, but closed, groups in both communities. Reaching out to their respective groups, each team member started conversations about the challenges confronting the area, and about how working with others could help in meeting those challenges.

Conversations took place in locations as varied as the Serbian Orthodox Church, the union hall, the country club, city hall, and the Italian-American Club.

The team members also recognized their good working relationships resulted largely from the leadership retreat they had all attended. So they started their own program to bring emerging leaders from both communities together. This program provided plenty of time for people to get acquainted while they addressed opportunities and challenges faced by both communities.

This was not easy. New ways of relating to others did not develop over night. Yet the team found the effort to be worthwhile. The communities' two Rotary Clubs held joint meetings. The Chambers of Commerce merged. The two Fire Departments signed a new agreement for expanded mutual aid. And the new industrial park and intercommunity lobbying group—changes that Anna cannot explain—became a reality.

Much has been written about social capital. As a practical matter for community leaders, however, there are three key ideas to keep in mind:

- Community action takes place through human relationships
- Social capital flows through networks
- Social capital comes in two forms—bonding social capital and bridging social capital[4]

Community action takes place through human relationships

When you want to get something done in the community, what do you do? You talk to people. You ask them to see things your way. You ask them to do things. And the better your relationships are with others, the easier it is to get them thinking and acting in ways that support your goals for a healthy community.

The same things are true when the government enacts a law or an international corporation decides to build a facility in your community. In each case, decisions are made and acted on by human beings who interact with each other. And what ultimately gets done depends on the quality of human relationships.

Social capital comes from the "stuff"—trust, reciprocity, durability—in human relationships that makes agreement and joint action possible. For example, the leadership team in Zirconia and Fawn Lake recognized that an effective economic development strategy was possible only by creating a web of relationships in which people trusted each other and knew they could count on each other in the future. The school bond committee described in an earlier community example was intentional about using its pool of good relationships to gain active support and get the bond approved.

[4] R. Putnam, *Bowling Alone: The Collapse and Revival of American Community* (New York: Simon and Schuster, 2000).

Both of these stories make a point: Social capital is like financial capital. You can draw on your account only if you have deposited something into it. Our ability to work together tomorrow depends a lot on how we treat each other today. Wise investors do not take their financial capital for granted. In the same way, wise community leaders do not take their social capital for granted.

Social capital flows through networks

Social capital flows through the community in patterns known as networks. Imagine that you need agreement and support from an individual or organization with whom you have no connection. You can use your social capital with people you *do* know to get *them* to influence that individual or organization. The more extensive and diverse your networks are, the more you will be able to tap community resources to which you have no direct access.

Social capital has been described as the resources available to people based on the networks their relationships give them access to.[5] And, as the school bond committee demonstrated, tapping diverse networks in a community can be critical to a project's success. Just as a skilled plumber knows how the water is piped throughout the house, a skilled community leader knows how social capital flows through the community.

Social capital comes in two forms

Bonding social capital and bridging social capital both require a sufficient level of trust, reciprocity, and durability. However, these forms of social capital represent somewhat different resources for getting things done in the community.

Bonding social capital holds groups together. It is most often found in groups that interact relatively frequently and that are based on

- Similar interests, for example, Rotary, antique car club, or bridge club
- Gender, for example, women and men's support groups, 100 Black Men, or Sigma Gamma Rho Society
- Ethnicity, such as a West Indian Social Club, Somali Mutual Aid Society, or Italian-American Club

Members of these groups tend to know a lot about each other's lives. They trust each other and know they will "be there" for each other when the need arises. They are allies for the long term, even if personal antagonism arises. In contrast, groups with little bonding social capital have a hard time reaching agreement or getting anything done.

[5] P. Adler and S.-W. Kwon, *Social Capital: Prospects for a New Concept* (2000). Retrieved October 25, 2005, from http://www.uky.edu/~skwon2/Social%20capital.pdf.

Bridging social capital connects or "bridges" diverse individuals and groups, making it possible for them to work together. Bridging social capital reduces the time and effort it takes to bring different groups together around an issue—an essential resource for getting things done in our complex communities.

Trust, reciprocity, and durability are part of any relationship that generates social capital. Compared to bonding social capital, however, relationships that produce bridging social capital involve less frequent interaction. The people involved do not know each other as well.

Here's a shortcut for remembering the distinction between these two forms of social capital: *Bonding* social capital develops among friends and allies. *Bridging* social capital develops between acquaintances.

The leadership team in Zirconia and Fawn Lake understood the value of both types of social capital. They knew that developing bridging social capital between their different communities was vital to their economic future. They also knew that little would happen until the various groups in both communities, each held together by their bonding social capital, got behind the idea.

The pro-bond committee for a new high school started with a small group of parents who had a high degree of bonding social capital that enabled them to quickly frame the issue and set a strategy. They then used their bridging social capital to garner support from others in the community.

In the welcoming community story, the mayor used her bridging social capital to pull together the initial task force of Somalis, Cambodians, Central Americans, and northern Europeans. Because of the intensity and duration of the work, the task force developed a good deal of bonding social capital. This enabled them to ask the "tough questions" about what values should guide the community as it dealt with a significant change in its population. Their answers set the tone for how people will live and work together in the community.

Mobilizing Resources

Mobilizing resources is the leadership competency of engaging a critical mass in taking action to achieve a specific outcome or set of outcomes. A **critical mass** is achieved when community leaders bring together enough people and resources to do what the community wants done. From a leadership perspective, mobilization is also about strategic, planned, purposeful activity to achieve clearly defined outcomes.

In each of the community examples mentioned so far, mobilization was critical. Many different resources had to be activated to get the bond issue approved, to create a welcoming community, and to create a new economic development strategy. Activities were directed by strategic thinking and workable action plans:

- The pro-bond committee was deliberate in tapping various community groups to win their support
- The welcoming community task force, coordinating committee, and the working groups all had well thought-out steps that activated different resources for different outcomes
- In Zirconia and Fawn Lake, the initial outcome was to form relationships and "sell" an idea. The leadership team carefully coordinated who was contacted, who made the contacts, and what messages were communicated

Remember that almost anyone can get resources moving. It takes leadership to get *enough* of the right resources moving toward the same target. The number of *interests* that you involve can be just as important as the number of *people* that you mobilize.

Mobilizing a critical mass requires strategic thinking, clear outcomes, and workable action plans. Four general strategies can be used to guide mobilization efforts in your community:

- Move others to speak and act in support of the goals
- Engage people who have access to key networks
- Directly involve large numbers of people throughout the community
- Remember the different points at which people adopt new ideas

Successful mobilization efforts often call for combining all these strategies.

Move others to speak and act in support of the goals

Successful mobilization requires that leaders stimulate conversations that move *others* to speak and act in support of the leaders' goals. This strategy was essential for the leadership team in Zirconia and Fawn Lake. As groundwork for their intercommunity economic development plan, team members recognized their ties with different groups and met with those groups. These leaders started conversations about the challenges facing the area and how working with the neighboring community could help meet those challenges. The conversations were intended not only to get people thinking about intercommunity cooperation, but also to get them excited about how cooperation could make things better.

Engage people who have access to key networks

Connecting with diverse networks plays a major role in building social capital. When using networks as part of mobilization, take into account the concept of leverage.

In its mechanical sense, **leverage** happens when you apply enough energy on one point (one end of a lever) to get another point to move (the other end of the lever). A good example of leverage is using a screwdriver to pry open the lid of a paint can. When you exert pressure on the handle of the screwdriver, the lid of the paint can lifts. If the screwdriver is too short and you can't get enough leverage to lift the lid, you then get a bigger screwdriver.

Community leaders need to ask two questions pertaining to leverage. The first relates to *where* the leverage is applied: Which networks will leverage the best or most resources? In other words, given the amount of energy it will take to mobilize this network, will the results be worth it? *Are we lifting the lid on the right paint can?*

If it is the right network, then the second question relates to the lever itself: Do we have the right person to tap this network? In other words, does this person have enough social capital in this network? Is this person credible with this network, or will he or she actually make it less likely that the resources in the network will be mobilized? *Do we have the right screwdriver?*

The pro-bond committee used the network strategy effectively to inform key groups of voters, organize neighborhood meetings, and develop the "get out the vote" phone bank. In large part, that strategy succeeded because those who formed the committee made sure they included people who had social capital with the critical community networks.

Directly involve large numbers of people throughout the community

All of the mobilization strategies are about engaging people. This particular strategy, however, is not just about getting people to speak favorably about your project or getting them to be a conduit to other resources. It is geared instead to get people to do the *work* that produces desired results.

In the welcoming community, for example, mobilization directly involved greater numbers of people in activities starting with the original task force and culminating with the work groups. In these groups, literally hundreds of people worked on projects they cared about.

Remember the different points at which people adopt new ideas

No matter which strategy you use, remember that you're mobilizing a critical mass in the community to make some sort of change. The outcome may be to create a new way to address an old challenge, such as intercommunity economic development. It may be to address a new opportunity, as in creating a welcoming community. Or it may be to build something new to replace something old, as in building a new high school. In any case, recognize that change is inherent in your intended outcome.

Social scientists have studied how changes are communicated and adopted in communities. This research reveals that some groups of people accept and act on a new idea fairly soon. Others do so at later times. Figure 2: Adopting Change Continuum, illustrates these different groups.

Figure 2. Adopting Change Continuum

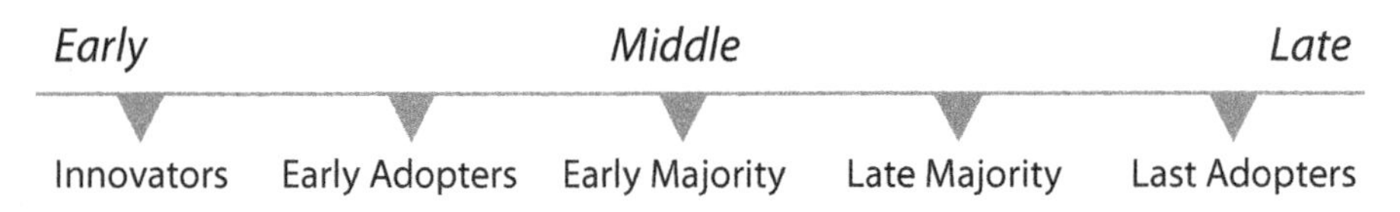

Recognizing several categories of **adopters** can help you to focus your efforts and to assess the progress of your mobilization effort:[6]

- **Innovators** come up with ideas. They are energized by an idea, see its value, and are willing to work for it from the outset. Innovators are usually a small group of people or a single individual. They may not always have extensive networks or support systems in the community.
- **Early adopters** may not initiate the change. Yet they are open to the new idea and "sign on" quickly. Early adopters are usually trusted opinion leaders with considerable social capital within their networks and groups. They maintain social capital by quickly backing ideas, programs, and projects that benefit their networks and groups. Because of their role as trusted opinion leaders, they are vital in mobilization efforts.
- The **early majority** are those most likely responding to the leadership of the innovators and the early adopters. Usually, many more people are in the early majority category than are in the innovator and early adopter categories combined. Mobilizing a sufficient number of the early majority usually creates the critical mass needed to achieve your outcome.

[6] E. M. Rogers, *Diffusion of Innovations* (New York: Macmillan, 1983).

- The **late majority** is mobilized because so many of their peers have signed on and they want to be on the winning side. Many people in the late majority may not become actively involved in your effort. However, they will no longer resist or oppose your effort.
- **Last adopters** are the final group to be mobilized. These people may actively resist your project in its early stages. Members of this group need to be certain that your efforts will succeed, and that any support on their part poses little risk for them. Like the late majority, many people in this category will not be highly engaged in helping to achieve your outcome. Nonetheless, mobilizing the late majority and last adopters can be important—not so much for their limited support but for their lack of resistance. They may not be your best advocates, but at least they are not your worst enemies.

You are probably in the innovator category because of the community changes you want to initiate. If that is the case, *your first mobilization task is to identify and recruit the right early adopters.* Focus on people with enough bonding social capital to energize the groups they belong to and enough bridging social capital to bring in other groups. These connections should involve the early majority, which can give you the needed critical mass.

Effective mobilization does not stop with the early majority. A community change can be implemented by the early adopters and the early majority. However, this *change may not be sustained until you get the broad base of support that is provided by the late majority and last adopters.*

Combining the Competencies

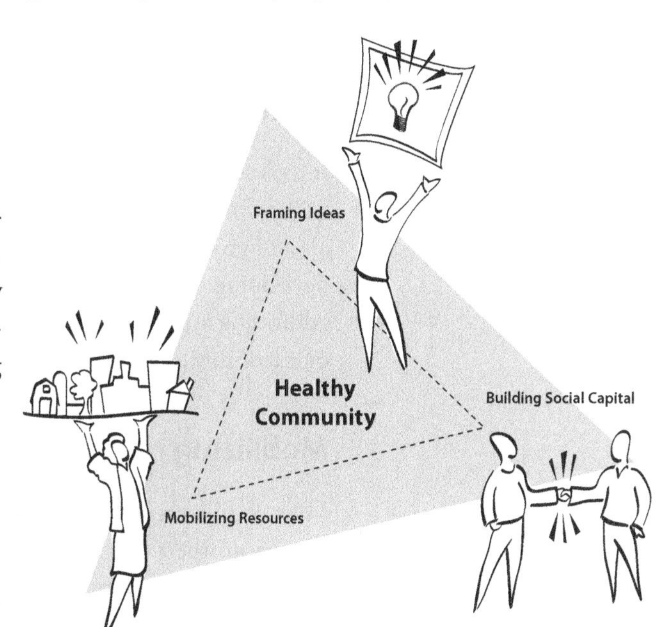

The three core competencies do not really ignite a community and get things done until they support each other. The effectiveness of one competency may depend on how the other competencies have been employed. The community examples described above illustrate the following points about ways that competencies interact.

Social capital helps people manage differences in framing

The task force that framed the welcoming community concept included representatives of the community's diverse ethnic groups, education systems, and major employers. Although task force members did not necessarily know each other, there was a reservoir of social capital based on their mutual trust in the mayor. As one group member put it, "I didn't know anybody else in the group, but I decided if they were OK with the mayor, I should give them half a chance."

Framing can increase or decrease social capital

If people feel excluded from the process of framing, they may find it hard to accept the framing or trust the intent of those doing the framing. Worse yet, people can be included in the process but feel that they are not being heard and their concerns are not being taken into account. In that case, they quickly lose the characteristics of trust, reciprocity, and durability in their relationship to those leading the framing.

When members of the pro-bond committee framed the issue, they held open forums and meetings with community groups to hear about what people wanted and did not want in a new high school. They discussed the pros and cons of the timing and the total amount of the bond issue. They then made sure that their framing addressed the major themes they had heard throughout the community. This process alone created community-wide trust in the committee and gave added legitimacy to their argument.

Effective framing makes it easier to mobilize resources

It is easier to mobilize resources around a clear focus that is relevant and achievable. The Zirconia–Fawn Lake leadership group was careful not to frame the issue as "How do we merge our communities?" Instead, the group focused on the immediate need in both communities to stop the downward spiral of the local economy. They framed outcomes that were achievable in a relatively short time.

Social capital is required to mobilize resources

It took a critical mass of support to generate the votes to approve the bond issue. The $10 million of welcoming community projects required the cooperation of many individuals and groups. The Zirconia–Fawn Lake economic development strategy was based on developing enough support in each community so that old rivals could risk a new way of addressing a common problem. In each case, achieving the outcome depended on webs of relationships that made it possible for people to act together on a common problem.

Mobilizing resources can increase or decrease social capital

How people are asked to share their time, talent, and networks can have a significant impact on their relationship with those doing the asking. When members of the pro-bond committee started the framing process, they went out of their way to create social capital throughout the community. When they started the mobilization phase, committee members not only used that social capital—they added to it by continuing to use processes that included more people. The citizens being mobilized to help design the block parties and the phone bank contributed much to the success of getting the bond issue approved.

Solve problems by looking at how competencies combine

Understanding the interplay of framing, mobilization, and social capital can help you think through problems. If you are having trouble in one area, look to one of the other competencies for an answer. Having trouble with framing? Then check to see if enough social capital has been built—that people trust each other enough to develop a common definition of the problem. Having trouble with mobilization? Check to see if the framing of the issue or strategy is clear enough so that people can respond.

Use tools to practice the competencies

This concludes the overview of core competencies for community leaders. The rest of this book is your toolkit—specific ways to frame ideas, build social capital, and mobilize resources. These tools will strengthen your ability to use each of the core competencies as you go about developing and sustaining the health of your community.

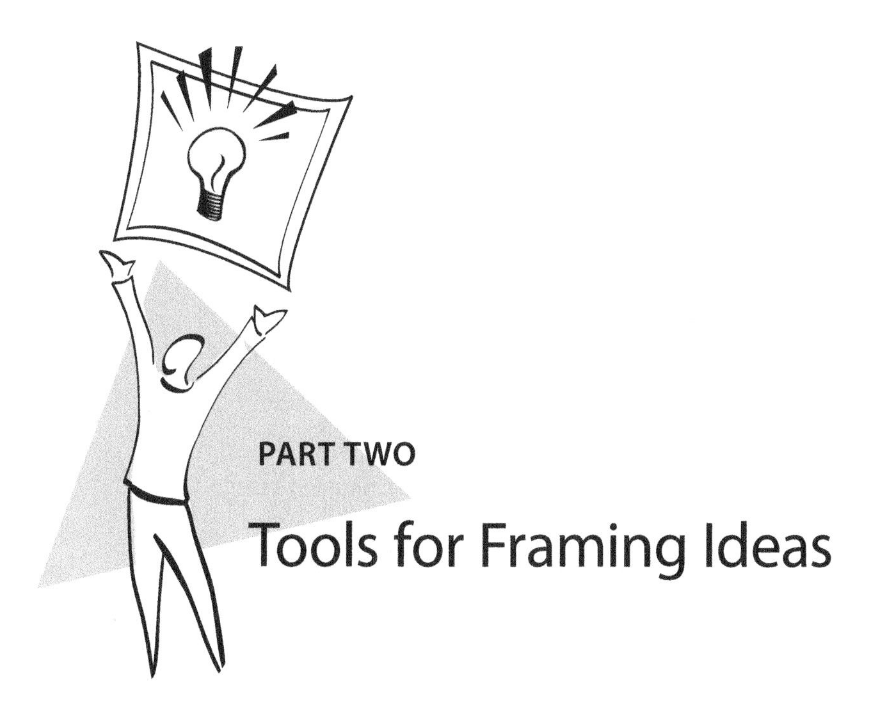

PART TWO

Tools for Framing Ideas

As described in Part One, *framing ideas* is the leadership competency of helping a group or community recognize and define its opportunities and issues in ways that result in effective action. Framing helps the group or community decide *what* to do, *why* it is important to do it, and *how* it is to be done. In addition, effective framing communicates all this in clear and compelling ways.

This part of the book includes the following tools:

1. **Identifying Community Assets** offers a process for pulling diverse parts of your community together to discover and build on its opportunities and strengths
2. **Analyzing Community Problems** presents steps for reaching agreement on what needs to be changed in your community
3. **Accessing Community Data** explains a number of ways to find relevant facts about your community
4. **Doing Appreciative Inquiry** breaks the cycle of frustration and discouragement by focusing on *what* is working in your community, *why* it is working, and *how* to maintain it
5. **Visioning** gives steps for producing a clear, compelling direction for your community's future
6. **Translating Vision into Action** helps you focus your efforts by choosing priorities, success indicators, and goals

TOOL 1. Identifying Community Assets

This Tool at a Glance

Why Use It
Identifying community assets offers an alternative to feeling helpless about problems. Using this tool helps you create energy for change.

When to Use It
Identifying community assets is useful when determining

- What resources are available to achieve goals
- What strategies will best leverage strengths
- How to best mobilize more people

You may find asset mapping to be most useful *after* you've completed the processes described in Tool 5: Visioning (page 57), and Tool 6: Translating Vision to Action (page 68).

How to Use It
Steps in identifying community assets include

- Clarify why you want asset information
- Create initial lists of assets
- Decide how to collect more detailed asset information
- Design your asset inventory and use it
- Map the assets you discovered
- Put your asset map to use

Where to Learn More
John Kretzmann and John McKnight. *Building Communities from the Inside Out* (Chicago: ACTA Publications, 1993).

This tool for framing opportunities is based on one suggestion: Begin community action by looking at your community's strengths rather than its weaknesses.

Community Example: Mercado Central

A small group of Latino immigrants wanted to increase family income for themselves and other Latino immigrants in their new community. It would have been easy to consider all the barriers they faced: limited proficiency in English, lack of marketable job skills, limited networks for job leads, lack of education, and more. But focusing on their needs would not move them forward economically.

Instead, Latino leaders from Interfaith Action, a faith-based community organization, conducted an "asset inventory" of their members. After church on Sundays, these leaders asked anyone interested in working on greater economic opportunities to answer some questions about their dreams, talents, and skills.

Their inventory uncovered a wealth of assets: the skills of artists, musicians, business operators, restaurateurs, booksellers, newspaper publishers, chefs, school teachers, and many more. They were a community rich with experience and talent. The next step was to connect these assets to create economic opportunity.

Community leaders reported their findings. They also invited community members to meetings to mobilize their assets and brainstorm possibilities for action. What resulted was a decision to create a traditional Latin American marketplace, or *mercado,* that would serve the Latino community *and* non-Latino people.

With a clear vision driven by community members, leaders created partnerships with developers, bankers, and others to create the Mercado Central. Within a few years, the Mercado Central operated with over forty-seven businesses and restaurants; over half of these were start-ups. The project had created over eighty-five new jobs and generated over $4.5 million in revenue.

About this tool

Assets are resources with economic or social value to the community. Examples are people with knowledge and talents that are relevant to your goals—anyone from a retired executive with accounting skills to a community volunteer who leads Alcoholics Anonymous meetings. However, assets can also include other aspects of your community, such as physical structures, natural resources, and organizations.

When community members decide to use their assets, they start by considering each part of the community and capturing information about the assets that exist there. This process is called **asset mapping.** You can do three major types of asset mapping:[7]

- **Targeted asset mapping** answers the question, *What resources do we have to achieve our goals?* A targeted asset map identifies people's skills and interests. It also uncovers organizational resources that can attract volunteers or become a basis for community partnerships. Use this type of asset mapping after your group or organization sets goals for what it wants to achieve in the community.
- **Visionary asset mapping** answers the question, *What strategies will best leverage our strengths?* Use it when your group, organization, or institution is revisiting its direction or planning new projects. This form of asset mapping also reviews the strengths and unique capacities of staff members, volunteers, members, affiliates, partners, and networks. You capture this information in order to choose strategies (such as tools in this book) that align such assets with your vision statement.
- **Mobilizing asset mapping** answers the question, *How can we get more people actively involved?* This map identifies the common interests, passions, and dreams of group members. The goal is to connect these people so that they can brainstorm ways to act together on their passions. Mobilizing asset mapping can build social capital and create new energy in local organizations.

[7] As defined by Deborah Puntenny and Luther Snow of the Asset Based Community Development Institute.

When asset mapping, you need to consider five key parts of community:

- Individuals
- Organizations
- Institutions
- Physical environment
- Methods of exchange

Figure 3: Community Assets offers more details about each item in this list.

Figure 3. Community Assets

Part of Community	Assets
Individuals Examples: elders, youth, adults, families	Skills, work experience, knowledge of culture, teaching ability, personal income, volunteer experience, life experience, technical know-how, hobbies
Organizations Examples: civic associations; block clubs; political, church, or sports groups; clubs; self-help groups	Group energy, mobilization of membership, knowledge based on group skills, professional and technical know-how, group trust, financial support, information, clout
Institutions Examples: libraries, schools, businesses, hospitals	Facilities, employees, volunteers, financial resources, expertise, clout, political voice, equipment, purchasing power
Physical environment Examples: land, water, buildings	Natural resources, location, facilities, infrastructure, flora and fauna
Methods of exchange Examples: income, loans, barter, grants	Income, financial instruments, bartering, loans, credit, community funds, pooled income

The data for asset mapping comes from brainstorming, informal research, and surveys that are often called **asset inventories.** Successful asset-mapping projects are customized to local communities. Therefore, this handbook does not offer a rigid model for developing and conducting an asset inventory. Instead it offers steps for you to consider and adapt.

Remember to use this tool as a guide and to spark creativity. You will find that conducting an asset inventory creates excitement. Asset maps offer a way to create a base of information from which leaders can promote economic growth, strengthen relationships, and raise the quality of community life.

Step 1. Clarify why you want asset information

Before you begin, clarify your goal for gathering information about community assets. State that goal specifically, and translate it into questions that will uncover relevant assets.

Suppose, for example, that a local organization sets a goal to support and grow entrepreneurs. This goal can be translated into a question, What are the entrepreneurial assets in our community? A possible follow-up question is, What barriers prevent entrepreneurs from achieving their dreams?

The questions you create in this step will guide you in creating more specific questions for your asset inventory (see steps 3 and 4).

Step 2. Create initial lists of assets

One way to begin asset mapping is to brainstorm a simple list of all the groups in your community. These can include businesses, associations, nonprofit organizations, self-help groups, clubs, and similar entities.

The key word at this point is *brainstorm*. This means to write down as many ideas as possible, without stopping to criticize or edit the list. Go for quantity, not quality. You can add details and fix errors later. Create a pencil-and-paper list, either individually or with members of your community group. Or use a computer for this step: Just open up a word-processing file and start typing.

Next, expand this list by consulting some easily located sources of information, such as

- Phone directories for your community
- Lists of businesses from your local chamber of commerce or a similar organization
- Newsletters published by local organizations
- Back issues of your newspaper that contain advertising supplements
- A librarian who can help you find lists of local organizations that have already been published
- Unpublished lists of organizations that have been compiled by your local newspaper, radio station, or television station
- Bulletin boards posted around your community that include meeting notices and advertisement for services
- Web sites for local businesses and other groups (check these for links to related organizations)

Now refine your list. Use spreadsheet or database software to create several categories of information about the groups on your list, such as name, location, size, product, service, profit or nonprofit status, or any other characteristic that interests you. If you're lacking information in any of these categories, go to the above sources another time to find it.

You'll probably finish this step with a list that's longer than you expected. If so, celebrate. You're beginning to get a clear picture of your community's assets.

Step 3. Decide how to collect more detailed asset information

Asset inventories can take you beyond the basic information you gathered in the previous step. An asset inventory is basically a survey, that is, a list of questions that you want answered.

Before you write up the questions to include in your asset inventory, think about how you will persuade people to complete it. Community groups get quite creative at this point. For example:

- A local church invites members to stay after service for coffee and donuts while filling out a one-page survey on parishioners' talents to support the church.
- A neighborhood group uses a community festival to offer neighbors a free hot dog or a raffle ticket for each completed asset inventory. (The group wanted neighborhood children to fill out the inventory along with their parents, and the hot dogs were a hit with the children!)
- A local community leader gathered a wide range of business owners and executives for a two-hour meeting. They identified potentials for business-to-business products and services.
- A local housing complex wanted to get residents involved in solving safety problems. The first one hundred residents submitting a completed asset inventory got one month of reduced rent in return.

Some key questions to answer at this point are

- Will you try to cover a specific geographic area with your inventory, such as a specific street, intersection, or neighborhood?
- How many people need to complete your inventory for you to get meaningful results?
- How will you present your inventory to people? You could mail it out, for example. Other options are to pass it out at community meetings, call people on the phone and ask them questions, or recruit volunteers to go door-to-door to conduct short interviews.

However you choose to gather asset information, do it in a way that's consistent with the culture and the capacity of the people involved in this task. Ask members of a local group in the community to conduct the inventory rather than using outsiders, such as consultants or college students from another region.

When completing this step, community members gain valuable insight about their neighbors. The process of collecting data can change people's perceptions. It can be exciting to do an asset inventory and hear your neighbors describe all the local talent, resources, ability, expertise, and know-how that they discover.

Step 4. Design your asset inventory and use it

Every asset inventory has three sections: introduction, survey questions, and follow-up information. Following are suggestions for creating each section and using them in door-to-door surveys conducted by community volunteers. However, many of these suggestions will apply even if you choose to conduct your asset inventory in a different way.

Introduction

Often a variety of people will conduct an asset inventory, each using their personal contacts to reach different sectors in the community. When using multiple interviewers, be sure they have consistent information about the purpose and use of survey information. This information comes in the introduction and should include

- **Who is conducting the inventory.** Provide the name of the organization, group, or affiliation that is gathering this information.
- **Purpose of the survey.** Identify why this group is interested in gathering information on local assets. This will most often be a goal that your group wants to achieve or a leading question to be answered.
- **How the information will be used.** Clearly state what will happen to the information that's gained. Will it be used in aggregate, or will you attempt to use specific names identified with assets? Linking names to assets may be difficult, depending on the community's level of trust in your group. Be sensitive to the interests and security of your neighbors.
- **Time commitment.** Let people know how long the interview will take.

Survey questions

Your asset inventory can include just two or three questions, or take up multiple pages. However, it is better to focus on getting useful information than to ask endless questions.

When designing survey questions, keep in mind that each one should

- Be clear
- Be easy to understand and answer
- Provide easy-to-use information

Make sure that people will understand what each question means without additional explanation. Also, you want the answers that people give to be easily tabulated and compiled.

Two survey samples follow (Worksheet 1: Community Talent Inventory, page 29, and Worksheet 2: Neighborhood Asset Inventory, page 30. Worksheet 2 was adapted from a worksheet called "Networking with Neighbors," which was developed by the Family Support Network, Inc., of Bothell, WA). You can use their questions as models for creating your own.

Consider taking your inventory questions through several drafts. Try out your first questions on a sample group of community members. Their reactions will help you determine whether any questions are confusing or irrelevant. Use this feedback to revise your inventory.

Follow-up

After people complete your survey, engage them in a conversation or give them a handout that covers three key topics:

- **How to get involved.** Provide information on how people can get involved in supporting your efforts. If they have assets, interests, and skills that align with your goal, they may well be interested. Share information on the next steps they can take to be part of further action.
- **Contact information.** Ask for their name, address, telephone number, and e-mail address. If your goal is to summarize asset information for a directory or other public use, then you must get respondents' permission to include their information. If you will not be publishing any public materials, you still may want their contact information to keep people informed about your organization's work.
- **Thank you.** Thank each person interviewed for their time. Remind them that sharing information helps to build a strong community based on the gifts of all its members.

The following worksheets offer two sample surveys that demonstrate the variety of ways that community groups map their assets. Additional samples can be found in *A Guide to Capacity Inventories: Mobilizing the Community Skills of Local Residents* by John Kretzmann, John McKnight, and Geralyn Sheehan.[8]

Use asset inventories as a vehicle to strengthen social capital and unite community members. When planning your inventory, establish a small group to draft the questions that will be asked. This helps people understand why you are asking each question and how the information gained will be used to answer the question generated by your overarching goal.

[8] Institute for Policy Research, Northwestern University, 1997. Available from ACTA Publications, 1-800-397-2282 or 773-271-1030.

WORKSHEET 1 Community Talent Inventory

Name: ______________________________

Address: ______________________________

City: ____________________ State: __________ ZIP: __________

Phone: ______________________________

E-Mail ______________________________

Please fill in answers to the following questions

1. What do you do well? For example, cooking, being a good listener, cross-stitching, public speaking, plumbing, etc. (We want to know practical skills and social skills.)

   Have you ever been paid for any of these skills? Yes No

   Which ones:

2. When you think about all of these skills, which would you say are the ones you are best at or enjoy doing most? Would you be interested in making money doing them or teaching someone else to learn them? (For example, a gardener selling produce, a quilter selling quilts at a craft fair, teaching carpentry skills, etc.)

   Which skills would you like to use to: Make money Teach others

3. Have you tried to make money on a skill and been successful? Yes No

   What skills?

   What happened?

4. Have you ever thought of starting a business at home or in the neighborhood? Yes No

   What kind of business would you start?

   Why haven't you started it?

   What would lead you to try?

5. What are some of the groups you belong to?

   Do you have a role in these groups? (chairperson, fundraiser, troop leader, etc.)

6. Can we list these skills in a published inventory for the community?

   Volunteer Skills Yes No

   Paid Skills Yes No

WORKSHEET 2 Neighborhood Asset Inventory

Fill in the following information. Please print.

Date: ______________________________

Basic Information About You

Name: ______________________________

Address: ______________________________

City: ____________________ State: __________ ZIP: __________

Home phone: ____________________ Work phone: ____________________

Cell phone: ______________________________

E-mail: ______________________________

Occupation: ______________________________

Languages spoken: ______________________________

Favorite volunteer experience: ______________________________

____

____

Your Skills and Interests

- ☐ Accounting
- ☐ Acupuncture
- ☐ Alterations
- ☐ Animal breeding
- ☐ Archery
- ☐ Architecture
- ☐ Athletic coaching
- ☐ Audio recording or production
- ☐ Automobile repair
- ☐ Backpacking
- ☐ Body work (such as therapeutic massage)
- ☐ Bookkeeping
- ☐ Bowling
- ☐ Bus driving
- ☐ Camping
- ☐ Canoeing
- ☐ Career coaching
- ☐ Career counseling
- ☐ Carpentry
- ☐ Carpet cleaning
- ☐ Child care
- ☐ Collecting cards, stamps, or other items
- ☐ Community organizing
- ☐ Competitive sports
- ☐ Computer programming
- ☐ Computer repair
- ☐ Construction
- ☐ Consulting (describe expertise)
- ☐ Cooking
- ☐ Counseling or psychotherapy
- ☐ Crime prevention
- ☐ Cycling
- ☐ Dancing
- ☐ Dentistry
- ☐ Electrical work
- ☐ Emergency health care
- ☐ Entertainment
- ☐ Environmental protection
- ☐ Event planning
- ☐ Financial advising
- ☐ Fire fighting or prevention
- ☐ First aid
- ☐ Floral sales or design
- ☐ Gardening
- ☐ Grant writing
- ☐ Graphic design
- ☐ Handy work or home repair
- ☐ Health care
- ☐ Home-based business
- ☐ Insurance
- ☐ Interior design
- ☐ Interpreting
- ☐ Interviewing
- ☐ Journalism
- ☐ Law enforcement
- ☐ Lawn care
- ☐ Lighting
- ☐ Managing people

(*continued*)

Worksheet 2 continued

- ☐ Managing projects
- ☐ Marketing
- ☐ Martial arts
- ☐ Mentoring
- ☐ Ministry
- ☐ Music performance
- ☐ Music teaching
- ☐ Nursing
- ☐ Pet sitting
- ☐ Philanthropy
- ☐ Photography
- ☐ Plumbing
- ☐ Printing
- ☐ Public relations
- ☐ Puppetry
- ☐ Reading
- ☐ Respite care
- ☐ Resume writing
- ☐ Sailing
- ☐ Sales
- ☐ Sign language
- ☐ Social work
- ☐ Speechwriting
- ☐ Strategic planning
- ☐ Theater
- ☐ Tutoring
- ☐ Video recording or production
- ☐ Visual arts
- ☐ Web design or production
- ☐ Writing or editing
- ☐ Yoga
- ☐ Other:
- ☐ Other:
- ☐ Other:

Supplies or Equipment You Can Share

- ☐ Aerator
- ☐ Air conditioning
- ☐ Audio or video equipment
- ☐ Bedding
- ☐ Blow torch
- ☐ Boat
- ☐ Bus
- ☐ Car, truck, or van
- ☐ Carpet cleaner
- ☐ Clothing
- ☐ Computer hardware
- ☐ Construction equipment
- ☐ Copier
- ☐ Fax
- ☐ Garden tools
- ☐ Hand tools
- ☐ Heating
- ☐ Housing (temporary)
- ☐ Lawn mower
- ☐ Leaf blower
- ☐ Lighting
- ☐ Limousine
- ☐ Paint sprayer
- ☐ Parachute
- ☐ Power tools
- ☐ Printer
- ☐ Pump
- ☐ Scanner
- ☐ Telephone
- ☐ Tent
- ☐ Trailer
- ☐ Wallpaper steamer
- ☐ Other:
- ☐ Other:
- ☐ Other:

This worksheet is adapted from a worksheet called "Networking with Neighbors" which was developed by the Family Support Network, Inc. of Bothell, WA.

Step 5. Map the assets you discovered

Now it's time to create your asset map. Here the word *map* refers to any visual device for representing the information you've collected in the previous steps. Again, be creative. Design your map in any way that presents your key data at a glance.

On a large street map of your community, for instance, use colored dots or push-pins to mark the location of assets such as natural resources, businesses, other organizations, or households with self-employed people. You could also draw a map by hand on a flip chart or poster board. Yet another option is to search the Internet for computer software that will help you create maps.

Instead of using a geographic map, you could also create a chart or diagram that summarizes the range of skills possessed by people in your community. Or your "map" might take the form of a published directory that lists people in your community along with their contact information (name, address, phone number, e-mail address) and a summary of their interests, skills, and experience.

Step 6. Put your asset map to use

If you completed the previous steps, you've achieved something valuable and unique. Many communities never get a clear picture of their assets. As a result, their potentials go largely unrealized.

Now take the next step: Take the information you gain from asset mapping and find ways for community members to access and use it. This step energizes people to take specific action and translate asset mapping into real payoffs for your community.

Let community members see what you've discovered and ponder what is possible. This is another place where creativity occurs. When sharing your asset data, identify ways to "mix it up." Ask open-ended questions, such as

- When you review the asset inventory data collected, what themes repeat?
- What assets are most exciting for you?
- Based on your new knowledge of local assets, where would you like to work to create something new for the community?
- What assets, if connected, could create new opportunities here?

The last question in that list deserves more comment. Use asset mapping as a mechanism to pull together diverse sectors in your community, and let those sectors have fun with making connections. This creates a nonthreatening way for different groups to bond over dreams for themselves and their community.

The possibilities for making connections are endless. Following are some ways to begin:

- Host a community meeting to present the asset map, inviting community groups or organizations that don't usually get together.
- Based on the patterns of assets in your community, target a particular area for economic development, for example, by assigning volunteers to help a cluster of local entrepreneurs create business plans, or by granting funds for storefront renovation up and down your town's "main street."
- Give your updated asset map to people who are deciding whether to open a new business in your community.
- Create a curriculum on asset mapping for use in local schools, allowing students to learn about their community and gain firsthand experience with this tool.
- Set up ways for members of your community to regularly exchange assets. This can be as simple as a list of people who are willing to exchange services or as complex as database of local organizations that are willing to share costs on certain types of projects.

Finally, consider that new assets are emerging in your community all the time. So set up a way to stay on top of these developments. For example, establish a paid or volunteer position for a "community asset coordinator" (or whatever term you wish to use). This person can take charge of updating your asset map each year, keeping records of asset exchange, and suggesting new ways for individuals and groups in your community to collaborate. In any case, you can make asset mapping a continuous process—and a regular way to renew your life as a community.

TOOL 2. Analyzing Community Problems

This Tool at a Glance

Why Use It

Analyzing community problems helps your community group clarify the causes, consequences, and nature of a problem *before* you try to solve it. Using this tool can help you avoid the wasted time and effort that often results when groups rush into action before making a careful diagnosis of current conditions.

When to Use It

Analyze community problems in the earliest stages of a project, before you develop priorities, set goals, or mobilize action. Along with this tool, consider Tool 1: Identifying Community Assets (page 22), Tool 3: Accessing Community Data (page 42), Tool 4: Doing Appreciative Inquiry (page 49), and Tool 5: Visioning (page 57).

How to Use It

Steps in analyzing community problems include

- State the problem as you see it now
- Describe why this is a problem
- Describe the causes and consequences of the problem
- Describe who is involved
- Identify information that you are missing
- Define the problem in one sentence
- Define the problem in manageable terms

Where to Learn More

Mihailo (Mike) Temali. *Community Economic Development Handbook: Strategies and Tools to Revitalize Your Neighborhood* (St. Paul, MN: Fieldstone Alliance, 2002).

Work Group on Health Promotion and Community Development, University of Kansas. *Community Tool Box: Chapter 17. Analyzing Community Problems and Solutions.* http://ctb.ku.edu/tools/en/chapter_1017.htm.

Sometimes it's hard to get the ball rolling on a community issue because no one agrees on what the problem *is*. This tool provides a step-by-step process for defining a community problem in such a way that people can do something about it. Analyzing Community Problems also helps prevent or resolve conflicts like the following one.

Community Example: Drug Abuse Prevention Task Force

"We've discussed everything and agreed on nothing. We are just spinning our wheels, and I, for one, am darn sick of it!" Peter said as he snatched up his coat and hurried toward the door. Elena nodded in agreement as she scooped her mound of papers off the table and said in a ringing voice, "We have talked this thing to death. Let's just fix it and be done with it. And," she added as she crammed her papers into her bag, "if you people would just stop and listen to me, we could have it fixed by now!"

Unfortunately, Peter and Elena were not the only members of the Drug Abuse Prevention Task Force who were frustrated and ready to leave the group. Everybody "knew" there was a growing drug problem. And based on how they defined the problem, everybody had a different idea of how to solve it. As a result, the group could not reach agreement on what strategies to recommend to the city council.

About this tool

To get the most benefit from this tool, keep several points in mind:

- **The way a problem is defined determines the type of solutions that will be developed.** For example, if a drug problem is defined in terms of a lack of discipline or lack of positive role models at home, the proposed solutions will focus on households and family life. If the problem is defined in terms of kids having too much time on their hands, the solutions will focus on providing youth activities. If the problem is seen as a matter of a lack of law enforcement, the solutions will focus on increasing police presence.
- **Problems usually have more than one cause.** For example, lack of positive role models, teenagers with too much free time, and limited law enforcement may all contribute to the drug problem.
- **The process of analyzing community problems runs against the tendency to think of solutions first.** This tendency runs strong in many, though not all, cultural groups. For many people, the habit of implementing solutions before understanding a problem is so ingrained that it becomes invisible.

When community leaders forget these three points, they often run into the following obstacles.

Equating problems and solutions

Consider what happens when a person says, "I need a drink of water" rather than "I am thirsty." He has described a problem (thirst) in terms of a solution (water). But water is only *one* way of handling the problem of thirst. Lemonade, soda, and iced tea can all be solutions to the problem of thirst.

Translate this idea to the above community example. A member of the Drug Prevention Task Force might say, "The problem is that we don't have enough squad cars on the street and enough good judges in the courtroom." He is describing the problem in terms of solutions he sees. Other possible solutions are missed. Even if inadequate law enforcement is part of the problem, there are possible solutions other than more squad cars and different judges. These include police practices, community liaisons, neighborhood watch programs, drug education programs, and many more.

Thinking in terms of solutions at the outset often prevents individuals and groups from identifying multiple causes of a problem. It also tends to limit creative thinking about alternate ways to solve a problem.

Insanity can be defined as repeating the same old behaviors and expecting them to produce new results. Analyzing community problems by starting with solutions can foster that type of insanity.

Rushing to action

When you go to a doctor, you don't expect her to start with surgery. You want a diagnosis first. Likewise, when your car develops a strange noise and you take it to a mechanic, you want him to just listen to the engine first and maybe ask a few questions. If he just opened the hood and started taking the engine apart, you'd be more than just a little upset.

Yet this often happens in community groups. People want to take action *before* making a diagnosis: *Let's just do something, and if it doesn't work, we'll try something else.*

A trial-and-error approach might work if you have abundant resources of time, energy, money, and community interest. But when resources are limited, you can't afford community efforts that fall short because they are misguided, failing to deal with the problem they were supposed to address.

People who do Community Problem Analysis find that time invested in carefully defining an issue pays off in time saved when people *do* take action. This tool prevents the "ready, fire, aim" syndrome that cripples many community efforts.

The steps in this tool are rigorous. They require following a certain logic. They call on us to look at information that we might otherwise ignore. Fortunately, the steps are few and fairly simple. The hard part is remembering to use the logic and gather the additional information.

These steps in Community Problem Analysis are designed for use in a group setting and are intended to

- Tap the diverse experiences, perceptions, and insights within the group
- Broaden and deepen the group's understanding of the problem
- Identify information that the group needs to adequately define the problem
- Help the group to frame the problem in a way that promotes constructive action

Read through all the following steps and think about what information your group may need to begin using this tool. Then get as much of it as you can *before* the first meeting.

Step 1. State the problem as you see it now

Start by asking your group, *What is the problem as you see it now?* This question gives group members a chance to get their definition on the table and have it acknowledged.

To have an effective discussion

- Alert the group to the drawbacks of thinking in terms of solutions at this stage. You can explain this idea using the above example about being thirsty versus needing water.
- Ask each group member to write down their definition of the problem.
- Next, ask each person to share their definition. Record the comments on a flip chart.
- Remind group members to listen without comment as each person speaks.
- After all definitions are recorded, let group members ask questions for clarification or offer additional information. At this point, the group does not need to reach agreement.

Step 2. Describe why this is a problem

Now ask the group, *Why is this a problem?* In other words, how does this situation keep us from being the kind of community we want to be?

Remember that situations are seen as problems because they are not the way we think or feel things should be. A problem is a *discrepancy* between what we want and what we have. For example, you may want teenagers in your community to abstain from alcohol until they're twenty-one. But suppose that a survey done at your local community college indicates that 40 percent of eighteen-year-olds enrolled there engage in binge drinking at least once per month. You have a problem.

This step taps the values and expectations of group members who are violated by the problem. The insights and feelings that surface during this step can motivate group members and other community members to *do* something to solve it.

Use the same process for this step that you used in the previous one (see the bulleted list above). Again, the group does not need to agree on why the situation is a problem. Community problems involve diverse expectations. This step gives your group a chance to identify shared values.

Step 3. Describe the causes and consequences of the problem

Next, ask, *What are the* causes *and* consequences *of the problem?* This helps the group get a sense of the problem's complexity.

Conversation during this step can help your group rank causes in order of importance. Focus on those that you can actually tackle and look for strategies that address more than one cause. Discussion about consequences can also take responses to the "why" question in Step 2 and make them more specific. This in turn creates motivation to identify key stakeholders and select solutions that deal with more than one consequence.

To facilitate this discussion, use a causes and consequences template like the one in Figure 4, which was created by the Drug Abuse Prevention Task Force. Write your template on a flip chart and record group members' ideas in the appropriate columns. Give participants a minute or two to think about their responses. It isn't necessary for each person to respond in turn, as in Steps 1 and 2. Just make sure everybody contributes.

You may find that the process goes faster if you deal with one column at a time, listing all the causes the group can identify and then all the consequences. If someone isn't sure whether an item is a cause or a consequence, ask group members to quickly decide. If they can't, list it in both columns and move on.

Figure 4. Sample Causes and Consequences Template

Cause	Consequence
Drugs are readily available	Kids failing in school
People make good money selling drugs	Increased violence at home, in school, and on the street • Property values dropping • Law enforcement costs rising
Drugs make you "feel good"	Individuals jeopardize their own health

Step 4. Describe who is involved

Now ask the group, *Who is involved?* More specifically

- Who is affected by the problem and how are they affected?
- Who gains from the situation the way it is now?
- Who loses?
- Who actually sees this as a problem?
- Who is doing something about the problem, and what are they doing?

This step generates a lot of information. Use Worksheet 3: Who Is Involved in This Community Problem on page 39 to record the group's input. Or prepare a wall chart using the same format as the worksheet, hanging five sheets of flip-chart paper side-by-side and labeling them. You may find it more productive to have the group work on questions A through C as a set first and then do D and E as a set. While these questions can be answered in an open discussion, make sure everyone gives their answers to all five questions.

Encourage group members to make their responses as specific as possible. Some may find it difficult to list responses for column B. Ask them to keep thinking, reminding them that any situation persists precisely *because* someone benefits from it.

WORKSHEET 3 Who Is Involved in This Community Problem

A	B	C	D	E
Who is affected and how?	Who gains from the current situation?	Who loses?	Who sees it as a problem?	Who is doing something about it and what are they doing?

This step begins the process of analyzing stakeholders. **Stakeholders** are people who *gain* from the current situation as well as those who *lose* from it. (For more information, see Tool 11: Analyzing Stakeholders, page 132.) At this time you can lay the groundwork for developing action strategies that take key stakeholders into account. Also consider adding new members to your community group at this point, seeking input from other groups, or doing both.

Step 5. Identify information that you are missing

Now ask the group, *What other information do we need?* This step challenges group members to identify gaps in their knowledge, including evidence they need to support their answers to the questions in the previous step.

After some discussion, your group may decide that it is missing crucial information. One possible solution is to add more members who can supply the missing data or experience. Also see Tool 3: Accessing Community Data, page 42, for ways to gather the information you need.

Before moving on to the next step, ask the group to revisit Steps 2 through 4 above. Check to see how the new information or new group members modify existing statements or add new ones.

Step 6. Define the problem in one sentence

Most community problems are complex. However, if your group cannot briefly state the essence of the problem—or some dimension of the problem—then it will not be able to take effective action. Taking action without a clear definition puts groups at risk for fragmenting their activities and scattering their energy.

To avoid such results, state the problem in one sentence. For example, a drug task force might use one of the following sentences to define its problem:

- Teenagers in our community can easily access alcohol if they want it.
- Teenagers in our community engage in binge drinking.
- Teenagers in our community use methamphetamines, undermining their performance in school and threatening their short-term and long-term health.
- Too many teenagers in our community are addicted to cigarettes or chewing tobacco by the time that they graduate from high school.

During this step, remember the difference between *describing* a problem and *defining* it. Describing is what takes place in Steps 2 through 5 above, where your group scopes out the current situation. Defining means focusing on some aspect of that situation that you *can* and *will* take meaningful action to change.

If your group is small (four to six members), ask group members to write out their one-sentence definitions and share them. Also ask people to state *why* they defined the problem in the way that they did. This may require you to review the definition of a problem given earlier in this chapter (a discrepancy between the current situation and the community's values) and the distinction between problems and solutions. Finally, help your group pull together the common elements in the individual statements. Negotiate until you "nail it" in one simple, declarative sentence.

If the group is larger than six people, have group members share their individual statements in teams of two or three people. Then ask each team to produce a problem statement and share it with the entire group, explaining why they defined the problem that way. Finally, negotiate to arrive at one single-sentence definition.

Step 7. Define the problem in manageable terms

This step is a reality check. It's now time for your group to ask, *Have we defined the problem in manageable terms?* And, *Why do we think so?*

Caution*:* If you try to include everything that everybody says into your one-sentence definition of the problem, you'll probably end up with something that's vague or overwhelming. Make sure that the group selects among the various ideas.

Consider this one-sentence definition of a community drug problem: *Our media promote a culture that glorifies drug use as a symbol of social status, an instant solution to problems, and a sure-fire way to deal with unpleasant feelings.*

This problem definition meets one key criterion: It consists of a single sentence. However, it points to more issues than any community group could tackle, let alone agree on: the state of the media, sweeping trends in our nation's culture, and longstanding attitudes toward drugs.

An alternative definition—such as *Teenagers in our community can easily access alcohol if they want it*—states the problem in manageable terms. The drug task force may not be able to reverse current trends in national culture. But it can take concrete steps to prevent teenagers from accessing alcohol, such as making sure that local merchants "card" customers who buy liquor.

The purpose of this step is to make sure that your community group focuses on areas where it really can make an impact. You want to know that your efforts make a difference—preferably one that you can measure. Once your group concludes that it has defined the problem in manageable terms, you can move forward to develop outcomes, set priorities, write goals, and develop action plans that lead to solutions. For more on accomplishing these tasks, see Tool 5: Visioning (page 57), and Tool 6: Translating Vision to Action (page 68).

TOOL 3. Accessing Community Data

This Tool at a Glance

Why Use It
Having adequate data about community conditions helps you persuade other people that a problem truly exists. Gathering data can also reveal how well your community group's strategies and actions are working. In addition, having accurate data boosts your credibility with community members and funders.

When to Use It
Accessing community data supports all the tools presented in this book. Be sure to use it with each of the tools for framing ideas included in Part One.

How to Use It
Steps in accessing community data include

- Decide what you're looking for
- Start locally
- Expand your search
- Determine what the data means
- Follow up on your research

Where to Learn More
Work Group on Health Promotion and Community Development, University of Kansas. *Community Tool Box: Section 4: Collecting Information About the Problem.* http://ctb.ku.edu/tools/en/section_1022.htm.

There is a saying that still rings true in community life: "In God we trust. All others bring data."

During a community meeting, questions such as these often arise: *What is really going on? How do we know if things are as good or bad as people say? Do we have any numbers to back this up? How does this compare with other communities?* Using this tool can help you find the "hard data" that provides answers.

Community Example: Community Action Program

As the executive director of the local Community Action Program, Monica was thrilled when her board of directors accepted her suggestion for the organization's vision statement: "No one in our community living below the poverty line."

She was convinced that this statement would generate all kinds of local activity to address the causes and consequences of poverty. Instead, the response was, "Look at all the good jobs we have here. There are no run-down neighborhoods. We have a good life here. Poverty really isn't that much of a problem."

After a few months of struggling to get other community groups interested in poverty, Monica shared her frustrations with one of the local pastors. His response, while sympathetic, was not what she was expecting to hear: "Monica, you have shown the rest of the community that you have passion about the issue of poverty. What you have not shown us is how big this problem is so that *we* can become passionate about it too. Other than your experience, what evidence do you have to show that poverty is really a problem?"

The next day Monica's staff went to work calling local and state agencies, exploring web sites, and visiting the public library. They gathered data about topics such as family income, poverty rates, dependency ratios, and labor force participation.

Once the data were collected, it became clear that although poverty was not highly visible in the community, it *was* a problem. Income statistics showed that the proportion of households living in poverty was higher than the state average. So were the teen pregnancy and suicide rates. However, the percentage of households with incomes over $100,000 was also higher than the state average.

Monica shared this information with the media and with a variety of community groups. She found she was stimulating the kinds of conversations that she originally wanted. Within six months, a coalition of leaders from the private and nonprofit sectors of the community had formed a coalition to address the challenge "No one in our community living below the poverty line."

About this tool

Your perceptions of a community challenge or opportunity may be valid, as Monica's were in the above example. However, others in your community need to have those perceptions backed by hard data. Had Monica gathered and shared those data earlier, her job would have been easier.

There are other advantages to gathering data. Having information on hand not only indicates the extent of a problem—it also helps you know whether your solution works. If your efforts at community leadership are making a difference, then the data you gather will probably reflect that. Also, gathering data helps you accurately monitor changes in your community over time and compare local conditions to those in other communities.

You can access two basic types of data:

- **Primary information,** which you gather directly from various stakeholders and other community members. This information is based on their personal experiences and perceptions. Other tools such as Tool 1: Identifying Community Assets (page 22), Tool 2: Analyzing Community Problems (page 34), or Tool 4: Doing Appreciative Inquiry (page 49) can uncover primary information.
- **Secondary information,** which is usually given in numbers that describe current situations and future trends. These data "measure" community conditions such as population changes, unemployment rates, and crime. Use the steps in this tool to gather secondary information that complements your primary information.

Data gathering is an essential part of all of the framing tools in this book. Remember that the meaning you give to the data will guide the decisions your group makes and drive the actions your community takes to solve any problem.

Step 1. Decide what you're looking for

You can access community data from a variety of sources, such as going online, visiting a library, or calling a local agency. To make these efforts more productive and less frustrating, answer the following questions first:

- What specific topic are we interested in?
- What data will help us know this about the topic?
- What specific time period (if any) does our data need to cover?
- Why do we want to know this about this topic?
- How will we collect the data?
- How will we know when we have enough data?

These questions boil down to a few key words. One is *what*—that is, what topic are you interested in, and what do you want to know about it? You might be interested in statistics, in opinions held by people in your community, in stories (such as personal testimonials or events in local history), or all of these. Deciding up front what you're looking for will save you time.

Another key word is *why.* What possible action will your group take based on your knowledge? Chances are that you're not collecting data just for the heck of it. The statistics, opinions, and stories that you gather might be fascinating, but finding them is not an end in itself. You are doing research with the intention of taking action to produce a specific outcome in your community. Remembering this point will help you gather the data you truly need, as opposed to piling up useless stacks of paper on your desk or clogging your computer's hard disk with useless files.

Finally, there's *how.* As a community leader, you might gather data yourself or delegate the task to someone else. That person could be a paid staff person or volunteer. If you have a lot of information to gather, consider asking several people to do it. Give them a list of specific questions to answer and a due date to complete their work. Whenever possible, assign the task to people with demonstrated skill in research, and give them enough time to get the task done.

Step 2. Start locally

Once you know what you are looking for and how you will use that information, start with local sources. Say that your issue is low rates of graduation from local high schools. Go to your local school district and ask what data they have about graduation rates.

Also, ask district staff members if they have data from state and federal agencies that can help you compare your local graduation rates with those in other communities.

Community leaders often overlook their local public or college library. Librarians can help you find many sources of information and access reams of data. Tapping a librarian's skills can save you hours of effort, and it may uncover information that's critical to your project.

Don't forget about other information sources. Think about who might collect the kind of data that you want. For example, a human services agency might have data about the number of people in your community who receive unemployment compensation or Medicaid benefits. And local hospitals might share statistics about causes of local injuries or accidental deaths.

Step 3. Expand your search

After making local inquiries, broaden your search. Potential resources include organizations at the local, state, and national level. Gale Research's *Encyclopedia of Associations* is a good source. You can find organizations specializing in almost any field, from Alzheimer's disease to tree planting to lead poisoning. And many such organizations have good web sites of their own.

Here are some specific online resources that may be useful to you. For a full description of each, see Community Data Resources in Appendix 2: Additional Resources (page 193). Also, note that many states have web sites with "community profiles" that give basic demographic and economic data about individual communities.

Remember that web sites are dynamic: They may be replaced, moved, renamed, or phased out over time. If you cannot access one of the sites listed below, ask a librarian about other ways to search for the information you want.

American Factfinder
http://factfinder.census.gov

Bureau of Labor Statistics
http://www.bls.gov

Career InfoNet
http://www.acinet.org/acinet

Centers for Disease Control and Prevention (CDC)
http://www.cdc.gov

County & City Data Book
http://www.census.gov/statab/www/ccdb.html

County Business Patterns
http://www.census.gov/epcd/cbp/view/cbpview.html

Economic Census
http://www.census.gov/epcd/www/econ97.html

Joint Center for Poverty Research
http://www.jcpr.org/index.html

State & County QuickFacts
http://quickfacts.census.gov/qfd/

U.S. Census Bureau
http://www.census.gov

U.S. Census Bureau Poverty Site
http://www.census.gov/hhes/www/poverty.html

USDA Office of Community Development
http://ocdweb.sc.egov.usda.gov

Keeping track of your sources

While gathering data, be sure to document the sources of any facts or quotations that you collect. Your aim is to be able to go back to the original source in the future, or to allow other people to access that source. Some key points to remember:

- When you find information in a published document, note the name of author or organization that created the document. Also note the time and place it was published, along with specific page numbers that you read.
- If you gather data by interviewing someone, note that person's name and the date of the interview. Strongly consider using a tape recorder or digital voice recorder during the interview so that you can capture the person's comments accurately.
- If you find information on the Internet, note the title of the web page you accessed, the date you accessed it, and the URL (the string of letters and numbers that follows *http://* when the page appears in your web browser). Also record the name of the person or organization who created the page.

Step 4. Determine what the data means

Your next challenge is to interpret the information you've accessed—to discover what it tells you about the issue and your community. To assign meaning to data, ask the following questions.

What type of information have we gathered?

Not all information is created equal. Sift through the research you've done and make distinctions between

- Facts, such as *Forty-eight percent of students who enter our local high schools don't graduate from them.*

- Inferences, such as *Students who do not graduate from high school will have a tougher time finding higher paying jobs than students with a college degree.*
- Opinions, such as *Kids fail to graduate because their parents don't know how to discipline them.*

All these types of information are potentially useful. Just remember that almost any fact can support more than one inference or opinion. Styles of discipline, for example, may be just one reason for low graduation rates. Perhaps mobility (the fact that many families stay in a community for a year or two and then move away) is just as important.

What is covered (and not covered) by the data?

The effort to discover meaning in data can reveal gaps in your research. Just knowing last year's high school graduation rate, for example, does not tell you whether that rate is an increase or decrease from previous years.

Research is a continuous process, not a one-time event. If you're missing key data, repeat the above steps to go out and find it. However, this is a matter of balance. Your group will have to decide how much data is enough. Too much data can lead to confusion and lack of action ("analysis paralysis"). Too little data can lead to poor decisions.

When you feel that you've answered the key questions about your issue, then you have gathered enough data. This does not mean that the members of your group have to be experts on the issue. It does mean, however, that your group has enough data to take focused action to produce a concrete change in your community.

How do the facts connect?

Discovering meaning is largely a matter of making connections. See if you can find out how graduation rates for your local high school students compare with those in other communities. Perhaps previous community groups tried strategies to raise graduation rates. What were those strategies? And did graduation rates change afterwards? Knowing the answers to those questions helps you make key connections. In turn, those connections could make a huge difference in what your group decides to do.

What is the context?

Getting reactions to data can put it in context and add another dimension of meaning. Find out how the data fit with the experiences of people involved in different aspects of an issue. Look for both of the following:

- **Insider reactions** come from people and organizations in the community that are directly involved in the topic of your research. For example, school administrators, faculty, students, and parents can help you connect high school graduation rates to other factors that they observe when working with students. They can tell you, from their perspective, what the data does and does *not* measure. And they can give real-life examples that go beyond the numbers, such as stories about what happened to local kids who dropped out of high school.

- **Outsider reactions** come from people and organizations in your community not directly involved in the issue. For example, people outside the school system—such as local business owners and religious leaders—can give their perspectives on the causes and consequences of low graduation rates. Outsiders offer a fresh outlook. They can provide insights or ask questions that do not occur to people who are immersed in a problem.

If your issue is particularly significant or sensitive, you may want to go even further "outside" and get reactions from people who do not live in your community. Someone from another city, county, or state may be seen as having more expertise, less bias, and greater freedom to "tell it like it is" than a local person or group. When seeking such reactions, look for people with expertise in the topic, training in data analysis, and a background in community work.

Step 5. Follow up on your research

Follow-up includes presenting your data and planning for future research. Members of your community group will want to know about the data you've gathered. Put your key discoveries in writing and present them at a meeting.

Also decide whether you want to present your data to the community as a whole. You can do this by setting up meetings that are open to the public and sending press releases to local newspapers. Sharing the fruits of your research now can help you build a base of support for your group's projects in the future.

Finally, plan for future research. After completing the above steps, you may decide that it's useful to collect certain types of data each month, each year, or at some other time interval. Doing this can help you stay on top of continuing developments. Having current data also makes it easier to apply for grants to fund your community initiatives. Most of all, accessing community data on a regular basis can tell you whether your group's strategies are making a real impact.

TOOL 4. Doing Appreciative Inquiry

This Tool at a Glance

Why Use It
Communities have more confidence and security moving into the future when they bring along parts of the past. Doing Appreciative Inquiry helps you define what is best about your community right now and how to preserve it. Using this tool breaks the cycle of frustration and pessimism that hampers many community efforts.

When to Use It
Use Appreciative Inquiry along with any of the tools for framing ideas presented in Part One of this book. It's especially useful in conjunction with Tool 2: Analyzing Community Problems (page 34), and Tool 5: Visioning (page 57).

How to Use It
Steps in doing Appreciative Inquiry include

- Conduct individual analysis
- Conduct two-person interviews
- Hold small group discussions
- Hold a large group discussion
- Choose how to follow up
- Experiment with an alternate form of Appreciative Inquiry

Where to Learn More
John Kretzmann and John McKnight. *Building Communities from the Inside Out* (Chicago: ACTA Publications, 1993).

Weatherhead School of Management, Case Western Reserve University. Appreciative Inquiry Commons. http://appreciativeinquiry.cwru.edu/.

Discussions about any given community change can become repetitive and discouraging. People constantly remind each other of what's wrong. They talk about how grim the future might be. Appreciative Inquiry breaks this cycle. This tool provides a framework for focusing on *what* is working and *why* it is working as the basis for planning for the future.

Community Example: Downtown Reborn

It all started with a front page editorial that ran the headline, "Retail Is Dead Downtown." The editorial pointed out that in the last five years the downtown area had lost two furniture stores, a department store, a men's clothing store, and a women's clothing store. It went on to challenge the community to "find a new purpose for the downtown area or pave it over."

A community meeting was organized as a response to that call for action. While nearly everyone in attendance knew that the downtown could never be the same as it had been, many were apprehensive about what would happen to the "old heart of the community" and did not want to see it abandoned.

The job of facilitating the meeting fell to Cheryl, the new executive director of the community's economic development corporation. As she prepared for the meeting, she, too, soon recognized that the downtown area would never be the type of retail center it had once been. She also realized that simply recognizing that fact would not necessarily lead to productive action—especially on the part of those who still cared a great deal for that part of town.

Cheryl opened the meeting by acknowledging the changes that the editorial had pointed out. Then she gave the assembled group the theme for the evening: "We are going to be in the future whether we like it or not. So let's decide what we want to take into the future with us." She then guided the group through a process to address three questions.

- What do you value most about the downtown area?
- How would you describe one of the best experiences you've had downtown and what made it that way?
- If you could take three characteristics of the downtown into the future, what would they be?

By the end of the evening, the group found itself energized and excited about the future of the downtown. They had identified characteristics that should and could be carried into the future: the historic character of the riverfront area, the "pedestrian-friendly" environment, and a culture of outstanding "hometown" customer service. These characteristics became the central themes for the visioning and strategic planning process that took place in the next few months.

Three years later, a new public library was under construction on the riverfront. A health club–fitness center was operating in what used to be one of the furniture stores. And the local community college had opened a customer-service training center where the men's clothing store had been.

About this tool

The process Cheryl used in that first community meeting is a good example of Appreciative Inquiry. As a framing technique, Appreciative Inquiry will help you discover what others see as the best of the past and present in your community. You'll gain a deeper understanding of what created community assets and identify which of these you want to carry into the future.

Appreciative Inquiry expands a community's conversation about itself. This tool opens up bold questions such as, *Imagine that we are immigrating to a new country. What is so valuable here that we would want to take it there?* What's more, Appreciative Inquiry invites new people to the conversation—residents who may not have had a public voice before. These can include residents who are turned off by local politics or who shy away from community organizations. People with any level of income, education, job skills, or physical ability can talk about what they appreciate in your community.

As you use this tool, remember that it's based on several key ideas:

- In every community, in every situation, there is something that works.
- What we focus on is what we act on. If we look only at what is not working as the basis for planning change, we may not develop strategies that will preserve and expand what is working.
- The scarcity model (there is not enough to go around) often becomes a self-fulfilling prophecy. That is, if people think there's a shortage of community assets, then this belief will shape their behavior. And as a consequence of their behavior, there truly will not be enough to go around.

Appreciative Inquiry opens a wide-ranging discussion that takes place in three contexts: with individuals, in small groups, and in larger groups. The steps below will guide you through each of these phases.

Step 1. Conduct individual analysis

Ask each member of your community group, working individually, to jot down answers to the following questions:

- What do you value most about this community?
- Describe one of the best experiences you had with this community.
- If you could take three characteristics or elements of this community with you into the future, what would they be? Why these three?

Depending on your goals, adapt these questions to refer to a specific situation in the community, or to a specific organization.

Step 2. Conduct two-person interviews

Now divide group members into two-person teams. For better results, pair participants with people whom they do not know well. Ask participants to interview each other about their responses to the three questions in Step 1. Hand out Worksheet 4: Questions for Appreciative Inquiry (page 52), so they can take notes on what their partners say. This is important, as participants will eventually share their partner's comments with a larger group.

WORKSHEET 4 Questions for Appreciative Inquiry

Instructions*: Interview your partner about how he or she responded to the following three questions. Use this worksheet to take notes on what your partner says. You will be sharing this person's comments with others.*

1. What do you value most about this [community, situation, or organization]?

2. Describe one of the best experiences you had with this [community, situation, or organization] and what made it such a good experience.

3. If you could take three characteristics or elements of this [community, situation, or organization] with you into the future, what would they be? Why these three?

Step 3. Hold small group discussions

This step takes place after the two-person teams finish their interviews. Ask these teams to form into small groups and pool their responses from Step 2. Instruct each group to find common themes in the responses—characteristics that group members agree should move forward into the future, and why.

You can explain this step to the group with the following instructions:

- Stay together as a pair and find three or four other pairs of people to work with, forming a small group.
- If you don't know each other, introduce yourselves.
- Select a group facilitator and someone else who will serve as recorder and spokesperson.
- Ask each group member, in turn, to share his or her partner's answers to the three questions. Check with your partner to make sure you've reported those answers accurately. Remember that this is not a time to agree or disagree with each other. Instead, use this time to clarify and understand what each person has to say.
- As a group, make a list of characteristics that all of you agree should be carried into the future, along with the reason for doing so. Your group does not have to agree on a single reason why a characteristic should be carried forward. In fact, you can list multiple reasons. Keep in mind that you will be sharing this list and your reasons with a larger group.

You can present these instructions as a handout or on a slide, or put them on a flip chart. In any case, ask groups to use Worksheet 5: Community Characteristics to Preserve for the Future, (page 54) or a flip chart in the same format to record their lists.

Step 4. Hold a large group discussion

This step brings the results of the previous steps into the large group, where participants identify the things that everyone wants to carry forward. To complete this step

- Ask the spokesperson for each small group to present their worksheet or flip chart from Step 3.
- As a large group, identify the common characteristics from the small group reports.
- Identify characteristics that were listed by at least one group but not by all groups. Decide as a large group whether these characteristics should also be carried forward, including reasons for each decision.

WORKSHEET 5 Community Characteristics to Preserve for the Future

Characteristic	Why important

Step 5. Choose how to follow up

Your group might already have a procedure for moving ideas into action. If so, tell other participants how their ideas from their Appreciative Inquiry will be used. Invite them to get involved in creating your group's vision and strategic plan, and in implementing them.

If your group does not have a process for following up on Appreciative Inquiry, see Tool 5: Visioning, and Tool 6: Translating Vision to Action. This is a good time to get the entire group, or part of it, involved in outlining the next steps.

Follow-up varies across community groups. But in all cases, lead your community group to take the results of Appreciative Inquiry and ask, What's next?

Step 6. Experiment with an alternate form of Appreciative Inquiry

While doing Appreciative Inquiry, you might find yourself among people with big differences in opportunities, political power, or access to community services. These differences may make it hard for them to focus on "what's working." Also, people who value a current feature of your community may fear that they'll lose it in the future.

Worksheet 6: Appreciative Inquiry Timeline (page 56), offers a tool for such settings. To use it, participants make several changes to the previous steps:

- In Step 1, individuals fill out Worksheet 6, listing what works well in their community or organization, what is not working, what they are afraid of losing, and what they aspire to achieve. Because the purpose of this worksheet is to describe changing conditions in your community over time, the worksheet includes spaces for three dates. Fill in these spaces with an appropriate date in the past, today's date, and an appropriate date in the future.
- In Step 2, the pairs interview each other about how they filled out the worksheet.
- In Step 3, the small groups combine the "in danger of losing" and "aspire to achieve" lists that the pairs report for the future.
- In Step 4, each small group shares these lists with the large group.
- In Step 5, the large group identifies common themes within these lists and then moves to next steps.

Worksheet 6 offers several benefits that help to overcome differences between people. It allows all participants to

- Name something about your community that works well
- Name something that is *not* working, enabling people from a more powerful social group to acknowledge any inequities that exist
- Describe their hopes for the future and discover common aspirations
- Express their fears of losing things they are most proud of as they move into the future

WORKSHEET 6 Appreciative Inquiry Timeline

1. **Date (in the past):**

   What works well in our community or organization:

   What does *not* work well in our community or organization:

   What our community or organization is in danger of losing:

   What our community or organization can aspire to achieve:

2. **Date (today):**

   What works well in our community or organization:

   What does *not* work well in our community or organization:

   What our community or organization is in danger of losing:

   What our community or organization can aspire to achieve:

3. **Date (in the future):**

   What works well in our community or organization:

   What does *not* work well in our community or organization:

   What our community or organization is in danger of losing:

   What our community or organization can aspire to achieve:

TOOL 5. Visioning

This Tool at a Glance

Why Use It

Visioning can produce

- A vision statement that gives a picture of an attainable future
- Clear reasons for why this picture of the future is important and worth achieving
- Hope for the future that translates into action

When to Use It

Use Tool 5: Visioning after completing a community assessment, such as those produced with Tool 1: Identifying Community Assets (page 22), Tool 2: Analyzing Community Problems (page 34), Tool 3: Accessing Community Data (page 42), or Tool 4: Doing Appreciative Inquiry (page 49). Make sure that your community group is ready to address the issues and opportunities identified by that assessment.

How to Use It

Steps in using this tool include

- Identify a coordinating individual or agency
- Form the steering committee
- Extend the invitations
- Hold a meeting to create the vision
- Draft the vision statement
- Gather reactions to the vision statement
- Share and market the vision

Where to Learn More

Emil Angelica. *Fieldstone Nonprofit Guide to Crafting Effective Mission and Vision Statements* (St. Paul, MN: Fieldstone Alliance, 2001).

To understand visioning, think of it as the process of answering two questions: *What do we want the future to be like?* And, *Why is it important that the future be like that?* This tool explains how a community or neighborhood group can answer those questions to create a clear, compelling direction for the future.

Community Example: Growing Jobs Through Education

Three state agencies and the regional planning agency had done economic studies. Several community sessions took place at which residents discussed local economic conditions. The facts were clear: People were leaving the area for better jobs elsewhere. And local employers were having a hard time finding trained employees.

As a consequence, small action teams were sprouting up like mushrooms throughout the community. Each had its own solution based on the immediate self-interest of its members. None had community-wide support. And all were competing for the same resources from state and local government agencies. A lot of activity was taking place in the community, but not much was getting accomplished.

After several months, a local restaurant owner—who in her own words "had enough of this"—called together a group of people. They represented the various action teams as well as other groups in the community. At the meeting she asked, "Do we know what all this activity will add up to? More important, do we really know what we want to be as a community in the next five to ten years?" As the group wrestled with the questions, they realized that the lack of a shared vision to guide their development efforts would lead them to waste time, energy, and money.

As a result of that meeting, the regional planning agency was asked to help the community create a vision of its economic future. After six weeks of intense community involvement, a vision statement was written, widely circulated, significantly revised, and finally agreed to. That statement, "Growing Jobs Through Education," centered on two key values that captured the sentiment of many in the community:

- We value quality jobs for everyone in our community.
- Everyone in the community should have access to education and training needed to qualify them for a quality job.

Also included was a description of "quality jobs" and what kinds of educational opportunities to create.

This statement is posted in the city hall, the local economic development agency, the school superintendent's office, and the office of the provost of the local state college.

Using the vision statement reduced competition among the action teams, increased public support and involvement, and sparked several new efforts in the community. Most notable was a collaboration between the local hospital and the college to create a medical-technical program. This program is designed to meet the hospital's employment needs *and* position the college as a major training center, drawing students from throughout the region.

About this tool

Visioning is the process of defining what you want. It recognizes the reality of current conditions and trends. At the same time, visioning taps the values and hopes of the community, motivating and guiding activities to build a desired future.

The words "vision" and "visioning" have been used in so many ways and so often that they may seem meaningless or clichéd. Yet visioning is critical to the leadership competency of framing, and this tool offers a step-by-step method for getting it done.

Characteristics of an effective vision statement

A vision presents your ideals. It completes this sentence: *If our community group succeeded in its efforts, our community would look like . . .* Remember, the word "vision" relates to being able to *see.*

An effective vision statement has two primary characteristics: It is clear, and it is compelling. This means that a vision statement should

- **Provide a shared picture of the common good.** That is, the vision should reflect more than just the special interest of some individual, group, or organization in the community.
- **Balance detail and clarity.** Vision statements should be detailed enough that people see "in their mind's eye" what the desired future would be like. On the other hand, the statement should not be so long that it obscures the essence of the vision, leaving people to "lose sight of the forest for the trees."
- **Balance possibilities with practicalities.** A vision statement should expand people's thinking about the future, excite their imagination, *and* be grounded in reality. Hope for the future is a precondition for positive community action. That is, without the hope that things can be better and the belief that our action can help make it better, not many people will be moved to act. If the vision statement frames a future that is totally unrealistic, it may produce cynicism rather than hope.

Many community groups and organizations capture the essence of their vision in a single phrase or sentence. For example:

- Our legacy is to be a welcoming community (see page 6).
- No one in our community living below the poverty line (see page 42).
- Healthy rural communities grounded in strong economies where the burdens and benefits are widely shared (Blandin Foundation).

Process is critical to product

A vision statement that does not get used (even if it is well crafted) is of little value. One of the most effective ways to ensure that a critical mass of stakeholders will use the vision is to make sure they are comfortable with the *process that generated the vision.* If people believe that the vision reflects their values and concerns, they will be more likely to act on it.

For some stakeholders, this means being involved in the visioning process from beginning to end. For others, it means having an opportunity to give their ideas at some phase of the process, and seeing those ideas reflected in the vision statement. For still others, it may simply mean knowing that they *could have* chosen to participate.

As you think about undertaking a visioning process, stay in touch with key stakeholders to learn about their expectations. For more suggestions, see Tool 11: Analyzing Stakeholders (page 132).

Step 1. Identify a coordinating individual or agency

The visioning process requires inviting many people, organizing meetings, circulating drafts of the vision statement, and more related tasks. For a smoother process, appoint an individual or coordinating group to manage such details. Choose a person or group viewed as unbiased about key community issues.

Step 2. Form the steering committee

While the purpose of the coordinator is to manage the details of the visioning process, the role of the steering committee is to guide its overall direction. This committee can also lend credibility to the process in the eyes of the community.

Specific tasks of the steering committee are to

- Set up the visioning process and make sure it's followed
- Schedule meetings
- Decide who will be invited to participate, how they will be invited, and who will make the invitations
- Determine who will know about the results of this process, and how those results will be shared
- Select a facilitator (or several) to conduct the visioning sessions

The steering committee should include people who can agree on the nature of visioning and what it will contribute to the community at this time. To give legitimacy to the process, members of this committee should also have considerable social capital with diverse groups throughout community.

Step 3. Extend the invitations

When inviting people to participate in visioning, there are three major areas for your steering committee to consider.

Whom to invite

The obvious answer is to invite people who represent key stakeholder groups. However, *who* those stakeholders are depends on the "territory" encompassed by the vision, which might be a single organization, a neighborhood, or an entire community.

So first determine the boundaries of the territory. Then decide who within that territory needs to be involved—preferably people who are highly respected and represent a range of opinions. Also consider whose support of (or opposition to) a vision statement could be critical. In most cases, the visioning process involves members from the local school district, churches, social and business organizations, and local governments (township, city, and county).

How to invite them

Your steering committee may decide to invite everyone in the defined territory and issue a public invitation. In that case, assign someone to work with the local media to get the word out in as many ways as possible. In addition, it may still be wise to identify key individuals or groups and contact them directly.

Given certain circumstances, such as size of the territory or focus on a specific issue, the committee may decide to invite only certain stakeholders. In this case, the invitation should be through direct contact, in both written and verbal form.

Clarifying outcomes

Everyone invited to visioning should know about

- What will be produced—a vision statement that will guide future projects in the community. Emphasize that a vision statement describes where the community or group wants to go. It is *not* an action plan for how to get there.
- How the statement will be used. For example, action teams will develop their priorities and goals based on the vision.
- The steps in the visioning process, how the participants will be involved, and how much of their time it will take.
- Why their participation is important.
- Who else is being invited to participate.

Step 4. Hold a meeting to create the vision

Outlined below are basic instructions for the person who facilitates the visioning meeting. These instructions can be adapted to fit your circumstances. Depending on the number and diversity of the participants, for example, your facilitator might choose to form small groups for part of the session and then have them share their results with the large group. (In fact, the following instructions are based on this option.)

Allow plenty of time for this meeting. Participants need to do four things:

A. Discuss "where we are now"

B. Discuss "where we want to go"

C. Frame the vision

D. Set next steps

When the group is fairly large, allow up to four hours to complete this session. If that is not feasible, then plan to complete these activities over several sessions.

A. Discuss "where we are now"

Before taking this step, your community group should complete an assessment of some sort. (For examples, see Tools 1 to 4 in this book.) At the beginning of the meeting, review and discuss this assessment so that everyone has a sense of the current situation and potential trends for the future. If the group at this meeting was not part of the assessment, the steering committee should make sure that they receive a summary of the assessment *before* the meeting.

B. Discuss "where we want to go"

Ask participants to keep in mind what the assessment reveals about the your community's current assets, challenges, trends, and possibilities. Based on that knowledge, participants can discuss what they want the community to look like within five, ten, or fifteen years.

For this discussion, split the participants into small groups. Using one of the process tools described below, encourage them to answer these questions:

- What is working now that should be carried into the future?
- What should be changed?
- What do we value most?
- What do we think the community should value?
- What would we like to see more of in the community?
- What would we like to see less of?
- How should this community be linked to relate to other communities, groups, agencies, or businesses outside of this community?

Use any of the following three exercises to generate responses to these "Where do we want to go?" questions.

- Snow cards visioning exercise[9]
- Community news visioning exercise
- "What do you want to see in the future?" visioning exercise

Ask meeting participants to do the exercises in small groups, and then have them report to the large group.

Snow cards visioning exercise. This process helps a group generate, organize, and prioritize its ideas for the future. Prepare for it by gathering square pieces of colored cardstock ("snow cards"), colored markers, and tape. Then have your facilitator follow these steps:

1. Ask each individual in the group to spend at least five minutes brainstorming as many answers as possible to the question, *What do we want for the future?* Ask them to record their ideas *individually.*

[9] Based on J. Bryson, *Strategic Planning for Public and Nonprofit Organizations: A Guide to Strengthening and Sustaining Organizational Achievement* (San Francisco: Jossey-Bass, 1995).

2. Ask participants to pick out their top three to five "best" or "priority" answers and write each one on its own "snow card" (a square piece of colored cardstock). Be sure to provide cardstock of uniform shape, size, and color. That way, each person's ideas will remain anonymous.
3. Shuffle the cards and then ask the group to tape them on a wall. Be sure the wall is long enough for the cards to be spread out, and that the texture is appropriate for taping the cards. The wall should also be accessible enough that people can walk up to any card taped on it.
4. Group the cards into general categories as defined and agreed upon by the group after reviewing the answers.
5. Organize the cards further into vertical formations of subcategories. Move cards around until they're grouped logically.
6. Create headings for each category.
7. Ask group members to identify their top priorities on the wall (which may be their own cards or someone else's), as well as any cards they don't agree with. Label these cards with small, colored dot stickers; for example, use green dots for priority cards and orange dots for cards with problematic answers. Continue the group discussion until participants reach general agreement on priority items.
8. Ask a spokesperson for the group to report these priority items to the larger group.

Community news visioning exercise. This exercise is a particularly effective way to generate ideas for visioning. To begin, distribute Worksheet 7: Imagine Your Community's Future (page 64), to participants and ask them to fill it out. You can also create your own worksheet, modifying the items according to the type of responses you desire. However, the dates used in the exercise should be no shorter than five years and no longer than fifteen years in the future.

"What do you want to see in the future?" visioning exercise. To begin this exercise, give each group member a pad of 3″x 5″ Post-it notes and a pen or felt-tip marker. Then ask your facilitator to guide the group through the following steps.

1. Explain that the purpose of this exercise is to create a description or "word picture" of what group members want your community to be like _______ years in the future. This process will involve some individual reflection, a chance for each individual to share those reflections, and a way for group members to identify the points they agree on. During the exercise, remind participants to consider the assessment of current community conditions and trends.

WORKSHEET 7 Imagine Your Community's Future

1. Imagine that you are watching a local television news program on this date: ____________________.

   Describe at least three events that could be reported during the program *if current conditions and trends in your community continue into the future.* For example, "Survey results released today reveal that fear of crime keeps shoppers away from downtown."

2. Now describe at least three events that could be reported on the same date *if conditions and trends in your community change in positive ways.* For example, "Today, a revitalized downtown lures shoppers away from outlying chain stores."

3. Meeting with members of your small group, share the events you described.

   As a group, select your top priority response to item 1. This represents the condition that your group *least* wants to see in the future. Describe this condition in the space below.

   Select your top three responses from item 2. These represent the conditions that your group *most* wants to see in the future. Describe these conditions in the space below.

2. Ask participants to describe the characteristics they would like to see in the community _____ years from now. To help participants identify those characteristics, write the following questions on a flip chart:

   - What do you want to see?
   - What don't you want to see?
   - What do you want to hear?
   - What don't you want to hear?
   - What do you want to see or hear more of?
   - What do you want to see or hear less of?
   - How should people and organizations in the community be connected and relate to each other?
   - Who should we welcome into our community and how should we welcome them?
   - How should we be linked to the world beyond our community?

3. Give participants a chance to think about their answers to the above questions. Then ask participants to write down these answers, recording each one on a separate Post-it note (for example, *More intergenerational activity* or *Less poverty*).

4. Ask participants to post their answers on a wall or flip chart. Use a "round-robin" process: One person puts up a note and explains why he or she chose that characteristic. Then someone else puts up a note and gives an explanation. Continue the "round-robin" until everyone has shared all their notes.

5. Rearrange notes into categories that make sense to the group—for example, *economic viability* or *valuing diversity.* If the group has some notes that do not fit easily into a category, then those notes can become categories in themselves.

6. Guide group members to decide which categories and notes they all agree on, and which ones they don't.

7. Ask a spokesperson for the group to report the categories they agreed on to the larger group, along with some notes to illustrate what the category is all about.

C. Frame the vision

After completing small group exercises, bring all participants back to the large group. Ask the spokesperson for each small group to report the results of their discussion by summarizing their ideas on a flip chart. Help the large group identify the common themes or elements in the small group reports.

Next, form another set of small groups and ask them to answer two questions: *What are the core values represented in the themes or elements? Are there core values that are not represented but should be?* Again, share summaries of these group discussions with the large group.

Finally, assist the large group to identify the values around which there seems to be the greatest agreement.

D. Set next steps

Explain that a smaller group (which could be the steering committee) or a designated individual will take the results of this meeting and write a draft vision statement. Explain how the draft will be circulated and how participants can provide their feedback on it (see Step 6, page 67).

Step 5. Draft the vision statement

Base the draft vision statement on the areas of agreement generated and values identified at the visioning meeting. Keep in mind that the vision statement is *not* a meeting summary. Instead, the authors need to remember the characteristics of an effective vision statement noted earlier in this chapter: The statement should be clear enough that people can say, *Yes, I see where we want to go.* It should also be compelling enough that they will say, *It's worth my time, energy, and resources to help get us there!*

Authors of a vision statement often feel pressure to please everyone and include every idea. As a result, the statement becomes so general that the unique assets of the community are lost or fade into the background. Remember, people are not likely to be motivated by a vision that could describe every other community in the state.

Variations on the visioning process

The visioning process explained in this book has been used successfully with groups of community leaders. If you research this subject, however, you'll discover other models of planning with markedly different instructions, such as

- In communities with a lot of cultural diversity, begin by meeting first with different groups of residents. Later, bring key people from these groups together to create the final vision statement.
- Create a vision that captures the community's ideals even if it is not achievable. A vision is different from a goal, which needs to be met over time. Human history has produced inspiring vision statements—such as peace on earth, liberty and justice for all, or Martin Luther King's "I Have a Dream" speech—that may never be fully attained. Yet these statements have moved people to take heroic action and make a lasting difference in the world.
- Instead of starting the visioning process with a community assessment that describes "where we are now," begin with "where we want to be." Think many years ahead—far enough to get current personalities and conflicts out of the picture. Create a clear and compelling picture of your desired future without reference to the present. Then look at where you are now and how to close the gap between the two conditions.

Remember that there is no single "correct" process for creating a vision statement or doing any type of long-range planning. The point is simply to enter a continuing conversation about your community's desired future—and then use that conversation to shape action in the present. Experiment with variations on the planning process and *use what works* for your group.

Step 6. Gather reactions to the vision statement

The vision statement you've created is only a draft. Now you need to gather reactions to it. Alternatives for gathering feedback include holding another meeting, sending the draft to key stakeholders, having the steering committee publish a draft in the newspaper for reaction, and posting the draft on an appropriate web site.

Whichever alternatives you choose, remind the people providing feedback that this is not an opportunity to simply nitpick and "wordsmith." Rather, feedback on the vision statement should answer these questions:

- Does the statement capture the essence of what the visioning group said?
- Is the statement clear and understandable?
- Does the statement seem attainable?
- Does the statement tap core values and give enough reason for hope so that people will be motivated to act?

If feedback shows the vision statement does not meet these criteria, continue to revise it until you are satisfied that you can say yes to all of the above questions.

Step 7. Share and market the vision

If the vision statement is to make an impact, people have to know about it. Moreover, they have to acknowledge it as important. Here are some ways to promote the vision:

- Send a copy of the vision statement directly to everyone who took part in the visioning meeting.
- Hold a community celebration to present the vision. Give newspaper, television, and radio reporters a special invitation to this event.
- Work with the reporters to do a story on the vision statement in which local leaders are interviewed.
- Include the vision statement in community newsletters, web sites, annual reports, press kits, letterhead, and stationery.

In addition, get buy-in from the community organizations that were involved in the process. Get the decision-making boards from these organizations to formally adopt the vision statement and consider it when making all decisions that affect the community. Publicize organizations in the community that officially adopt the vision.

Above all, use the vision statement as a blueprint for further action. Your steering committee can ensure that community action teams use the statement to establish priorities and set goals. The committee can also devise a long-range strategy to provide key stakeholders (and the entire community) with progress reports on what is being done to turn the vision into reality. These reports can explain strategies to achieve the vision or even how the vision statement is modified as the community itself changes.

TOOL 6. Translating Vision into Action

This Tool at a Glance

Why Use It

A primary task for community leaders is to prevent group energy from being wasted on nonproductive tasks. That's the purpose of translating vision to action, which includes framing priorities; developing indicators of success; and setting clear, measurable, and attainable goals.

When to Use It

Before using this tool, take your community group through at least one type of assessment (see Tools 1 through 4 in this book) and through the steps described in Tool 5: Visioning (page 57).

How to Use It

Steps in using this tool are

- Revisit the vision
- List key tasks needed to achieve the vision
- Choose criteria for setting priorities
- Set priorities
- Develop indicators of success
- Explain the SMART goal concept
- Review the vision, prioritized tasks, and success indicators
- Brainstorm goals
- Use the SMART criteria to state final goals

Where to Learn More

Bryan Barry. *Strategic Planning Workbook for Nonprofit Organizations.* (St. Paul, MN: Fieldstone Alliance, 2001).

Work Group on Health Promotion and Community Development, University of Kansas. *An Overview of Strategic Planning or "VMOSA" (Vision, Mission, Objectives, Strategies, and Action Plans).* http://ctb.ku.edu/tools/en/sub_section_main_1085.htm.

An effective visioning process and a clear, compelling vision statement can generate a lot of energy and enthusiasm in the community. Use the tool described in this section to help your group focus its efforts on tasks that will best advance your vision.

Community Example: River Flats Library

The flood damaged almost every house in the River Flats Neighborhood. Most of the public facilities were in such bad shape that they could not be salvaged. As community members recovered from their shock and grief, they began to wonder what would replace that which they had lost.

As part of the recovery effort, the local residents invested a lot of time and energy in creating a vision for rebuilding their community. Two facilities generated the most excitement and interest. One was a major new complex on the river that would combine retail space, a community center, and a recreational area that would serve as an anchor for downtown. The other facility was a new library.

In spite of the initial positive reaction to both ideas, the downtown complex was not built. Today, however, the new library bustles with activity and is a source of community pride.

Why did one idea become a reality while the other did not? Unlike the supporters of the downtown complex, the librarian and a group of community leaders (officially known as Citizens for the Library) were able to target their energy and that of others in strategic ways:

- They set priorities for what needed to be done: get a library up and running on a temporary location to give people hope, then involve the community in discussing a permanent location
- They established indicators of success for each priority, such as reaching a consensus on the permanent site by using a process that involved diverse community groups
- They set specific, achievable goals for each priority, for example, *The temporary site will be operational by June 1st.*

About this tool

In the example above, Citizens for the Library used the leadership competency of framing to bridge the gap between vision and action. This involved three group processes: prioritizing tasks, developing indicators of success, and setting goals. Figure 5: Processes to Translate Vision into Action, shows the order of these processes as they relate to translating vision into action.

Figure 5. Processes to Translate Vision into Action

Prioritizing tasks, developing success indicators, and setting goals could each be seen as tools in themselves. For ease of explanation, this section takes you through all three with a single list of steps. Your group may be able to complete all these steps in one meeting.

For larger or more complex projects, however, you might choose to use this tool over several meetings—perhaps one devoted to prioritizing tasks, another for developing success indicators, and a third one for setting goals. Following is an overview of each process.

Prioritizing tasks

Achieving a vision means dealing with complexity. This is true whether the vision has a single focus, such as building a library, or involves something more comprehensive, such as becoming a "welcoming community" (see the Community Example on page 6). For most community projects, there are multiple stakeholders to consider. Various types of resources will be needed. And not everyone is going to see the vision as a good idea. While you have to start somewhere, complexity makes it impractical to start everywhere.

So where do you start? By setting priorities that give your activities focus. This is the purpose of the first steps in visioning, where you use the community's wisdom to choose the tasks that need to get accomplished. Doing this invites people to "buy in" to the vision and ensures that the pros and cons of various activities are considered.

Developing success indicators

Once your group has prioritized its list of tasks, ask, *How will we know that we've succeeded with each priority?*

One obvious answer to that question is that you got each task done. However, community life is not that simple. It's not just *what* gets done that matters, but *how* it gets done. The process used to accomplish a task might leave the community divided or deplete social capital. Ultimately, this process may make it more difficult for the community to come together on other issues in the future.

When looking at indicators of success, effective community leaders think in terms of two dimensions. One is **product**, or *what* concrete, specific things are produced—for example, funding was secured, and the library was opened. The other is **process**, or *how* those things get produced—more friends were created than foes, for instance, and most people feel that the process was fair.

When your community group examines its list of tasks, be sure that both the process used and the task accomplished *improve the health of the community.* Specifically, the group needs to name indicators of success for each priority—that the end product was indeed accomplished, and that the process used helped the community build social capital.

Setting goals

After your group has prioritized tasks and identified success indicators, your next job is to develop realistic, measurable goals.

When it comes to the leadership competency of framing, goal setting is probably the most familiar element. Many community members set goals related to their work and personal lives, leading to great variety in approaches to planning.

Since it is both intuitive and fairly well known, we suggest the concept of SMART goals as a reasonable approach for everyone to use. This acronym reminds us that effective goals are Specific, Measurable, Achievable, Resourced, and Time-bound. SMART goals give community groups the clear direction and specific results they need to produce in making their vision a reality. You'll find more about SMART goals later in this chapter.

Step 1. Revisit the vision

Ideally, the people who shape the vision of a community group are the same people who translate the vision to action. In such cases, a simple review of the vision and a reminder of the processes used to create it are all that's needed before starting to set priorities.

This is not always the case, however. If the priority-setting group includes many people who were *not* involved in earlier assessments and creation of the vision, then schedule enough time to review these processes. Emphasize the role that the community played in shaping the vision. Though now is not the time to revise the vision statement, be sure that a majority of participants buy in to it.

Step 2. List key tasks needed to achieve the vision

In this step, your group identifies the key tasks or major actions that have to occur to achieve the vision.

This process is something like putting together a complicated puzzle. You begin by finding the "chunks," or major pieces, and putting those in place as part of your plan. In the case of the vision for the new library, for example, the "chunks" included finding a site, getting city council approval, and obtaining funding. Once you've clarified such key tasks, you can fill in the rest of the planning puzzle by listing smaller-scale actions that support the major tasks.

During this step, some groups get bogged down in arguments over the details of those smaller actions. Remind the group that such details can be worked out later. This step is a "big picture" discussion that focuses on major priorities, and a chance to get a lot of ideas out for consideration.

Having this discussion with a large group can be difficult. If your group has more than ten members, consider breaking into smaller teams; then have each team report its ideas to the large group. Again, remind everyone to focus on the big chunks, not the details.

If group members do generate items that are tactical details, either record these under the heading "for future reference" or list them under the big chunk to which they relate. For example, "select a site for the new library" is a big chunk. "Find out if old mill can be renovated to library space" is a related tactical detail.

Step 3. Choose criteria for setting priorities

After creating a list of key actions, your group's next step is to organize those actions into priorities. If your community has a vision that people are excited about achieving, this step will help them identify where to productively focus their attention first.

At the beginning of this step, remind your group that there are two critical concepts in deciding which tasks should get acted on: leverage and sequence.

- **Leverage** means choosing actions that will give the greatest payoff for the energy and effort invested. In Part One of this book, the concept of leverage is illustrated by describing the use of a screwdriver to lift the lid off a paint can: You can try to pry the lid off with your fingers. Or you can place a screwdriver under the lip of the lid, apply pressure, and—with a lot less effort—lift the lid.

A similar notion applies in setting priorities. For example, completing a single task (such as gaining the support of the community group with the most financial resources) might move a project forward with a lot less effort than completing a long list of other tasks. This is leverage as applied to community projects.

- **Sequence** involves a question: *Will achieving certain tasks first make it easier to achieve other things later?* Selecting the site for a new library, for instance, makes fundraising easier. In addition, giving priority to things that are more easily accomplished can give your project the early success it needs to build momentum.

Sequence is not necessarily about logic. Sometimes the most logical way to organize tasks ignores the value of getting a quick, publicly visible success or avoiding a difficult battle at the beginning of a project. The wisdom of community groups will usually identify these important influences on sequence.

Through experience, we have developed a set of questions for discovering the important leverage points and sequence. These are listed in Worksheet 8: Rate Tasks (page 73). Hand this worksheet out to every member of your group. Discuss the criteria that are listed and make sure that everyone understands them.

Next, discuss and decide on any other criteria the group wants to add. Assign each of these a letter and add them to the worksheet. Note that the group may also choose to remove criteria from the existing list. In our experience, however, these questions usually do pinpoint the key points of leverage and sequence.

After everyone understands and agrees on the final list criteria, ask the group members to take the tasks from Step 2 and list them in the "Task" column on Worksheet 8. Then let everyone work individually to fill out the rest of the worksheet. Finally, bring everyone back into the main group and move on to step 4.

WORKSHEET 8 Rate Tasks

List the tasks to be prioritized in the first column. For each item, check the box under the letters of the criteria you think the item best meets.

	Criteria									
Task	**A**	**B**	**C**	**D**	**E**	**F**	**G**	**H**	**I**	**J**
Example: Finding a site	*X*	*X*		*X*	*X*					

Criteria

A. For which items is there currently a sense of urgency—a feeling that this issue or opportunity needs to be acted on soon?

B. Which items have already generated interest and enthusiasm in this group or community?

C. Which items are already being addressed by someone?

D. If you could achieve or make significant progress on certain items, would this make it easier or more likely for you to accomplish others?

E. Which items could be achieved with the resources this group already has?

F. Which items could be achieved with resources beyond this group that could be easily accessed?

G. Which of these items makes best use of the community's strengths and assets?

H. Additional criterion set by the group:

I. Additional criterion set by the group:

J. Additional criterion set by the group:

Step 4. Set priorities

Your group should now discuss the actions listed in the "Task" column of Worksheet 8 and note which criteria each task meets. Groups often find it most productive to take one task at a time, discussing *which* criteria it meets and *why* it meets those criteria.

If your group has more than ten members, break up into smaller teams for this step. Meet in different teams than you formed in Step 2.

When discussing Worksheet 8, participants may have a tendency to simply count up the number of boxes that get checked for each item, and then assume that the items with the most checks are the highest priority. If this occurs, remind the group that it is not just the number of boxes with checks that determine the priority. Equally important is *why* each item meets the criteria. Through this discussion, the most important order of tasks should begin to appear.

After group members finish talking about their responses, ask each person to number the items on the task list in their preferred order of priority. You may find it helpful to have them rank in order their top three priorities.

Finally, help the group reach a final consensus on the top priorities. There are various ways to do this. One is to write the list of tasks on a flip chart and then give everyone three stickers to place on this chart as they wish: three stickers on one task, or two stickers on one task and one on another, or one sticker on each of three tasks. When everyone has posted their stickers, you'll get a sense of the group's read on the most important tasks.

Though in most cases the priorities will need some further discussion and reorganization, this method will quickly move the group toward consensus around the overall ordering of tasks. If there are ties, then ask the group to decide if these items should be addressed at the same time, or if more discussion is needed to break the tie.

Step 5. Develop indicators of success

In this step, group members apply the concepts of product and process to the prioritized items. Review the meaning of product and process as defined earlier in this chapter under About this tool (page 70). Make sure that the group has a clear understanding of what the terms mean and why they are important. It may help to take some hypothetical tasks unrelated to your current project and discuss indicators of success for them. For examples of such tasks, refer to the Community Example at the beginning of this tool or others throughout the book.

Your goal for this step is to list indicators of success for each of your prioritized tasks. Develop indicators for both product and process that are realistic and have the group's support. Make copies of Worksheet 9: Indicators of Success (page 76), and give one to each group member to fill out during this discussion.

Your group may find that its list of indicators becomes quite specific. Up to a certain point, this can help you set goals later. If the group gets bogged down over details, however, remind participants to stay at a more general level.

As before, you may want to divide groups of over ten people into smaller teams for discussion. If you have a long list of priority tasks, assign only a few priority items to each team. Then have the teams report their list of indicators to the larger group. Allow enough time so that people can explain their choice of indicators and their reasons for each choice.

If there is a serious disagreement over an indicator, help the group find the source of the disagreement and choose how to deal with it. The basic options are summarized in the following statements:

- We can't go forward right now because of this disagreement.
- We can go forward, but only on those items on which we have agreement.
- We need more information to resolve this disagreement.
- We will issue a report that lists the minority's choice of indicators.

Once the group has agreed on indicators of success, take a blank copy of Worksheet 9 and create a master sheet as a record. Use this list of success indicators throughout your project to ensure that the group is accomplishing goals *and* building social capital.

Step 6. Explain the SMART goal concept

This step can help you produce goals that are realistic and measurable. A SMART goal is:

S Specific: focused on one priority item and a particular aspect of that priority

M Measurable: with indicators that tell you when the goal has been accomplished, including conditions that you can observe or quantify

A Achievable: stated in a way that allows a reasonable chance of success, focused on things that the group can reasonably expect to influence while "stretching" a group to greater efforts.

R Resourced: that is, the means to achieve the goal are identified and accessible

T Time-bound: stated with a clear deadline for achieving the goal that provides enough time to get the job done, but not so much time that people lose interest and motivation

Explain the SMART concept to your group and use it as checklist to assess the goals that you write.

WORKSHEET 9 Indicators of Success

For each priority item, list what you would look for as indicators that your efforts are successful in terms of product (what is produced) and process (how it is produced).

Priority	Product	Process
Example: Finding a site for the new library	*Site is (a) accessible with (b) ample space for parking*	*(a) Site location is decided in six months; (b) there is increased public support for the library*

Citizens for the Library, for example, selected this as one of its goals: *To secure a site for the new library that is at least an acre in size at a cost not to exceed $50,000 by June 15, 2008.*

This is definitely a SMART goal—specific, measurable, achievable, resourced, and time-bound. The goal addresses one of the priorities for Citizens for the Library and specifically states that the group will not just locate a site but also secure it. In this goal, both size and cost are measured. Because securing a site is a local decision, it is an achievable goal for a local group like the Citizens for the Library. Furthermore, the key resources needed for securing the site—information, public support, initial funding—are primarily local and accessible. And finally, the deadline is clearly stated, making the goal time-bound.

Step 7. Review the vision, prioritized tasks, and success indicators

If your group is completing all of the other steps in this tool during one meeting, you can skip this one. But if you use this tool across several meetings, be sure at this point to remind the group of its vision statement, prioritized tasks, and indicators of success. Recap the process you used to create these, making sure that everyone is clear about the agreements you reached and truly buys in to them. Do these things *before* you go on to the next two steps, which translate your vision, priorities, and indicators into goals.

Step 8. Brainstorm goals

By now, your group will be fairly effective at generating ideas. Meeting either as a large group or as smaller teams that report to the group, generate a list of goals related to *each* priority task. List these goals on a flip chart or erasable board that's visible to everyone in the group. Or, if the time and equipment are available, take a break to key the goals into a computer file, print them out, and distribute them to every member. If you develop too many goals to accomplish, take a moment to combine goals or eliminate some.

Step 9. Use the SMART criteria to state final goals

Now ask each member of your group, working individually, to use Worksheet 10: SMART Goals Checklist (page 78) to evaluate each of the goals you brainstormed. You may copy this worksheet and distribute it, or enlarge and project it on a screen for the group to see.

Next, convene again as a group. Reframe each goal so that it meets the SMART standards. If the goals are complex or your group is large, consider assigning this task to an individual or smaller group to complete outside the meeting. Then schedule another meeting to discuss and approve your final list of goals.

WORKSHEET 10 SMART Goals Checklist

Put your goal in writing. Then use the following checklist to determine how well your goal is stated.

Goal Statement:

- ☐ **Specific**

  This goal is focused and clearly relates to a priority task.

- ☐ **Measurable**

  The outcome of the goal is stated as conditions that we can observe or quantify.

- ☐ **Achievable**

  The goal is based on factors that we can influence.

- ☐ **Resourced**

  This group has or can access the resources needed to accomplish this goal.

- ☐ **Time-bound**

  The deadline for completing this goal allows enough time to get the job done but not so much time that those involved lose interest and motivation.

PART THREE

Tools for Building and Using Social Capital

Leadership that develops and sustains a healthy community is based on three core competencies: framing ideas, building social capital, and mobilizing resources. Each of these competencies is needed for getting things done *and* for getting them done in a constructive way. It's only when the competencies are combined that the community becomes healthier.

Part Two of this book presents a set of tools to help you frame ideas. In Part Three, you'll find tools for building social capital. This core competency involves developing and maintaining relationships that allow people to work together and share resources as they address community opportunities and issues. Having social capital means we can call on and depend on each other to get things done. Relationships that yield social capital are marked by

- Trust: belief in and reliance on the honesty, integrity, and reliability of the other party
- Reciprocity: a mutual, fair benefit from the relationship over time
- Durability: lasting over time through stress and changing circumstances

Social capital comes in two forms: *bonding social capital,* which is formed in closely knit groups and between friends; and *bridging social capital,* which is formed between diverse groups and acquaintances.

Part Three includes the following tools:

7. **Building Social Capital Through Effective Communication** provides a model of speaking and listening that increases shared meaning and builds trust

8. **Managing Interpersonal Conflict** lays out a format to help you understand sources of conflict and consciously choose your responses in these situations
9. **Building Social Capital Across Cultures** offers practical guidelines for building social capital in situations where cultural differences make trust, reciprocity, and durability more difficult to establish
10. **Mapping Your Social Capital** gives you a tool to assess your group's social capital and discover the resources that your social capital makes available

As you read this section, you will find references to tools and techniques located in other parts of the book. Following up on these references will help you combine the core competencies to achieve the results that you desire.

TOOL 7. Building Social Capital through Effective Communication

This Tool at a Glance

Why Use It
Effective communication is essential to each of the three core competencies for community leadership. This tool appears in the context of building and using social capital because of the special role that interpersonal communication plays in this competency.

When to Use It
Apply the suggestions in this tool to all your work as a community leader. Set aside a few hours specifically to study the model of communication that follows and to go through the tool's three major steps. Note that you can use the exercises in this tool to diagnose a current problem in your speaking with or listening to a specific person.

How to Use It
Steps in using this tool are

- Identify ways to create shared meaning
- Evaluate your communication skills
- Plan to develop your communication skills

Where to Learn More
Beth Gilbertsen and Vijit Ramchandani. *The Fieldstone Nonprofit Guide To Developing Effective Teams* (St. Paul, MN: Fieldstone Alliance, 1999).

Simply put, social capital requires trust. And trust requires communication. If you can't communicate successfully with others, then you won't work successfully with them. This tool provides a model of communication you can use in all your work as a community leader.

Community Example: A Dynamic Duo

The awards banquet had just concluded. Bill, the director of the local food shelf, and Adriana, the chair of the food shelf's board of directors, were all smiles. The governor had just recognized their program as one of the most innovative in the state. In his remarks, the governor had made a point of saying that the success of the program was due in large part to how well Adriana and Bill worked together.

What the governor did not point out, however, was that it had not always been that way.

Adriana, who was well known in the community for her work on multicultural issues and her role as director of the Family Violence Survivors Center, had been on the food shelf board for only two years when she was elected chair. At that time, Bill was in his eighth year as director, a job he took shortly after he retired from the Army where he held the rank of master sergeant.

Experience had taught both Bill and Adriana that if they were to fulfill their roles, they would have to be in regular contact with each other about the food shelf. Unfortunately, it seemed that the more they tried to communicate, the more difficult things became and the less they trusted each other.

Adriana would make a comment such as, "We need to be more accountable to the entire community." Bill would reply, "We already account for everything we take in and how it was used." Or Bill would say, "We need more volunteers who can follow procedures." Adriana would respond, "No, we should be empowering volunteers and helping them develop a sense of ownership in this program."

The breakthrough in their ability to work together came when both were selected to attend a retreat about leadership. As they engaged in the retreat's activities, they discovered that, in spite of their different backgrounds, they both cared deeply about the food shelf and the people it served.

They also discovered that, because of their different backgrounds, words often meant different things to them. For example, when Adriana talked about "being accountable to the entire community," she meant that they should do a better job of reaching out to underserved populations. What "being accountable" meant to Bill was using good accounting and inventory control procedures.

As they made these discoveries, something became painfully clear: While they had been talking to each other a great deal, they had created very little shared meaning between them. Their relationship and the work of the food shelf were suffering as a consequence.

By the end of the retreat, Bill and Adriana had developed a plan to use a checklist for creating shared meaning. Little did they know at that time that their plan would result in the governor referring to them as the "dynamic duo."

About this tool

Communication in this tool is defined as the creation of shared meaning. And communication, as Bill and Adriana found out, is not just a matter of sending and receiving messages. Instead, communication creates a common *understanding* of those messages.

So what constitutes shared meaning? It happens when the "picture in my head is the same as the picture in your head"—and when we each know how the other feels about that picture.

The communication continuum

The creation of shared meaning almost always requires interaction and is a matter of degree. Communication occurs on a continuum, or range, from no shared meaning to maximum shared meaning. Figure 6: Degrees of Shared Meaning, illustrates this continuum.

Figure 6. Degrees of Shared Meaning

No Shared Meaning	The experience of no shared meaning is like speaking different languages. Speakers can't understand each other.
Minimal Shared Meaning	With minimal shared meaning, speakers get a glimpse of the "pictures in each other's heads." For example, you understand that I want something to change in the way that we run the food shelf, but you don't know what I want changed.
Partial Shared Meaning	With partial shared meaning, the pictures in the speakers' heads are taking shape for each other, although the details have not been filled in. For example, you know *what* I want changed, but you don't know *why* I want it changed.
Maximum Shared Meaning	The pictures are complete and shared. Speakers can "see" the other's picture and also understand how they feel about or value that picture. For example, you know *what* I want changed in the way the food shelf operates, *how* I think it should be changed, and *why* I think it should be changed.

Complete shared meaning is not always possible—and not always necessary. For example, you may never totally understand the depth of my reaction to the way things were being done at the food shelf, and you may not need to. All you need is enough understanding to realize *what* I want and *why* it is important to me.

There is a danger of assuming greater shared meaning than really exists, especially in long-term relationships. At the retreat with Bill and Adriana were two members of the city council who had grown up as neighbors and had been on the council together for ten years. When discussing the concept of shared meaning, one council member pointed to the other and said, "Oh, we know each other so well I finish her sentences for her!" To which the other member replied, "Yes, and you always get it wrong!"

An effective communicator is not necessarily someone who sends the most messages. It's someone whose messages are "heard" the way they were intended. An effective communicator is anyone who succeeds at creating shared meaning.

Three common challenges to creating shared meaning

There are many barriers to creating shared meaning. For example, technical language, or jargon, can get in the way. Opportunities for interaction may be limited. Distractions can disrupt the process.

In community work, three challenges to creating shared meaning are common and deserve special attention:

- **We assume that sending messages equals sharing meaning.** Many times we think we've created shared meaning by sending someone a written message, leaving a voice message, or speaking directly to them. Later on it becomes obvious that there was little or no shared meaning. In response, we say: "But I sent you a memo." "Didn't you get my voice message?" I told you at the end of the last meeting!" Effective communicators do not automatically assume that shared meaning exists. They check with the other person to see what meaning the message has for them.
- **We forget that meanings are held in people, not in words.** This is not to say that you can throw your dictionary away. But it does serve as a reminder that words can mean different things to different people. For example, the word *accountability* meant different things to Bill than it did to Adriana. Common words such as *leader, community, alcohol, babe, boy, girl,* or *citizen* can have a range of meanings to the people in your community.
- **Communication is not about the speaker's intended message—it is about what the listener perceives.** It is not what the speaker says that gives meaning to the speaker's words, it's what the listener hears. For example, Bill may ask, "Why do we have this procedure at the food shelf?" because he wants to do it correctly. But in these words, Adriana may perceive disapproval of the procedure, and she could feel hurt.

An interactive model of communication

Use the model of communication on page 84 to be more aware of how people arrive at meaning, and to be more intentional about that process. This model is based on two assumptions:

- The first step in creating shared meaning is to recognize that everyone comes to a conversation with tendencies to assign certain meanings to messages—and those tendencies are not necessarily the same for everyone.
- The process of creating shared meaning requires people to rapidly switch back and forth between the role of speaker and listener.

Figure 7: Interpersonal Communication, presents the model in detail.

Figure 7. Interpersonal Communication

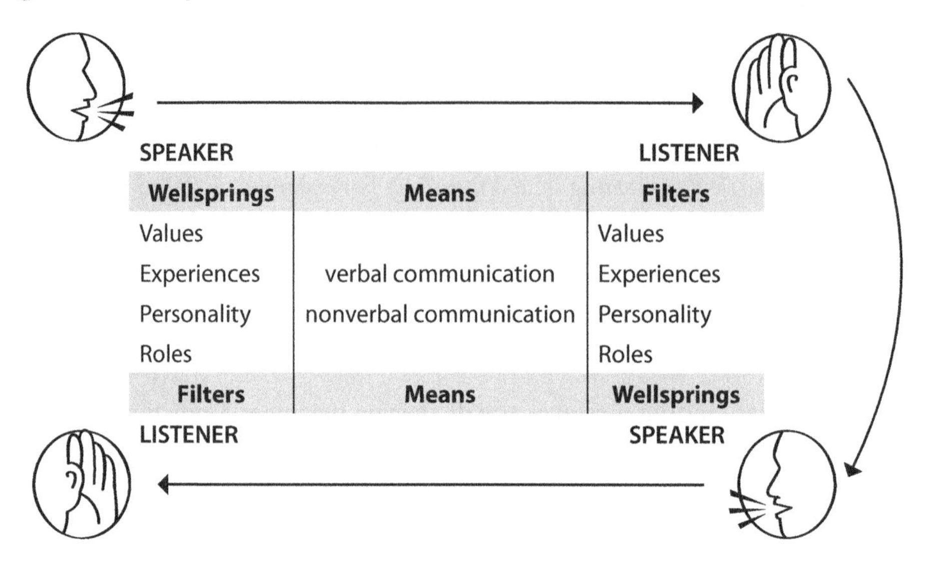

Key terms

Means The form of communication—verbal (words) or nonverbal (body language, gestures, tone of voice).

Wellsprings The tendencies that guide us as we create meaning in the messages that we send. Our wellsprings lead us to *encode* our messages in certain ways as we speak or write.

Filters The tendencies that guide us as we assign meaning to the messages we receive. Our filters lead us to *decode* messages in certain ways as we observe, listen, or read.

Values The deeply held beliefs we have about the way things should be, about what is right and what is wrong.

Experiences Our past, which comes to us through our family, gender, ethnic background, work, travel, and education. In this figure, the term *experiences* refers to the ways that our personal history gives meaning to what we say and hear.

Personality Our psychological makeup, especially as it relates to creating meaning. For example, some of us create meaning through details. We provide a great deal of detail in our messages and expect the same in messages from others. On the other hand, some of us find meaning in general patterns and create our messages accordingly.

Roles The social "hats" that we wear in different circumstances—for example, boss, mayor, teacher, parent, or concerned citizen. People may hear messages about education differently depending on whether they are listening in their role as a parent, as a taxpayer, as a teacher, or as a school board member.

In real time, the model unfolds like this. Adriana creates a message by saying something to Bill, the food shelf director: "Let's make sure that whenever the food shelf is open, somebody will be there who speaks Spanish. That way, we can be more helpful to our newer families who may not be bilingual." Her message came out of her *wellsprings,* which are listed in Figure 8: Bill and Adriana's Interpersonal Communication. Bill, in turn, receives the message and passes it through his *filters,* which are also described in the figure.

Figure 8. Bill and Adriana's Interpersonal Communication

Adriana → Bill

SPEAKER | LISTENER

Wellsprings	Means	Filters
Values: *Adriana highly values inclusiveness in community service.*		Values: *Bill also values inclusiveness.*
Experiences: *In the Peace Corps, she learned what it felt like to be excluded because she could not speak a language fluently.*	verbal communication	Experiences: *He has tried to make sure that there is always a Spanish speaker on-site, but the food shelf is staffed by volunteers and there are times when Spanish-speaking volunteers are not available.*
Personality: *Adriana thinks in big picture terms and does not often focus on the details.*	nonverbal communication	Personality: *Bill needs a lot of detail.*
Roles: *Adriana is the executive director of an agency and chair of this board. She is used to speaking with authority and expects her recommendations to be "heard" as board chair.*		Roles: *After a career as a master sergeant, Bill is used to being in charge. In his role as the director of the food shelf, he feels personally responsible for its strengths and limitations.*
Filters	**Means**	**Wellsprings**

LISTENER | SPEAKER

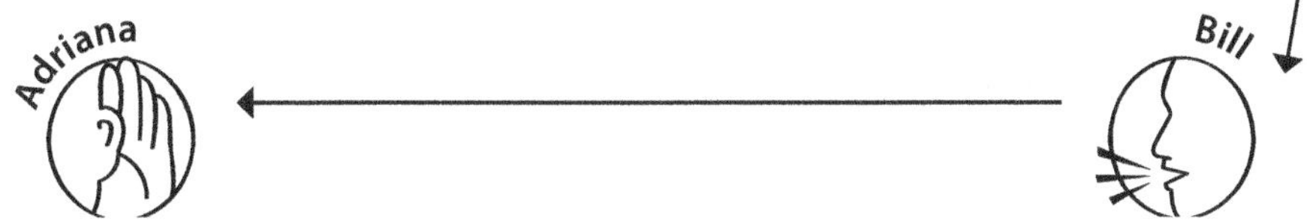

Adriana ← Bill

Having passed Adriana's message through his filters, Bill can switch from being the receiver to being the sender. He could say, "I think that having a Spanish-speaking person on site is a good idea, and I agree with it. But I have tried to do that in the past and, in spite of everybody's best efforts, I was not very successful. If you have some specific suggestions about how to get this task accomplished based on your experience, I'll take them into consideration." Adriana could pass Bill's message through her filters and respond directly to his request, adding further clarity. Ideally, the process would continue until they reach maximum shared meaning.

As a result, Bill and Adriana increase their shared meaning by adapting to each other's wellsprings and filters. They recognize that effective interpersonal communication is a bit like a dance—a step-by-step process in which two partners continually adjust to each other.

Given the nature of this dance, what are some of the basic steps that make you a good partner and help to build social capital? Two things are needed: speaking skills and listening skills. Use the steps presented later in this tool to become more effective at both.

Speak to create shared meaning

Success at creating shared meaning means being intentional about the ways that you frame your messages. Take into account your own wellsprings and filters as well as those of your listener. Get feedback on how your message is received and adjust accordingly. Use the following suggestions as a checklist for what to remember.

Understanding your filters, experiences, personality, and roles

It is not easy to gain insight into how you speak and listen. Asking the following questions can help you take the model of communication in this tool and apply to your own experience.

Regarding values*:* What are some of your values and how do they affect the way you speak about or listen to statements about certain topics?

Regarding experiences*:* What key life experiences shaped the way you listen and the way you speak? Are there negative or positive experiences you try to avoid or re-create when communicating?

Regarding personality*:* What are some aspects of your personality that affect the way you create meaning? Do you see the world in black and white or shades of gray? Are you more task-oriented (concerned about getting things done) or people-oriented (concerned about what others think and feel)? Do you like to think out loud when trying to create shared meaning, or do you need some time to think things through before you speak?

Regarding roles*:* What roles are you used to playing? What "hats" are you wearing when you try to create shared meaning? What impact do those roles have on the ways you send your messages and receive messages from others?

Be specific

- Be concrete: find words that give the most precise description.
- Be complete: answer key questions that people might ask about your message, such as Who? What? Why? Where? When?
- Be concise: avoid distracting clutter and tangents. Stick to the point. Do not litter your message with repetitive words such as "you know," "well," "OK?" and "uhhh."

Take responsibility

- Be clear about what *you* think or feel by saying, "I think" or "I believe." Beware of expressing your concerns with statements such as "You have a problem" or "This group has a problem." Statements like these are usually heard as judgmental, accusatory, or demanding. "I" invites dialogue; "you" invites rebuttal.
- Unless people ask you to speak for them, avoid phrases such as "We all know . . ." If you have a concern, say something like: "I don't know about anybody else, but I think there is a problem with . . ."

Be adaptable

- Be aware of words that may have several meanings in a given situation. For instance, you might say, "We will all have to sacrifice something for this issue," referring to a task that will use up time and energy. Some of your listeners could be offended by this comment, however, because for them, sacrifice means backing away from strongly held values. Remember that meaning is in people, not in words, and adapt your messages to the perception of your listeners.
- Acknowledge your wellsprings and filters. Which habits in the way you send and receive messages will be activated in different situations? How will your messages change as a result? If your wellsprings and filters are having a major impact, say so. For example: "As business owner, I . . ." "Having gone through this myself, I . . ." "This is really important to me because one of my core values is . . ."
- Adjust for the receiver's possible wellsprings and filters based on gender, age, occupation, and cultural background.

Check for accuracy

- Ask for feedback about how your message was heard. Ask questions such as, "What did you understand me to say?" "Does this make sense to you?" "Is there anything that is not clear to you?"
- If feedback shows that your message was not heard, keep reframing it until you are sure it's understood.
- Remember, the biggest danger in communication is assuming that it has taken place—that shared meaning has already been created.

Listening for understanding

Community leaders often try to create shared meaning in situations where there is disagreement and argument. In these situations, the task of creating shared meaning becomes more difficult.

This happens, in part, because those involved have a tendency to listen for *agreement* rather than for *understanding*. That is, we are prone to listen only for things that we agree (or disagree) with. We become cautious about how active we seem to be listening, because we do not want it to be taken as a sign that we agree with everything a speaker says. However, listening for agreement rather than understanding increases the likelihood of conflict, diminishes shared meaning, and leads to the loss of social capital.

To listen for understanding

- Check the other person's meanings before determining agreement or disagreement. Many potential conflicts will never develop as you discover that your differences lie in your use of language, rather than in your values or opinions.
- Remember that you can listen to ideas and feelings that you don't agree with. *The act of listening is not the same as the act of agreement.* Listening demands an open mind, not agreement. When you hear someone out, even though you disagree, it creates greater shared meaning as you come to understand what shaped that person's point of view.
- Understanding (shared meaning) does not ensure harmony. You may understand someone else's position and why they think or feel that way, and still disagree. But now you disagree based on a real understanding, rather than a lack of understanding or lack of shared meaning.
- The heart of listening for understanding is to listen to learn, not to judge the speaker or to force people to adopt the same viewpoints.
- The skills of paying attention, motivating the speaker, and clarifying messages are especially important in listening for understanding.

Listen to create shared meaning

Listening plays a powerful role in creating shared meaning. And as noted earlier, what gives meaning to a message is the listener's perceptions—not the speaker's intentions. The listener must be able to "read" or "decode" the speaker's message accurately. An active listener can be a skilled dance partner for the speaker, actively creating clarity in the speaker's message. Following is a checklist for effective listening.

Be attentive

- Concentrate on the speaker. Stay focused on what people say and how they say it.
- Demonstrate interest nonverbally. Make eye contact in ways that are culturally appropriate. Lean forward and focus on the speaker. Do not check your watch, sort your mail, or look for something in your pockets while you listen.

Motivate the speaker

- Ask open-ended or clarifying questions. Avoid questions that can be answered yes or no. Ask questions such as, "What do you think?" "What are your feelings?" "Could you give me more detail?" "Could you describe for me . . . ?"
- Avoid interruptions. Wait your turn to respond to the speaker, and respect the other person's right to speak. Do not insert your story in the middle of someone else's. If you feel an overwhelming urge to interrupt, count to ten before you speak.

Provide clarification

- Paraphrase. Describe what you heard without evaluating or interpreting the message.
- Summarize: "So the key points that I heard you make are . . ."

Step 1. Identify ways to create shared meaning

Use Worksheet 11: Checklist for Creating Shared Meaning (page 91), especially if you are having difficulty in achieving shared meaning with someone. The worksheet gives you a template to state your own wellsprings and filters and to discover those of the other person. It also offers a format for planning how to use your speaking and listening skills.

Step 2. Evaluate your communication skills

Worksheet 12: Evaluate Your Communication Skills (page 93) will help you determine how effectively you are speaking and listening. It also suggests basic steps for planning to improve your communication skills.

Step 3. Plan to develop your communication skills

After you have ranked yourself on all of the skills mentioned in Worksheet 12, identify those on which you scored two or less. Did the particular situation you were in place limits on your use of that skill? Or do you struggle with this skill at other times?

Choose the skills you want to work on and create a plan for developing each skill. Answer the following questions.

- **Why is developing this skill important to you?** For example: I want to improve my ability to be concrete and specific. My lack of detail confuses the other committee members. I can't get my point across and I'm really frustrated.

- **How will you develop the skill?** For example: I will write the important details down before I go to the meetings. I will ask for feedback on how I am doing from the committee chair.
- **What indicators will tell you that you are getting better at this skill?** For example: I'll know I've improved when I spend less time backtracking, trying to provide details I've missed and that people have had to ask me about.

You may also want to create a development plan for skills on which you scored three or four, if improving those skills is critical for you. As part of your plan, find a way to create a video recording of yourself in a one-to-one conversation or a small group setting. This recording will give you powerful feedback on your speaking and listening skills.

The greater your ability to understand and use the skills described in this chapter, the better your ability to communicate with other community members—and to build the social capital that is essential for your role. Keep reminding yourself of the following key points:

- Communication is an interactive process in which the people constantly move back and forth between the role of speaker and the role of listener
- The speaker's job in this process is to adjust for the listener's wellsprings and filters and to check for accuracy
- The listener's job is to adjust for the speaker's wellsprings and filters and to actively listen for understanding
- The basic building block of good communication is the assumption that every person is unique and of value

WORKSHEET 11 Checklist for Creating Shared Meaning

Use this worksheet to prepare to engage with someone in creating shared meaning about an issue, idea, or situation. You can also use this worksheet to diagnose a difficulty in achieving shared meaning.

1. **Identify the wellsprings and filters**
   In this situation,
   Which of *your* wellsprings and filters will come into play? Name them below.
   - Values
   - Experiences
   - Personality
   - Roles

   Describe how these wellsprings and filters might affect how you *formulate and send messages.*

   Describe how they might affect how you will hear the other person's messages.

   Which of the *other person's* wellsprings and filters are likely to come into play? Name them below.
   - Values
   - Experiences
   - Personality
   - Roles

   Describe how these wellsprings and filters might affect how the other person will formulate and send messages.

   Describe how these wellsprings and filters might affect how the other person will hear your messages.

2. **Check your speaking skills**
   Be specific.
   What are some words that you can use to give a precise description of what you are talking about?

   What are some examples you can give to help the other person understand?

   What detail do you need to include about who, why, where, how, and when?

Worksheet 11 continued

What can you omit?

What "I" statements will you use to describe how you think or feel, or to name things you are concerned about?

Be adaptable.
Given what you know about your wellsprings and filters and those of the other person, what are some words that might have a different meaning for your communication partner than they do for you?

How will you acknowledge your wellsprings and filters and how they affect you in this situation?

How will you recognize and adjust for the other person's wellsprings and filters?

Check for accuracy.
How will you ask for feedback about how your messages are heard?

3. **Check your listening skills**
Be attentive.
What could get in the way of your concentrating on the speaker and the speaker's message?

How will you deal with this?

Motivate the speaker.
What kinds of open-ended questions will be most helpful for the other person as he or she tries to make a point?

When are you most likely to interrupt the other person? Why?

How will you handle your urge to interrupt?

Provide clarification.
When you listen, what will tell you that it is an appropriate time to paraphrase or summarize what the other person has said?

WORKSHEET 12 Evaluate Your Communication Skills

This worksheet will be most helpful to you if you focus on a specific communication situation or episode. With that situation in mind, use the five-point scale to rate how effective you were in using each skill. (5 = very effective; 1= not at all effective). In the appropriate spaces, write down why you rated yourself the way you did for that skill.

Before beginning, take a moment to imagine a specific episode. Give it a name here to help you remember it:

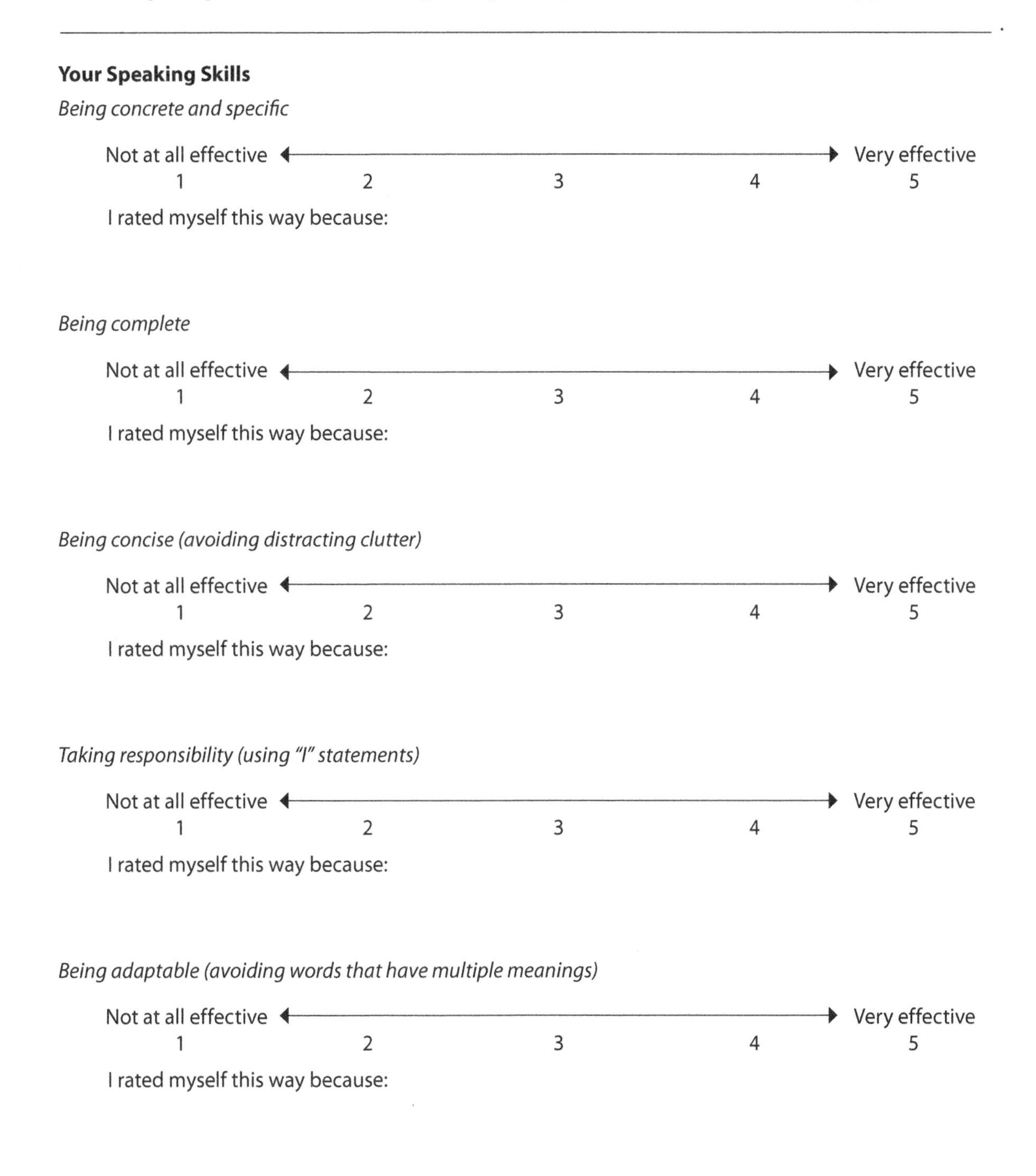

____ .

Your Speaking Skills

Being concrete and specific

Not at all effective ◄——————► Very effective
1 2 3 4 5

I rated myself this way because:

Being complete

Not at all effective ◄——————► Very effective
1 2 3 4 5

I rated myself this way because:

Being concise (avoiding distracting clutter)

Not at all effective ◄——————► Very effective
1 2 3 4 5

I rated myself this way because:

Taking responsibility (using "I" statements)

Not at all effective ◄——————► Very effective
1 2 3 4 5

I rated myself this way because:

Being adaptable (avoiding words that have multiple meanings)

Not at all effective ◄——————► Very effective
1 2 3 4 5

I rated myself this way because:

Worksheet 12 continued

Recognizing and acknowledging your own wellsprings and filters

Not at all effective ◄——► Very effective
1 2 3 4 5

I rated myself this way because:

Adjusting for the other person's wellsprings and filters

Not at all effective ◄——► Very effective
1 2 3 4 5

I rated myself this way because:

Asking for feedback about how my message was heard

Not at all effective ◄——► Very effective
1 2 3 4 5

I rated myself this way because:

Your Listening Skills

Concentrating on the speaker

Not at all effective ◄——► Very effective
1 2 3 4 5

I rated myself this way because:

Demonstrating interest nonverbally

Not at all effective ◄——► Very effective
1 2 3 4 5

I rated myself this way because:

Worksheet 12 continued

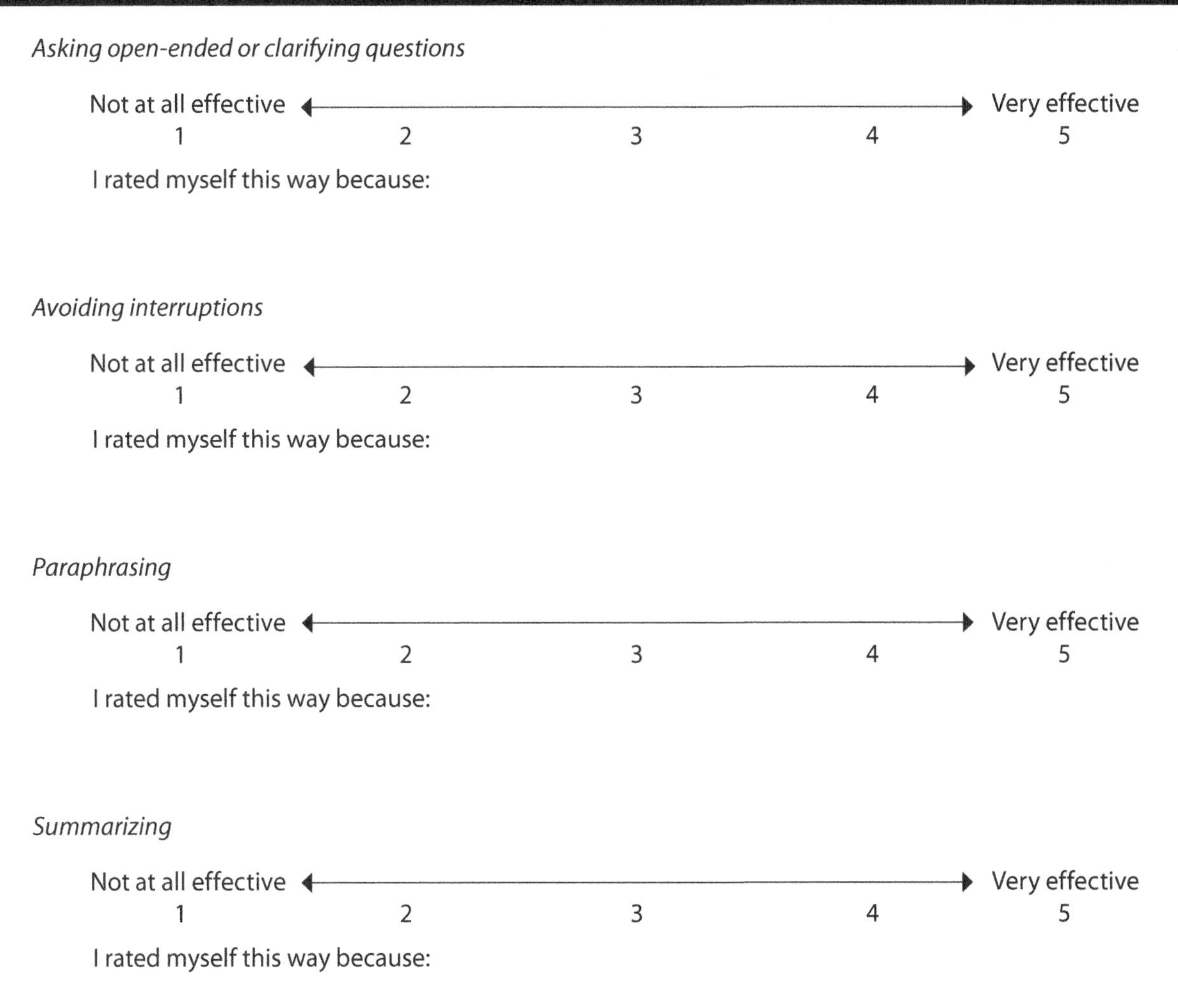

Asking open-ended or clarifying questions

Not at all effective ←→ Very effective
1 2 3 4 5

I rated myself this way because:

Avoiding interruptions

Not at all effective ←→ Very effective
1 2 3 4 5

I rated myself this way because:

Paraphrasing

Not at all effective ←→ Very effective
1 2 3 4 5

I rated myself this way because:

Summarizing

Not at all effective ←→ Very effective
1 2 3 4 5

I rated myself this way because:

TOOL 8. Managing Interpersonal Conflict

This Tool at a Glance

Why Use It
Use this tool to understand, manage, and prevent the kinds of personal conflict that drain community groups of energy and decrease their social capital.

When to Use It
Apply the suggestions in this tool to all your work as a community leader. Set aside a few hours specifically to study the model of conflict management that follows. Note that you can use this tool to diagnose a current conflict in your work as a community leader and then consciously choose your responses.

How to Use It
Steps in using this tool are

- Reflect on your skills in managing conflict
- Plan to gain skills in managing conflict

Where to Learn More
Marion Peters Angelica. *Resolving Conflict in Nonprofit Organizations: The Leader's Guide to Finding Constructive Solutions* (St. Paul, MN: Fieldstone Alliance, 1999).

Developing and sustaining a healthy community is about change—initiating it, managing it, guiding it, or resisting it. And dealing with change means dealing with conflict. This tool will help you select strategies to manage conflict in ways that are less likely to deplete your social capital.

Community Example: Shouting Match

No one could remember a planning and zoning commission meeting quite like it. The session just seemed to disintegrate as the conflict between two of the commission members, Shante and Paul, raged out of control. In fact, the conflict carried over after the meeting to a shouting match between the two in the hallway, which was witnessed by the mayor and the editor of the newspaper, among others.

It all started two meetings before, when the commission considered a request to rezone an area on the edge of town to accommodate a proposed hazardous waste disposal and recycling plant. The facility would primarily serve industries located in a city about eighty miles away. When the plant became fully operational, it would add fifty jobs to the local community's sagging economy.

Shante had long been associated with groups concerned about protecting the local environment. At the earlier meeting, she raised questions about the potential risks of bringing hazardous materials into town. Paul was new to the commission and had just completed a term as the chair of the local economic development corporation. He spoke at length about the boost the new facility would give to the local economy.

The commission ended this meeting by voting to postpone making a decision about the plant. Commission members felt that they needed more information about how the plant would affect local traffic patterns. They also wanted to find out if the site met state standards for soil conditions and drainage.

At the next meeting, the commission learned that the site would meet the standards. Also, while traffic would be increased near the plant, it would not be disruptive. Paul presented detailed information about the economic impact of the fifty new jobs, and said that the facility owners had pledged to "buy locally" as much as possible. He closed his presentation by looking directly at Shante and saying, "This plant is good for the community, and the role of this commission is to support community progress, not block it."

Shante responded by giving a detailed analysis of the toxic nature of the materials that would come to the facility. She also pointed out that trucks hauling the material would pass directly in front of an elementary school, and that in the last two years there had been three major accidents at the intersection by the school. She concluded her remarks by looking across the table at Paul and declaring, "I agree that our job is to help promote progress in our community. I do not consider endangering the environment and putting grade school children at risk to be progress!"

The chairperson tabled the discussion until the next meeting when representatives from the state environmental agency and the firm proposing the new facility would be present. After the meeting, the chairperson called both Shante and Paul and asked that they get in touch with each other before the next meeting to "clear the air."

Shante and Paul declined to act on that suggestion. Instead, they each used the time between meetings to lobby other commission members. Unfortunately, these lobbying efforts were not focused on clarifying the issue but on undermining each other's credibility and integrity.

By the third meeting, the conflict had become very personal for both Paul and Shante. In spite of the presence of both state officials and company representatives, the meeting was so rancorous that the company withdrew its request.

Epilogue: A year later the plant was built in a community thirty miles away. Given the location of the facility, however, the materials are still transported through this community via a route that passes within a half-mile of the elementary school. Many community residents blame both Paul and Shante for a situation that brings no economic benefit and exposes the community to environmental risks that it cannot control. Shante and Paul do not speak to each other outside of commission meetings.

About this tool

The conflict described in the example above was legitimate and not unusual. Unfortunately for their community, Paul and Shante seemed to be locked into a competition that ruled out other options. Yet they could have managed the conflict in ways that produced different results.

This tool is intended to help you avoid some of the pitfalls that trapped Paul and Shante. Use all of the suggestions that follow, or incorporate some of them into your current approach to managing conflict.

The basic model presented in this tool is an equation. It says that effective conflict management flows from three factors: recognizing that the conflict exists, setting criteria for effective management, and choosing a strategy that matches the situation:

recognition + criteria + strategies = effective conflict management

This model is based on several key assumptions:

- **Conflicts are a normal part of life.** It is not the presence or absence of conflict that determines the health of a community or relationship. What matters is how the conflict is managed.
- **Not all conflicts can be resolved, but most can be successfully managed**. Conflicts based on differences over deeply held beliefs are not likely to disappear. People may experience value conflicts and never reach agreement on a specific issue. However, even these conflicts can be managed in ways that allow people to work together on other issues on which they *do* agree.
- **You are part of the equation**. Interpersonal conflict requires at least two people. You are one of them, and the approach to conflict management explained in this tool starts with you. Though you may try to influence the behavior of other people, remember that the only person you can really control is yourself. The first questions for you as an effective conflict manager are not *How am I going to fix the other person?* Or, *How am I going to get this person to give up?* Instead, ask, *What is causing the conflict? What do I want to happen and not happen?* And, *How am I going to conduct myself in this conflict?*

Things to remember about managing conflict

- Conflict is a normal, healthy part of community life
- How conflict is managed determines its impact on the community
- Effective community leaders can use more than one conflict management strategy
- In building a healthy community, it is often more productive to win an agreement than to win an argument

Recognition: When is it a conflict?

Increasing your effectiveness as a conflict manager means *naming the conflict early.* The sooner you recognize a conflict, the more options you're likely to have for managing it. If Paul and Shante had acknowledged their differences at the first meeting, their conflict may not have escalated to a shouting match in the hallway.

To name a conflict, remember the following definition:

> **Interpersonal conflict** is a situation in which two *interdependent* people *perceive* incompatible *goals;* achieving one person's goal means that other person's goal will not be achieved.

This definition rests on several key terms:

- **Interdependent:** People who are in conflict are also in some kind of a relationship with each other. Shante and Paul were interdependent in that they both sat on the zoning commission.
- **Perceive:** This word refers to understanding or regarding something in a particular way. If two people understand their goals to be incompatible, they will act accordingly. What if this perception is wrong and the goals are not really incompatible? Is it still a conflict? Yes, as long as the people *believe* their goals are incompatible and act that way.
- **Goals:** This term refers to any desired outcomes. The issue in any conflict gets down to incompatible goals. In the conflict between Paul and Shante, the issue centered on rezoning part of the community for a hazardous waste facility. Paul's goal was to rezone it. Shante's goal was to prevent the rezoning. These two outcomes were clearly incompatible.

Conflict, in other words, is *any* situation in which people who are linked together want different things, and both cannot have it their way. Note that this definition does *not* describe conflict in terms of individuals feeling angry, upset, or frustrated. Those emotions are not what make the situation a conflict. What creates a conflict is interdependence and incompatible goals. The emotions are signs that the conflict is escalating and is not well managed.

If you can recognize and name the conflict before there is a lot of emotion and history attached to it, you will have more options to manage it. Ask the following three questions:

- **What are the incompatible goals?** Answering this question allows you to name the conflict. For instance, Shante could say: "Paul wants the area rezoned so the hazardous waste facility can be built. I want to prevent the rezoning."
- **What are the key causes of the conflict?** For example: "Paul and I seem to value different things. He sees the facility primarily in terms of its economic benefit. I see it in terms of its potential threat to our health and safety. We have different ideas about what progress really is for this community." Remember that labeling other people in

negative ways and blaming them can cloud your ability to identify the root causes of a conflict.

- **What are the consequences of this conflict?** Consider how the conflict affects you, the other person, and the community. Paul and Shante gave little thought to the consequences or outcomes of their conflict. Paul could instead say: "The stakes are high. I find myself getting more and more upset and I sense that Shante is getting angry with me, just like I am with her. I'm afraid we could end up not being able to work together in the future *and* create a deep division within the commission."

Criteria: What is a well-managed conflict?

Effective conflict managers set criteria—explicit signs that tell them whether the conflict is being well managed. Having the conflict "resolved" may be one sign. But also consider *how* you achieved the resolution. Are the consequences of that process acceptable to you?

In the above example, Paul could have set these criteria for managing his conflict with Shante: "The zoning commission will be able to make a decision by the end of the month. There will be no personal attacks either in private or public. Also, Shante and I and the rest of the commission will be able to work together on issues in the future."

A well-managed conflict will allow you to maintain—and even increase—your social capital with your conflict partner and others who may be affected. In most cases, signs that conflict is being well managed include the following:

- **The people involved do not lose their sense of self-worth.** This means that you will not do anything that causes others to lose their self-respect. It also means that you will avoid losing respect for yourself. Shante and Paul forgot about this criterion. Neither of them felt good about themselves after their public shouting match in the hallway.
- **The conflict stays focused on the issue.** Conflicts that are not well managed lose sight of the issue and become personal attacks. This can harm the community as well as the people who are directly involved—*and* leave the issue unresolved. Even if the conflict centers on someone's behavior, remember that it's about what that person *does,* not who they *are* or whether they are worthy of respect.
- **The interests of the conflict partners are identified, acknowledged, and taken into account.** The *issue* in a conflict is about incompatible goals. However, people have *interests* in a conflict that go beyond the issue. These matter greatly to the people involved and affect their behaviors during the conflict. Such interests can include fear of losing self-esteem, worries about what other people will say, and concerns about violating a value or principle. Often the interests are the underlying reasons for the situation—the "why" of the conflict—and they generate more energy and emotion than the issue itself. Had Shante and Paul been able to discuss economic development along with environmental safety, they might have created a plan that took *both* interests into account.

Strategy: How can I manage this conflict?

Few conflicts can be managed with only one strategy or even one general approach to conflict management. Effective community leaders do not depend on a "one size fits all" approach. Instead, they have a variety of options for managing conflict and are flexible in using them.

The approach to conflict management presented in this tool is unique, and some of the suggested strategies may surprise you. Read about them with an open mind, remembering that there is no single "correct" model of conflict management and no fail-safe way to resolve any conflict. Test any suggested strategies in your daily experiences with community groups. Combine these approaches to conflict management with other perspectives and discover what truly works for you.

Consider that every conflict involves two factors that can guide you in choosing strategies. First, conflicts are between people who are linked in one or more ways, meaning that they are interdependent. In other words, every conflict involves people who have some type of *relationship*. Second, conflicts occur when there are incompatible goals, meaning that in every conflict there is an *issue*.

When choosing strategies to manage a specific conflict, consider these two factors and ask yourself how they play out in the situation. Figure 9: Factors in Choosing Conflict Management Strategies, illustrates the interaction of relationship and issue.

Figure 9. Factors in Choosing Conflict Management Strategies

RELATIONSHIP

LOW ⟷ HIGH

- What is our relationship (friend, fellow committee member, spouse, coworker . . .)?
- How important is this relationship to me?

ISSUE

LOW ⟷ HIGH

- What is the issue (the focus of the incompatible goals)?
- How important is the issue to me?

In the discussion that follows, we present a model that allows you to choose from four strategies for managing conflict. There are many strategies for managing conflict. Moreover, it may take a combination of strategies to manage any given conflict. Community leaders can plug whatever strategies they want into the grid in Figure 10: Conflict Management Strategies (page 103). We use these four to illustrate how to use the model.

- Avoidance, when neither the issue nor the relationship is very important to you
- Accommodation, when the relationship is more important to you than the issue
- Competition, when the issue is more important than the relationship
- Compromise, when both the relationship and the issue are important to you

Avoidance. With this strategy, you simply stay away from your partner in the conflict. If you're walking down a street and see this person coming toward you, for example, you cross to the other side to avoid a meeting. You don't name the conflict—in fact, you don't talk about it at all.

Avoidance is the most effective option when neither the relationship nor the issue is particularly important to you. It can be an especially useful short-term strategy if

- You or the other person need time to calm down before discussing the issue
- You are both tired and need time to recuperate
- You want to avoid a situation where you cannot successfully manage the conflict

Avoidance can also be an effective long-term strategy as long as the issue and the relationship remain relatively unimportant to you. However, overusing this strategy can lead your conflict partner and others to see you as uncaring and uninvolved.

Accommodation. In this conflict management strategy, you "give in" on the issue so that you can maintain or enhance your relationship with your conflict partner. Unlike avoidance, accommodation usually involves naming the issue and dealing with it. You may disagree with this person's position, but the importance of the relationship outweighs your need to take a firm stand on the issue. One person "wins" on the issue, but both people "win" on the relationship.

This strategy is effective as long as the issue is unimportant to you. When used to manage conflicts about issues that matter to you, however, accommodation can cause problems. You run the risk of being seen as a "doormat"—someone who will not stand up for what you believe. Accommodation can be particularly inappropriate if the issue centers on a core relationship between two people, such as a marriage that involves verbal or physical abuse.

Competition. Use this strategy when the issue is so important that you're willing to win even if it costs you the relationship with your conflict partner. Competition can be valid in value-driven conflicts that affect the health of the community—for example, about an issue that involves equal access to quality education. However, remember to focus competition on the *issue,* not on the other person. The goal is not to make that person a loser but rather to gain what matters to you.

People who overuse this strategy often compete on relatively minor issues and feel they must win no matter what. As a result, they may "win the battle but lose the war" and waste social capital.

Compromise. Sometimes both the relationship and the issue are important to you. In these situations, compromise is often most effective. This strategy entails giving up some (but not all) of what you want on the issue while at the same time maintaining the relationship. You and the other person both win and lose a little on the issue. And to a certain extent, both of you might also win and lose on the relationship.

With compromise it can be difficult to determine the acceptable level of wins and losses and negotiate them. In order for this strategy to work, both people must see the wins and losses as fair, even if they are not equal. Be honest about what wins you need and what losses you will tolerate. Otherwise, you can end up escalating the conflict and losing a great deal of social capital.

Choosing a strategy. Figure 10: Conflict Management Strategies, illustrates a way to choose among the four strategies just described. Looking at this grid will reveal immediate applications. To begin, determine the importance of your relationship with the other person. Also determine how important the issue is to you. Then plot these factors in appropriate places on the grid to find an appropriate overall strategy. For example, if you do not have a close relationship with the other person but the issue is important to you (relationship is low, issue is high), you might find competition to be most effective.

Figure 10. Conflict Management Strategies

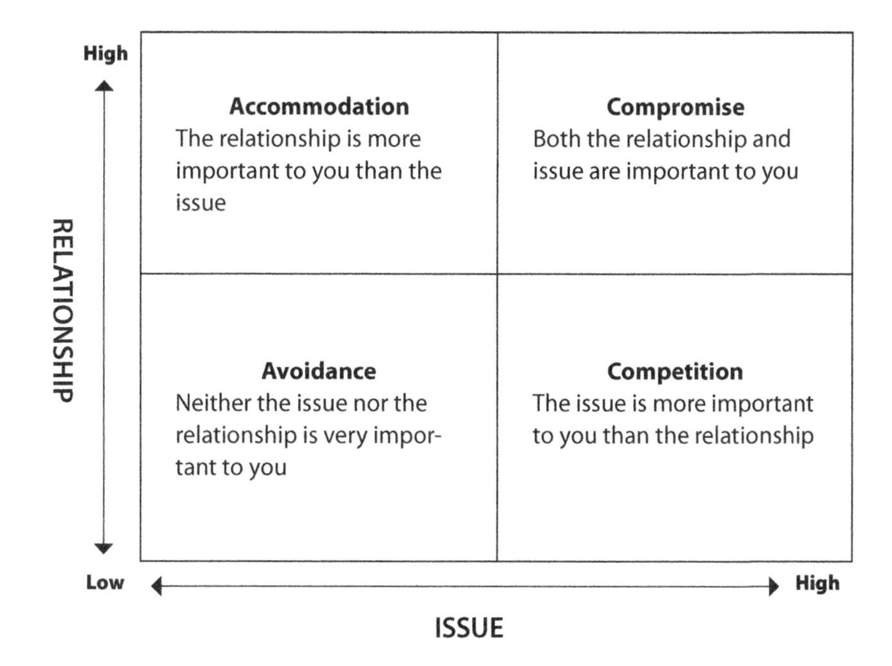

You can also use the grid by completing the following two sentences, or use the sentences as basic structures to guide your thinking:

- **Given the relationship and its importance, and the issue and its importance, the overall strategy for managing this conflict I will use is . . .** Example: "Given Paul's value of improving the economy, which is important for the health of the community, and given my concern for protecting the environment and the safety of our children, which is also important for community health, and recognizing that Paul and I both want to be on this commission for some time, we should not spend the next ten years canceling each other's vote out. Compromise is the best overall strategy."
- **The first thing I will do in implementing this strategy is . . .** Example: "Both Paul and I respect the city administrator. I will call him tomorrow and ask him to set up a meeting this week for the three of us where Paul and I can explain our positions to each other. The city administrator can help us clarify our positions and help us explore alternatives that take into account our differing concerns about the future health of our community."

Note: Collaboration (another possible strategy for managing conflict) is not included on the grid above. Because there's so much to say about this strategy, it's presented in more detail as part of Tool 12: Building Coalitions (starting on page 140). You are encouraged to learn about collaboration and look for ways to use it in managing conflict whenever appropriate.

This section has covered a lot of material about managing conflict. To remember the key points and apply them in your community work, complete the following steps.

Step 1. Reflect on your skills at managing conflict

Learning to be more effective at managing conflict starts with becoming aware of your current skills in this area. Worksheet 13: Conflict Styles Checklist (page 106), is designed for this purpose. It includes eight scenarios that describe common situations in community groups. Read them and then choose one conflict management strategy from the list that follows each scenario. You may find it helpful to refer to Figure 10: Conflict Management Strategies (page 103), before doing this worksheet.

To get the most benefit from Worksheet 13, follow up by completing Worksheet 14: Scoring the Conflict Styles Checklist (page 107). As you do, keep the following points in mind:

- You may find that none of the options described in Worksheet 13 describe exactly how you would deal with the conflict. In that case, choose the option that comes *closest* to what you would do.

- Worksheet 14 lists "correct" strategies for managing conflict in each of the scenarios in Worksheet 13—that is, the *recommended* strategies based on the *particular* model of conflict management described in this tool. No strategy for managing conflict is absolutely right or wrong in all circumstances. In fact, you might ultimately choose an alternative to the strategies recommended in Worksheet 14. Before you make that choice, however, take some time to understand how this model on conflict management works.
- If a scenario raises strong feelings about a particular issue based on your experiences, simply notice those feelings and put them aside for the time being. Base your responses only on the facts presented in the scenario.

Step 2. Plan to gain skills in managing conflict

Use Worksheet 15: Managing Interpersonal Conflict (page 111), to identify a current conflict that concerns you. This worksheet can also help you develop a plan for managing the conflict in ways that may be more effective than your current style.

WORKSHEET 13 Conflict Styles Checklist

Place a check mark by the option that comes closest to what you would do in a similar situation.

1. **A long-time high school principal has announced his retirement.** He was respected by his students and loved by his staff and community. The superintendent and school board want to fill the position with someone of equal caliber. To help with this process, the superintendent is putting together a task force of 21 community and school personnel to review and make recommendations about candidates for the position. You have lived in the community for six years, but you do not have strong relationships with the superintendent or members of the community. Moreover, you do not have strong feelings about the school district or who becomes the next high school principal. The superintendent has asked you to lead the task force, but there are a number of other things that you would rather be doing. How would you respond to his request?

   ☐ A. Thank the superintendent for the opportunity but respectfully decline.

   ☐ B. Lead the task force.

   ☐ C. State that the selection of the new high school principal is the responsibility of the superintendent and school board and that a task force should not be part of the hiring process.

   ☐ D. Tell the superintendent that you do not have time to lead the task force, but perhaps you could become a member of the group or help them in other ways.

2. **A group of teenagers and parents have been raising funds for the construction of a local teen center.** The leader of the fundraising effort is also a good personal friend of yours. You do not have any children still at home and you are more or less indifferent to the new facility. However, some other members of the community think a new teen center will only cause problems, and they have started writing letters to the local newspaper to get citizens to stop contributing money to the construction project. Because you are a prominent member of the community, your friend has asked you to write a letter to the editor in support of the teen center. What would you do?

   ☐ A. Tell your friend that you are not a very good writer and are very busy over the next few weeks.

   ☐ B. Write the letter.

   ☐ C. Join the group who oppose the teen center.

   ☐ D. Negotiate a compromise with your friend. Tell her you don't have time to write the letter, but you will "spread the word" with the groups you belong to.

3. **Your local school district has been facing declining enrollment over the past ten years.** To deal with shrinking budgets, the school board has decided to close two of the five elementary schools in the district. This would save the district a considerable amount of money, but your two children would need to take a bus instead of walk to school. In addition, their class sizes would increase from an average of 18 to 31 students per class. One of the key reasons you moved into the neighborhood was because of its proximity to and the reputation of the nearby elementary school. Because you are relatively new to the community, you do not have strong connections with school board members or school administrators. How would you deal with this conflict?

   ☐ A. Not say anything to the school board or administration and accept the fact that your children would be bused to school.

   ☐ B. Tell the school board and administration that they had a tough decision to make and you support their decision.

   ☐ C Organize a group to campaign against the closing of the local school.

   ☐ D. Work with the school board and administration to develop some sort of compromise—to reconsider the timing of the closure or to develop alternative funding to keep the school open.

Worksheet 13 continued

4. **Your community is approaching its centennial celebration.** As an active member of the community and city council, you have often expressed concern that the city is starting to show its age. You are worried that former residents returning home for the celebration will be disappointed with the community's appearance. You want the city council to set aside $50,000 for a city beautification project. One of your good friends, another city council member, believes the $50,000 would be better spent improving the community's infrastructure. How would you handle this conflict?

   ☐ A. Vote to spend the $50,000 on something completely different than the beautification project or infrastructure upgrade.

   ☐ B. Pass up the beautification project and support your friend's infrastructure initiative.

   ☐ C. Garner enough support to get the majority of city council members to vote for the beautification project.

   ☐ D. Work with your friend to see if there is a way to split the funding between the projects or find alternative funding for one or both of the projects.

5. **A group of individuals has been trying to recruit new members to their service organization.** You know very little about the organization, and right now most of your free time is taken up doing volunteer work at one of the local nursing homes. An acquaintance of yours, someone you see socially once or twice a year, has asked if you would be interested in joining the service organization. The reality is that this is something you have little time for and you do not want to give up your volunteer work at the nursing home. How do you respond to his request?

   ☐ A. Ask the person to give you some literature about the service organization and tell him that you will get back to him later with an answer.

   ☐ B. Join the service organization.

   ☐ C. Tell the person that you are too busy doing volunteer work at the nursing home and not interested at this time.

   ☐ D. Try to spend a little time with the service organization and a majority of time doing volunteer work at the nursing home.

6. **Your community has seen little economic growth over the past few years, and your mayor has been working very hard to attract new businesses into town.** He recently got a sportswear manufacturing company to consider building a facility in town, but only if the community provided $60,000 worth of property and infrastructure necessary for the building. You have been working in the community for the past 12 years and have a very secure job, and you have no firm position on this economic development project. The mayor is a close personal friend of yours, and she has asked you to come to the next city council meeting and speak in support of the project. How would you respond to the mayor's request?

   ☐ A. Tell the mayor that you have a previous engagement that evening but that you wish her luck with the upcoming vote.

   ☐ B. Attend the city council meeting and vocally support the new business.

   ☐ C. Tell the mayor you think there are better ways to spend $60,000 of taxpayers' money.

   ☐ D. Ask the mayor if there is any other way you could support the new business venture without showing up at the city council meeting.

Worksheet 13 continued

7. **A large meat-processing facility recently moved into your community.** The company is the area's largest employer; as a matter of fact, people commute from over 30 miles away to work for the company. The facility is such a large employer that the town has seen a tremendous influx of new people—largely refugees, immigrants, and ethnic groups new to the town. To better accommodate the new members of the community, the city council has proposed building a large affordable housing complex a few blocks from your home. It is very likely that the complex will drive down the value of your home by at least 30 percent. You were looking forward to selling your home and retiring out of state in five years. Now you are not sure if you will be able to do this if the affordable housing complex is built. A group of neighbors have banded together to pressure the city council to withdraw its proposal for the complex. One of your neighbors has asked you to join the group, and you feel strongly that the complex should not be built in your neighborhood. You do not have strong relationships with anyone on the city council. How would you respond to your neighbor's request?

   ☐ A. Tell your neighbor you will give it some thought, but that you do not want to get involved with the group.

   ☐ B. Tell your neighbor that the affordable housing complex needs to be built somewhere and it might as well be in your neighborhood.

   ☐ C. Join the neighborhood group.

   ☐ D. Approach the city council and see if it is possible to either delay the construction or change the location of the complex.

8. **Your community has a small downtown dominated by family-owned businesses.** A large discount retailer recently approached your community about setting up a store next to the main highway on the outskirts of town. The new store would likely lower prices on a number of consumer goods and would provide an additional 250 jobs to the local economy. You own the local hardware store, and this new store would directly affect your sales. You are adamant that the new store not be built, and you are leading a group of local citizens and businesses to oppose its construction. Several key community leaders are your good friends, and they support the building of the new store. There is a meeting on the issue tomorrow. How should you resolve the conflict that is likely to occur in the meeting?

   ☐ A. Avoid the meeting altogether, and use the local media and other community groups to help fight this battle.

   ☐ B. Decide that the relationships you share with these community leaders outweigh the negative impact on your business. Attend the meeting but say little, as a highly public fight would only ruin these relationships.

   ☐ C. Go to the community meeting with your group and wage a highly public battle to defeat the new store.

   ☐ D. Work with the community leaders who favor the store and representatives of the retail chain proposing the store to find a compromise solution, such as delaying the building of the store or reducing the size of the store.

WORKSHEET 14 Scoring the Conflict Styles Checklist

There are two different scores for the Conflict Styles Checklist—one for your preferred conflict styles and another score for your recommended conflict styles.

Your Preferred Conflict Styles

This score indicates your predominant ways for dealing with conflict. Everyone tends to have one or two ways they prefer to handle conflict, and as a result they also tend to overlook using other ways to deal with conflict. It is important for community leaders to be aware of their preferred and less preferred conflict styles as they decide how they will manage a particular conflict.

To score your preferred conflict styles

1. Record the number of A, B, C, and D responses to questions 1–8 in the space below:

   A: _____

   B: _____

   C: _____

   D: _____

2. In each column, put an X in the box that represents the total number of times you chose that response.

Preferred Conflict Styles

8				
7				
6				
5				
4				
3				
2				
1				
0				
	A Avoidance	B Accommodation	C Competition	D Compromise

Your Preferred Conflict Management Style is the one you most frequently chose. People who are highly skilled at resolving conflict and maintaining or building social capital are adept at using all four styles. In other words, the plot on their graph is relatively flat. Those who overuse or underuse certain conflict management strategies tend to have plots with peaks and valleys. At the end of this section is information about the advantages and disadvantages of each style, and when to use the different conflict styles.

Worksheet 14 continued

Your Recommended Conflict Styles

Next you will find the recommended conflict style for each of the situations described in the Inventory. These recommendations are explained below, but first check your answers against the following answer key.

Situation	Recommended Style
1	A—Avoidance; low relationship importance, low issue importance
2	B—Accommodation; high relationship importance, low issue importance
3	C—Competition; low relationship importance, high issue importance
4	D—Compromise; high relationship importance, high issue importance.
5	A—Avoidance; low relationship importance, low issue importance
6	B—Accommodation; high relationship importance, low issue importance
7	C—Competition; low relationship importance, high issue importance
8	D—Compromise; high relationship importance, high issue importance

1. Record the number of times you chose the recommended style: ________

2. Benchmark your score using the scale below:

   6–8 You do a very good job adapting your conflict management styles to the demands of the situation. You will likely be seen as someone who does a good job resolving issues and maintaining relationships.

   4–5 You do a reasonable job matching your conflict management style to the demands of the situation. But it is likely that one or more preferred styles are being overused and interfere with your ability to successfully resolve issues and maintain relationships.

   1–3 You likely are overusing one or two preferred conflict management styles. You probably need to adopt more styles into your repertoire to be a more effective community leader.

Does your score and its benchmark description fit the way you usually manage interpersonal conflict?

To find out why certain styles are recommended for each situation, see Figure 10: Conflict Management Strategies on page 103. This model identifies four conflict management styles, each of which has a time and a place for use: avoidance, accommodation, competition, and compromise.

Revisit the situations described in each conflict situation, and study them for where they belong on the grid. For example, in situation 1, the school principal issue, you have little relationship with the superintendent and the community, and the issue is not important to you. This is why the "correct" choice was *avoidance:* you thank the superintendent for the opportunity but respectfully decline his offer. Study each situation carefully and you will see that cues are provided as to the importance of the relationship and the importance of the issue. These cues signal an effective choice in conflict management.

WORKSHEET 15 Managing Interpersonal Conflict

Recognition: Is it a Conflict?

1. Name the conflict. That is, what are the incompatible goals?

2. What are the key causes of the conflict? Remember, labeling people in negative ways and blaming them for the conflict can cloud your ability to identify root causes of a conflict.

3. What are the consequences of the conflict? How is the conflict affecting you, the other person, and your community?

Criteria: What Is a Well-Managed Conflict in This Situation?

What signs or indicators will tell you that this conflict is well managed? Having the conflict "resolved" may be one sign. But also consider how you achieved the resolution and whether the consequences of that process are acceptable to you.

Strategies: How Will I Manage the Conflict?

Review the Conflict Styles Grid below. Then select your strategy for managing this conflict. Remember, your natural preference may not be the preferred style for the situation.

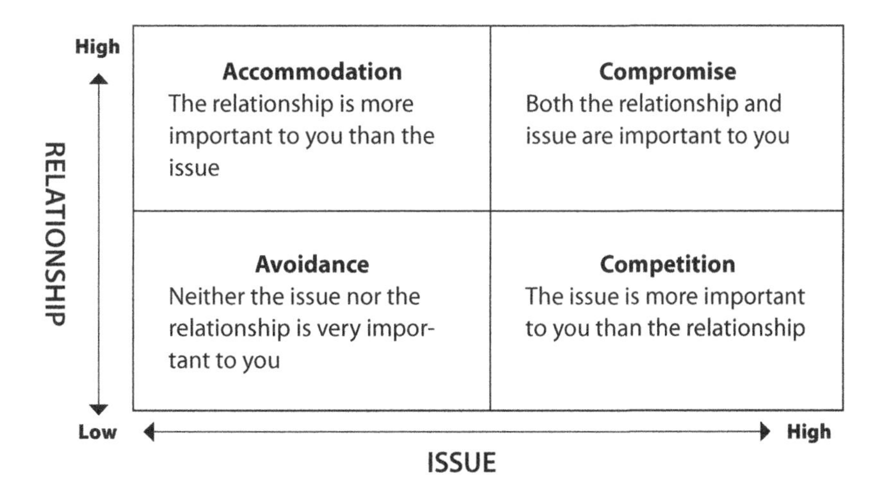

1. Given the relationship and its importance, and the issue and its importance, the overall strategy I will use to manage this conflict is . . .

2. The first thing I will do in implementing this strategy is . . .

TOOL 9. Building Social Capital Across Cultures

This Tool at a Glance

Why Use It
Creating and sustaining change in most communities takes people who understand the importance of building social capital across cultures.

When to Use It
During any community initiative, taking time to build relationships across cultures can determine whether your project succeeds or fails. This is especially important when significant differences increase the chances for misunderstanding.

How to Use It
Steps in using this tool are

- Acknowledge differences in culture
- Frame differences as assets
- Create opportunities for people of different cultures to interact
- Pay attention to power dynamics
- Establish healthy patterns of negotiation and conflict management
- Find common goals
- Continually build and rebuild trust

Where to Learn More
Paul Mattessich and Barbara Monsey. *Community Building: What Makes It Work* (St. Paul, MN: Fieldstone Alliance, 1997).

Work Group on Health Promotion and Community Development, University of Kansas. Chapter 27. *Cultural Competence in a Multicultural World.* http://ctb.ku.edu/tools/en/chapter_1027.htm.

Communities today include an increasing variety of racial and ethnic groups, adding to the complexity and the richness of neighborhood life. Understanding how to navigate significant cultural differences is critical to building the kind of social capital that mobilizes and engages all citizens.

Community Example: Diversity Day

A small community was shocked when, for the first time in decades, a racially motivated incident gained widespread media attention. Several young white boys were taunting a Somali woman for wearing a veil in public. Her brother and two cousins responded by beating the boys with sticks. One of the boys required hospitalization.

City council members decided to take positive action by declaring May 5 "Diversity Day" in the community. They declared a theme for the day—"Our Common American Heritage"—and invited leaders from the Mexican, Somali, and Hmong communities to discuss the details. Council members drafted a detailed agenda for this meeting that spelled out the proposed activities: a meet-and-greet pancake breakfast, speeches by elected officials praising the progress already made by minority populations and stressing more tolerance, plus an ethnic food fair and games for the children.

The Council scheduled an organizing meeting to discuss the day. Unfortunately, only one leader from the Mexican immigrant community showed up. And nobody from the Hmong and Somali communities attended.

Stunned by the lack of response, the council cancelled the event due to "lack of interest." Many white community members felt that they had made an effort, but that the community's minority populations were just not interested in being good citizens.

Bob Owens, one of the local business owners, had been an exchange student to Mexico years ago and had made friends with Mexican families while serving as a volunteer translator. Bob took it upon himself to try to find out what went wrong. He asked his friend Juanita to gather some key members of the Mexican community at a local café to discuss it.

To Bob's surprise, nine people showed up. This included two members of the Hmong and Somali communities who were invited by Mexican friends. All passionately and energetically shared their viewpoints on what went wrong.

Bob listened and heard no evidence of the lack of commitment or passion for community life that the white community had been complaining about. Instead, he learned that

- Many people felt that the written invitation sent to a handful of ethnic organizations was impersonal and almost offensive in its expectation of attendance with no personal contact.
- Both the organizational meeting and the Diversity Day had been completely planned by the council, with no input from anyone else.
- All of the ethnic groups present were still concerned about escalating verbal abuse and violence toward minority populations. People felt angry that the council was choosing to gloss over the recent incident with a "Diversity Day" event.

Bob asked the group if anyone would be willing to organize a meeting to which he could invite council members and other interested members of the majority community. At this meeting, people of all ethnic groups would be able to voice their perspectives and figure out some first steps for addressing the challenges of intolerance. Two members of the group volunteered, and everyone left the gathering feeling like there was hope for creating a community in which they could all participate.

About this tool

In our example, it took just one personal relationship between two cultural "bridge-builders" to get the community moving in a positive direction. There are a number of reasons to place such bridge building high on any community's agenda.

- **Social capital is required for a healthy community.** Our definition of a healthy community is "a place where all people can meet their economic, social, physical, cultural, and spiritual needs; work together for the common good; and participate in creating their future." A community cannot be considered healthy if some needs are being met and not others, if some people are working together but not others, and if the community's future is created without the participation of entire populations or groups.
- **Communities need a reservoir of bridging social capital.** Bridging social capital consists of relationships that allow diverse individuals and groups to work together. This form of social capital reduces the time and effort needed to mobilize resources and is essential for getting things done in communities with many cultures.
- **Our communities need to engage all their resources to reach their full potential.** When it comes to tackling tough social issues such as drug use, low high school graduation rates, or escalating violence, we can succeed only by mobilizing resources across the entire community. Challenging issues such as these typically involve the community as a whole. They also require a solution from the community as a whole.

Building social capital across cultures requires a basic understanding of the concept of culture and how it relates to human behavior. The following three points are especially important.

People are individuals first

Individuals, not culture, are primary to creating social capital. Ultimately, people seek understanding and respect as individuals. So, in building social capital across cultures, we need to look first at individuals and understand cultural influences in that context.

To understand this context, remember that all human beings start with some things in common—a kind of universal code that comes automatically programmed in their mental software. These universals include the ability to feel fear, anger, joy, love, and sadness; the need to associate with others, to play, work, and exercise; and the ability to observe the environment and discuss it with others. While we all have these basic needs and feelings, what we do with them and how we express them differs greatly by culture.

Culture refers to patterns of thinking, feeling, and acting that we learn from other people. We acquire most of these patterns in early childhood, when we are most easily influenced. However, cultural conditioning continues throughout our lives in our neighborhoods, in the workplace, in religious forums, and through the multitude of media messages that bombard us every day. Culture is mental software that we learn rather than inherit, and this software modifies the ways we express our basic needs as human beings.

However, individuals are more than the simple sum of their universal software and cultural conditioning. Each of us possesses a unique set of characteristics, behaviors, experiences, and reactions to those experiences. The bottom line: We first must treat people as individuals, knowing that their cultural conditioning is only part of who they are.

Culture is complex and largely invisible

Once we see the importance of treating people as individuals first, we can use the concept of culture to understand and bridge some of our deepest differences. In fact, cultural understanding and respect can be just as important to some people as individual understanding and respect.

One reason for the complexity of culture is that its most significant aspects are not easy to observe. We tend to notice the most physical manifestations of culture—differences in clothing, food, languages, and the like. Deeper and often more significant aspects of culture (such as values and basic assumptions about life) cannot be seen. When these deeper aspects go unexpressed or unquestioned, we risk running into them full force during a conflict.

Building social capital across cultures requires acknowledging, understanding, and negotiating the differences that are easily observable as well as those that require deeper knowledge and exploration.

We are all multicultural

Most of us belong to a number of different groups over our lifetime. As a result, we carry within ourselves several layers of programming, each corresponding to a different dimension of culture, such as

- Age
- Nationality
- Ethnicity
- Religion
- Language
- Gender
- Generational level: our roles as grandparents, parents, and children
- Social or economic class, associated with educational opportunities and occupation
- Sexual orientation
- Physical ability
- For those of us who are employed, formal and informal expectations about how to behave at work

Everyone has a set of cultural assumptions that are truly unique. While culture in a general sense is still a useful tool for understanding our deepest programming, always consider how our multiple cultures interact.

Given the complexity of culture and its influence on us as individuals, what can we do to most effectively build social capital? The following steps reflect key learnings of participants in Blandin Community Leadership Programs.

Step 1. Acknowledge differences in culture

Many people believe that acknowledging cultural differences serves only to make the problem of intolerance or misunderstanding worse. In our experience, however, only relationships that are based on admitting the differences between individuals and cultures have any hope of being sustained. When differences are smoothed over or ignored, the majority perspective tends to take over as the unspoken norm. Eventually, other racial or ethnic groups simply disengage.

Step 2. Frame differences as assets

Communities have completely reshaped their view of cultural differences by surveying new members and discovering their assets. This involves a critical shift in perspective: seeing people who are multicultural and multilingual in terms of what they *bring* to a community rather than by the challenges they pose.

Putting a dollar figure on the contributions of immigrant populations to the local economy is one quick way to make their assets clear. You can do this, for example, with census data about the number of immigrants in the local workforce and their record at starting businesses. For suggestions about how to find such information, see Tool 3: Accessing Community Data, page 42.

You can also do surveys to identify the skills, civic contributions, volunteer capacities, and entrepreneurial experiences of various cultural groups. Tool 1: Identifying Community Assets, page 22, explains how to create and conduct such a survey, called an asset inventory. Following are some questions to include in your inventory and be answered by members of each cultural group:

- How many bilingual members do we have?
- How many bicultural members do we have?
- Who has the capacity to offer language classes?
- Who has the capacity to offer translation services?
- How much money do we spend in the community?
- What other financial resources do we control?
- What skills and capacities does our population possess?

- What skills are we currently contributing to the labor force?
- Which skills might we offer as volunteers?
- Which skills might we be willing to teach others?
- Who has experience in starting or running a business?
- Who is currently operating a business that employs others?
- Who has civic or community-based experience?
- Who has experience in government office?

Once the information has been gathered, it should be widely distributed through the media, town meetings, and the various civic and business organizations in the community.

Step 3. Create opportunities for people of different cultures to interact

One of the most effective community interventions is creating opportunities for informal contact among members of different cultures. Personal contact can effectively break down the barriers between "us" and "them." When people reveal personal information about themselves, they are more likely to be seen as individuals rather than as members of a category.

Also, sharing personal information often leads to the discovery that others previously considered as "them" have some of the same feelings, concerns, and ambitions as "us." This helps to break down barriers between in-groups and out-groups.

Organize special events. Your community group can organize events that bring people of different cultures together, such as a National Night Out in diverse neighborhoods or ethnic fairs. In your survey of various groups, get information about their traditional celebrations, especially those that could be opened to the public.

Increase your own cultural competence. As a community leader, you can profit by increasing your own cultural competence during special events. This term refers to your ability to form personal relationships with people from different racial and ethnic groups. Some ways to do this are

- Pick a specific culture and learn everything you can about it through reading, taking courses, or learning another language.
- Put yourself in culturally diverse environments—anything from restaurants and other informal gathering places to public meetings where you find yourself in the minority based on your ethnic group or race.
- Ask people questions about their culture, based on what you've learned.

- If you accidentally offend someone with a question or comment, apologize and learn from the incident. Don't let a fear of making mistakes stop you from creating new relationships.
- When discrimination affects someone of another ethnic group or race, take a public stand against it.

Use "story starters." Giving people an opportunity to tell something of their life story enables you to build relationships and learn about other cultures at the same time. You can build this activity into regular meetings of your community group, or set aside a retreat or workshop for this purpose. Doing so will build social capital and recognize participants as individuals, not just as representatives of a group.

Use questions such as the following to stimulate the sharing of life stories:

- Share the complete story of your name.
- Describe your family's recipe for treating the common cold.
- What experiences make you feel close to nature?
- If your shoe could tell its story, what would it say?
- Describe your mind picture for the word "home."
- Tell about a childhood friend.
- Describe something your parents taught you that is very important to you.
- Tell about a person who has significantly influenced your life.
- What has been your most embarrassing moment?
- Did you ever have a nickname? How did you acquire it?
- Tell a fond memory you have of your grandparents or other favorite relatives.
- How were you disciplined as a child?
- Tell about the naughtiest thing you ever did as a child. Did you get caught? If so, what were the consequences?
- Tell about the worst storm you have survived.
- What was your favorite meal as a child?
- What was the first movie you ever saw, and what was your reaction to it?
- Tell about your very first love, date, or kiss.
- What was your favorite subject in school? Who was your favorite teacher? How did these affect your current vocation?
- Describe a favorite place you like to go to be alone.
- Did you have any pets? Tell about your favorite animal.
- Did other kids ever tease you? What did they tease you about?
- How did you choose your career or vocation? Who influenced you?

- What is your favorite time of year and why?
- Describe your household chores as a child
- Have you had any broken bones or other injuries? How did the injuries happen?
- What is the best book you ever read and why?
- Did you or your family have any superstitions? What were they? Do you still believe them?
- What was your biggest childhood fear?

In an ongoing community project, you will get the best results by using story starters at the beginning of several consecutive meetings. Do this until the sharing of personal stories and exploration of cultures become part of your group's culture. At that point, you'll notice members of the group spontaneously sharing their stories and asking questions of each other. The formal story-starting process will no longer be necessary.

Step 4. Pay attention to power dynamics

This step means being aware of where minority populations do and do not have a voice—whether their interests are represented, whether they sit on decision-making bodies, and whether their concerns are reflected in your community group's policies, procedures, and reward systems. In cases with a long history of discrimination or exploitation—as with African Americans or Native Americans—majority populations need to make clear and concerted efforts to ensure the full and fair participation of minority groups.

The following are steps that every community can take to increase the inclusiveness of their systems and structures. Which steps has your group taken?

- Establish written recruitment strategies for reaching underrepresented populations to serve on boards and in elected offices
- Establish training about cultural diversity and antiracism issues
- Identify community leaders in various cultural groups and invite them to meetings of your group
- Develop relationships with key people in organizations serving minority populations to obtain feedback, establish referrals, and build credibility
- Provide financial support to organizations or programs serving minority populations
- Locate key community programs in geographic areas accessible to people of all cultures
- Whenever possible, hold meetings in places that are close to key neighborhood centers and accessible by public transportation or walking

- Publicize your meetings in a variety of ways—by phone, mail, word of mouth, public service announcements on radio and television, announcements at neighborhood meetings, and flyers posted in churches, schools, day care centers, laundromats, grocery stores, and other public areas
- Rewrite job descriptions to value experience, competence, and sensitivity in working across cultures
- Review volunteer recruitment strategies (recruitment, retention, networking) to ensure they are sensitive to and accessible to people of all cultures and languages
- Develop advisory committees that reflect the racial and cultural composition of service area
- Publish organization brochures in all relevant languages
- Develop policies that ensure the use of culturally diverse vendors
- Regularly monitor the staffing and use of all community facilities to ensure they reflect the multicultural composition of the community

Step 5. Establish healthy patterns of negotiation and conflict management

Communities with a healthy approach to negotiation and conflict management tend to embody three key characteristics:

- **A shared understanding of controversy and difference is a natural part of community life.** Controversy is necessary to make informed and democratic choices. To enable people to weigh the advantages and disadvantages of alternatives, there must be debate in the community. In communities where controversy is accepted, people can disagree with each other and still respect each other. They address problems and do not become defensive or cast blame.
- **Conflict is depersonalized and "deculturalized."** This means that those who disagree with a particular position are seen as doing so not out of deficiencies but because of honest differences. We can discuss issues, lay out various arguments, and still see each person as having a unique viewpoint as a human being.
- **People give as much attention to process as they do the ultimate outcome.** Considerable energy is paid to giving all people equal airtime and treating all perspectives as legitimate.

Communities that embody these characteristics are often able to anticipate and speak about conflicts before they actually arise, and consider suggestions for their resolving them early on. Your group can use the following process to sort out misunderstandings or conflicts related to culturally driven behaviors:

1. Name the behavior in nonjudgmental terms. For example, "David speaks loudly and uses large hand gestures."
2. Describe the meaning that behavior has in your cultural context. "It seems like David is angry much of the time."
3. Explore different cultural interpretations that could be occurring. "This behavior means I care what we're doing," or, "That's how I always speak in groups; it's a way of getting people's attention."
4. Negotiate (without judgment) behaviors that will allow for the greatest expression of everyone in the group.

Step 6. Find common goals

Perhaps the highest impact community intervention of all is framing what we might call "superordinate goals." These are goals that rise above cultural differences, embody the desires and values of many cultural groups in the community, and demand the efforts of everyone to succeed. Examples include many issues that your group can tackle—anything from reducing crime to bringing high-speed Internet access to rural areas. When people work together to achieve goals they all value, prejudice can be set aside in the interest of achieving higher aims.

Step 7. Continually build and rebuild trust

We wouldn't do justice to this topic if we didn't recognize that efforts to build social capital across cultures take place in a historical context of racism, segregation, and broken promises. European and Anglo populations stole land, broke promises, upheld slavery and segregation, and often placed economic interests before basic human rights.

This means that many community building efforts across racial and cultural lines start from a place of distrust. Many efforts to developing bridging social capital fail due to a lack of recognition of this history and its implications. This history must be recognized rather than ignored, and specific strategies must be put in place to overcome the trust deficit.

Even in cases where there is not a history of distrust, none of us can know other cultures so well that we will always behave appropriately. So many specific cultural differences exist that no one can be expected to know them all. People can make mistakes, experience misunderstandings, and leave intercultural interactions with bad feelings about what occurred. Sometimes they can understand the reasons if they examine cultural differences.

This is why issues of trust are so critical to developing and sustaining bridging social capital. In a multicultural community, trust is built through a history of intentional and consistent behavior that reflects the following key values:

- **Consistency and fairness.** People need to know that principles or policies will be applied consistently across racial, cultural, and ethnic lines.
- **Promise fulfillment.** Promise fulfillment occurs when people say what they will do and do what they say. Broken promises are the quickest route to patterns of distrust.
- **Availability and receptivity.** In trusting relationships, people feel they have equal access to power and decision-making structures and know their needs and interests will be heard.

Communities that are most effective at increasing their bridging social capital are those that recognize existing trust deficits and intentionally and consistently work to build trust across cultures. It can be helpful to create specific guidelines for behaviors that build trust in your community group. While each group should develop its own norms, following are examples from one group that succeeded in building a high level of trust:

- We will do our best to be respectful of others at all times and create positive feelings in our interactions with others
- We realize and accept that we cannot behave perfectly in all intercultural interactions, and we will make mistakes
- We will assume goodwill on the part of others (until proven otherwise)
- We will tell each other if we have been offended and offer suggestions to help each other learn
- We will stay focused on our mutual goals

TOOL 10. Mapping Your Social Capital

This Tool at a Glance

Why Use It
Doing a detailed analysis of your group's social capital will help you develop strategies for working with key stakeholders and mobilizing resources throughout the community.

When to Use It
This mapping exercise is particularly powerful when used with Tool 11: Analyzing Stakeholders (page 132).

How to Use It
Option A (individual exercise):

- List the relevant groups and organizations
- Determine the strength of the ties
- Determine the resources represented
- Analyze the map
- Set next steps

Option B (group exercise):

- List the relevant groups and organizations
- Determine the strength of the ties
- Determine the resources represented
- Combine the individual lists
- Analyze the map
- Set next steps

Where to Learn More
Kim Bobo, Jackie Kendall, and Steve Max. *Organizing for Social Change* (St. Paul, MN: Fieldstone Alliance, 2001).

Paul Mattessich and Barbara Monsey. *Community Building: What Makes It Work* (St. Paul, MN: Fieldstone Alliance, 1997).

Social capital comprises the relationships that make resources available for your community initiative, including the larger networks that you can access through those relationships. This tool will help you create a clear picture of those relationships and networks.

Community Example: Pro-Bond Committee

The committee was so effective that, in spite of many odds, it mobilized a city of 100,00 people to approve a school bond referendum by a two-to-one margin. Critical to this success was a strategy that the committee used throughout the campaign: mapping its social capital.

At its initial meeting, the original committee members decided to identify and recruit new members—people who had a great deal of social capital with diverse networks in the community. This expanded committee met to analyze the social networks and ties that it now had to other individuals and groups. This information was assembled into a chart called a social capital map.

Based on this analysis, committee members got "assignments" to get in touch with specific people. This effort allowed the committee to communicate its key messages directly to key groups of voters, pull together neighborhood meetings, and develop the volunteer pool for the "get out the vote" phone bank.

About this tool

This tool suggests ways to measure relationships in terms of strong ties and weak ties, discover the benefits and limitations of these ties, and analyze networks in terms of the strength of their ties. First, remember that relationships with high social capital are marked by

- Trust: the belief in and reliance on the honesty, integrity, and reliability of other people
- Reciprocity: a mutual, fair benefit from the relationship over time
- Durability: lasting over time through stress and changing circumstances

The concepts of strong ties and weak ties refer to relative degrees of trust, reciprocity, and durability. You can use these concepts to assess the strength of a relationship and its potential social capital. Mapping your group's pattern of ties will help you access your current social capital and identify where to develop more social capital.

While it may be convenient to use strong ties, the resources needed for a community initiative to succeed usually require you to also use weak ties. Be careful not to underestimate the value of your weak ties.

Characteristics of strong ties

Relationships that are high in trust, reciprocity, and durability tend to produce **strong ties.** These ties often involve a high level of emotional investment in the relationship, as in *I really like that person.* We tend to "go to" people with whom we have strong ties for a wide variety of resources and support, often involving more than one aspect of our life. Strong ties are often associated with bonding social capital and tend to be formed with those with whom we have much in common.

Strong ties offer several benefits. For one, they are the easiest to tap. They also directly provide resources for a variety of needs, including the need for emotional support.

However, strong ties can have limitations as well. Because they are usually formed with people who are similar to us, strong ties tend to decrease our access to diverse knowledge, perspectives, or resources. And strong ties tend to provide links to networks that we can already access.

Characteristics of weak ties

Weak ties exhibit the following characteristics:

- They are formed in relationships that have lower levels of trust, reciprocity, and durability and that tend to have little emotional investment
- We tend to "go to" those with whom we have weak ties for a specific resource to address a specific need
- They are often associated with bridging social capital and tend to be formed with those with whom we have fewer things in common

- Benefits include access to a greater diversity of knowledge and perspectives; access to a wider range of networks and their resources than you, yourself, already have; and the fact that they set the groundwork for a broader base of support and sense of ownership for a community initiative
- Limitations include that they are harder to tap; they can usually be tapped only for specific, limited purposes; and they provide little emotional support

Mapping your social capital

The social capital mapping exercise that follows is designed to be done either by an individual (Option A) or by a group (Option B). Either option will help you create a "map" of your connections and networks—a table listing who you know, the type of tie you have to the person or network (strong tie or weak tie), and the resources that each person or network can access. For either option, use Worksheet 16: Social Capital Map (page 128).

Option A: Individual exercise

Use this exercise to map your social capital in general, or to analyze your social capital with key stakeholders or potential partners for a specific community project.

Step 1. List the relevant groups and organizations

Use Worksheet 16: Social Capital Map (page 128), for this step. In the first column of this worksheet (Group or Organization), list the groups and organizations with which you are linked. For example, you might be a member, serve on staff, or participate as a board member or volunteer. You might also do business with some of these groups or have a personal connection with their leadership.

If you are doing the exercise to map your general social capital as a community leader, be selective about the organizations that you list. Focus on those that play some sort of community role.

If you are doing this exercise to map your social capital for a particular initiative, list the groups or organizations that are most relevant to it. Include organizations inside *and* outside your community.

Step 2. Determine the strength of the ties

In column two of Worksheet 16 (Strength of Tie), write an S to indicate groups with which you think you have a strong tie and a W for those with which you have a weak tie. Remember that

S = Strong ties = higher levels of trust, reciprocity, and durability

W = Weak ties = lower levels of trust, reciprocity, and durability

Step 3. Determine the resources represented

In the Resources column, write down the resources that each group represents. Resources include money, information, votes, volunteers, and access to other groups and networks.

Step 4. Analyze the map

Now analyze your map by answering the questions included in Worksheet 17: Social Capital Analysis (page 129).

Step 5. Set next steps

After you have finished the analysis, identify how and when to use the results.

Determine what actions you will take in response to the questions in Worksheet 17—especially how you will strengthen ties, build new ties, and leverage existing ties to increase social capital.

Option B: Group exercise

You can use the same basic process described in Option A with a group. The group process is essentially the same, with the addition of an extra step to combine lists from individual members.

Option B can be used to map your group's general social capital in the community, though this may be a cumbersome process. You may find it more productive to map your group's social capital for a specific community initiative.

Step 1. List the relevant groups and organizations

Give each group member a copy of the social capital map and ask them to fill in the Group or Organization column. In this column, people should list all the groups with which they have a link as a general member, board member, staff member, volunteer, client, or customer. If any of your members have a personal connection with a group's leaders, that group should also be listed here.

Step 2. Determine the strength of the ties

Ask each of your members, working individually, to complete the Strength of Tie column by writing an S for those groups with which they think they have strong tie or a W for those groups with which they think they have a weak tie.

S = Strong ties = higher levels of trust, reciprocity, and durability

W = Weak ties = lower levels of trust, reciprocity, and durability

Step 3. Determine the resources represented

Still working individually, each group member should now fill out the Resources column. Resources can include money, information, votes, volunteers, and access to other groups and networks.

Step 4. Combine the individual lists

For this step, display the combined social capital of your group members in a visual way. Some groups use a spreadsheet software program for this purpose. Others create a tally sheet on pieces of flip-chart paper hung side-by-side on a wall. Whatever technology you use, make the display large enough to be seen by the entire group.

The format that most groups use for their map is a grid with space to list each group member's name in the left-hand column and groups or organizations across the top of the grid. For example:

	School	Lions	AARP	Hospital
Juan	S	W	S	
Alice	W	W	S	S
Marty		W		W
Jemal	S	W		W
Veronica	S	S		S
Celeste		S	W	

This example does not have a column for resources, as that makes the grid unwieldy. However, your group will discuss resources in step 5.

The names of your group's members can be filled in on the grid ahead of time. If you know some of the relevant community groups that are very likely to be named, they can also be filled in on the grid before doing this step. Ask each group member to go the grid, and, in the row with their name on it, write an S to indicate organizations or groups with which they have a strong tie and a W for those with which they have a weak tie. If they have links with groups not already on the grid, they should add that group to the grid and indicate the strength of these ties.

You may wish to try some variations on this step:

- Create a large grid and then fill it in as a group. Ask each of your members to state the groups with which they are linked and the strength of each tie. Your facilitator can record this information on the grid.
- Use colored circles or squares to represent the strength of the ties—for example, red for strong ties and blue for weak ties.
- Fit this step into a meeting break. Group members can leave the room after writing their individual information on the grid.

Step 5. Analyze the map

When your map is finished, analyze it by answering the questions included in Worksheet 17: Social Capital Analysis (page 129).

Step 6. Set next steps

By completing and analyzing the social network map, your group will have a clear picture of

- Resources to which your ties provide access
- Where ties need to be strengthened
- Where ties need to be created
- Whom you are most likely to influence
- The people whom others in your group are most likely to influence

After your group has finished mapping social capital, discuss how and when you will use the results. Choose what actions you will take in response to the questions in Worksheet 17, especially how you will strengthen ties, build new ties, and leverage existing ties to increase social.

WORKSHEET 16 Social Capital Map

Group or Organization	Strength of Tie	Resources

WORKSHEET 17 Social Capital Analysis

1. What resources do your strong ties give you access to?

2. What resources do your weak ties give you access to?

3. Are there ties you want to strengthen? If so, how will you strengthen them?

4. Are there relevant groups with which you lack social capital (that is, they do not appear on your map)? How will you access the resources of these groups?

5. How can you leverage your ties to have access to more groups, organizations, and resources?

PART FOUR

Tools for Mobilizing Resources

Leadership that effectively develops and sustains a healthy community is based on three core competencies: framing ideas, building social capital, and mobilizing resources.

As noted in the earlier chapters, each of these competencies is necessary for getting things done, and for doing them in such a way that the community becomes healthier as a result. However, no one competency is sufficient in and of itself to accomplish this. It is only when the competencies are used in combination that a healthy community results.

This section contains tools to help you increase your effectiveness in using the core competency of mobilizing resources—engaging a critical mass of people, resources, and interests in taking action to achieve a specific outcome or set of outcomes. From a leadership perspective, mobilization is not just about activity. It is about strategic, purposeful activity involving others to achieve clearly defined goals.

Part Four of this book includes the following tools:

11. **Analyzing Stakeholders** offers a detailed picture of the people who feel they have something to gain or lose from your community project

12. **Building Coalitions** presents a technique for organizing diverse groups around their mutual self-interest

13. **Building Effective Community Teams** gives a model for forming effective groups and improving their performance

14. **Recruiting and Sustaining Volunteers** provides techniques for attracting the right volunteers to the right roles and helping them to succeed

As you use these tools, you will see references to tools and techniques located in other parts of the book. Following these references can help you combine the core competencies in powerful ways.

TOOL 11. Analyzing Stakeholders

This Tool at a Glance

Why Use It
If you want to create the critical mass of support needed for the long-term success of a community project, then stakeholder analysis is a critical first step.

When to Use It
Before you begin a stakeholders analysis, your group needs to have clear outcome in mind. Use this tool after completing Tool 5: Visioning (page 57), and Tool 6: Translating Vision into Action (page 68).

How to Use It
This tool is meant to be used with a group. In doing the analysis, your group will create a stakeholders map and fill out a grid to determine each stakeholder's attitude and power relative to your project.

Steps in using this tool are

- State the key outcome of your proposed project
- List stakeholders
- Assess each stakeholder's attitude toward the outcome
- Identify each stakeholder's power relative to the project
- Determine the linkages
- Fill out the Power and Attitude Grid
- Decide how you will deal with each set of stakeholders

Where to Learn More
Linda Hoskins and Emil Angelica. *The Fieldstone Nonprofit Guide to Forming Alliances* (St. Paul, MN: Fieldstone Alliance, 2005).

It takes time and energy to overcome resistance and mobilize support for any community initiative. Unfortunately, many worthwhile projects limp along or fail because the interests and concerns of key stakeholders were missed or not addressed in time. Use this tool to prevent such outcomes.

Community Example: Mobilizing Support for a Community Center

As a visitor, one of the first things you notice about this community center is how much activity is going on. People are in the hallways, almost every meeting room is being used, and the offices are full. Although it is attached to the high school, the center is run by the city.

This is a large facility. Within its walls are a gymnasium, hockey rink, senior citizen center, caterer's kitchen, large meeting rooms, small meeting rooms, and the city's administrative offices. Four full-time employees are required to staff the center. It is located in a town with a population of 4,800, yet on busy weekends over 5,000 people will come to the community center for one purpose or another.

The idea for this joint city-school district center originated with the school superintendent and the city administrator. However, the decision to actually do the project was not theirs to make. The use of city resources and school resources for the center required two separate public votes—one for the city's expenditures and one for the school district's.

Mobilizing support for the two referendums was not easy. But those involved say the effort was manageable—and ultimately successful—because of a thorough stakeholders analysis. The analysis identified stakeholders ranging from the local Senior Coalition to the Visitors and Convention Bureau. Representatives from the city and the school met with each of the key stakeholders, explained the project, and listened to their concerns. Many of these conversations led to changes in the center's design, which increased public support for the project.

One city official summarized the process: "We put a lot of effort into this. And at the beginning, I thought we were spending way too much time on the stakeholders analysis piece. It turned out, instead, to be time well spent. It made us think about what we were doing. It got us talking to the right people, including the local tribal government, at the right time."

About this tool

Analyzing stakeholders will help your group produce the following outcomes.

Find out who is a stakeholder and why

The term **stakeholder** refers to everyone who has a vested interest in your project and its outcome. This includes people who stand to gain if your group's goal is successfully achieved—*and* those who believe that they'll lose something as a result. Using this tool allows you to identify both sets of stakeholders as early as possible.

Determine the type of power that stakeholders have over outcomes

For the purposes of stakeholders analysis, **power** means the ability to take action or block action. There are two types of power:

- **Initiation power** gets a project started
- **Maintenance power** keeps it moving

Any community initiative requires both types of power.

A project may achieve initial success but fail in the long run because key stakeholders who control resources needed for the project's future were not taken into account. Consider this statement, for example: "We got the project started with a foundation grant and we were doing a really good job, but the project died after three years because the agency's board wouldn't pick up our budget." In this case, a community group had stakeholders with initiation power but failed to line up stakeholders with maintenance power.

Discover two types of links

Using this tool will help you discover your group's links to stakeholders and the links that stakeholders have with each other. You'll need this information to determine which stakeholders can influence other stakeholders.

Step 1. State the key outcome of your proposed project

Part Two of this book includes a number of tools to help you frame your community project. These include Tool 5: Visioning (page 57), and Tool 6: Translating Vision into Action (page 68). Use these or a similar process, but make sure that your group defines a clear outcome for your project *before* trying to analyze stakeholders.

Take some time to review the nature of this outcome and how you arrived at it. If the group conducting your stakeholders analysis includes the same people who defined the outcome, then this step will take little time. If new members are present, however, it is important to bring them up to speed.

Note: Before you proceed to the next steps, pass out copies of Worksheet 18: Stakeholders Map (page 135), and Worksheet 19: Power and Attitude Grid (page 139). Also select a group member who will participate in the discussion while recording ideas on a flip chart.

Step 2. List stakeholders

As a group, on a flip chart, list all the stakeholders who will be affected by the outcome you reviewed in step 1. Be as specific as possible. For example, listing "businesses" as a stakeholder is too general, because your outcome may affect different businesses in different ways. Instead, name each business and list it separately.

When you've finished the list, take a moment to organize the entries. Then ask group members to write the names of stakeholders on their individual copies of Worksheet 18. They will fill in other sections of this worksheet during the following steps.

WORKSHEET 18 Stakeholders Map

List the desired outcome for your community project. Then list stakeholders who will be affected by the outcome, how they might respond, and why.

Rank each stakeholder's attitude toward the outcome by using the following scale:

Strongly Favor the Outcome	++
Favor the Outcome	+
Neutral to the Outcome	0
Opposed to the Outcome	–
Strongly Opposed to the Outcome	––
Don't Know	?

Rank each stakeholder's power in the appropriate column by using this scale:

Very Powerful	VP
Powerful	P
Not Powerful	NP

Desired Outcome:

Stakeholder	Attitude	Objectives and Values Motivating Their Attitude	Stakeholder's Power		Linkages	
			Initiation	Maintenance	Who Influences Them	Whom They Influence

Step 3. Assess each stakeholder's attitude toward the outcome

There are two parts to this step. Group members work individually; then they share and discuss their work.

First, ask group members to quickly go through the list of stakeholders on Worksheet 18 and predict each stakeholder's attitude toward the outcome. Be sure that group members assess the outcome *through the eyes of each stakeholder.*

It's important to be realistic during this step. To think through the effect of your desired outcome on stakeholders, describe their current situation and contrast it with their possible situation *after* your outcome is achieved. If you don't have enough information to do this, consider collecting it outside the meeting through informal discussions with stakeholders, or by using research techniques. For more information about this kind of research, see Tool 1: Identifying Community Assets (page 22), especially Steps 3 and 4.

Worksheet 18 includes a scale for ranking the probable attitude of each stakeholder. Ask your group members to fill out the Attitude column on their copy of the worksheet. Then share and discuss the rankings as a group. Talk about the objectives and values that might motivate each stakeholder's attitude.

At this point, honesty is critical. Be sure to use the Don't Know rating if the group cannot predict a stakeholder's likely response.

Step 4. Identify each stakeholder's power relative to the project

Note that Worksheet 18 divides power into two categories: initiation and maintenance. This is a key distinction. For example, a mayor or council member may be powerful in starting a project but have little influence when the project is implemented. On the other hand, local residents may exercise a lot of power during implementation, but they may need to form a special group to lobby the council to approve the project.

As a group, discuss each stakeholder's power, classifying it as initiation power, maintenance power, or both. Then fill out the Stakeholder's Power column in Worksheet 18, ranking degrees of power from Very Powerful (VP) to Not Powerful (NP).

Step 5. Determine linkages

A stakeholder's influence can rise or fall, depending on that person's linkages and social capital. Worksheet 18 includes two categories of linkage: who influences the stakeholder, and whom he or she influences. Using your group's wisdom, list the individuals or groups the stakeholder influences or is influenced by.

Step 6. Fill out the Power and Attitude Grid

A Power and Attitude Grid sorts stakeholders by their attitude toward your project and their degree of power. (See Figure 11 for an example.) By sorting stakeholders in this way, you can focus your group's energy in productive ways; create appropriate strategies to communicate with stakeholders; and, in some cases, choose how to mobilize them.

Figure 11. Power and Attitude Grid

ATTITUDE

POWER

1. Positive attitude with much power	2. Negative attitude with much power
3. Positive attitude with little power	4. Negative attitude with little power

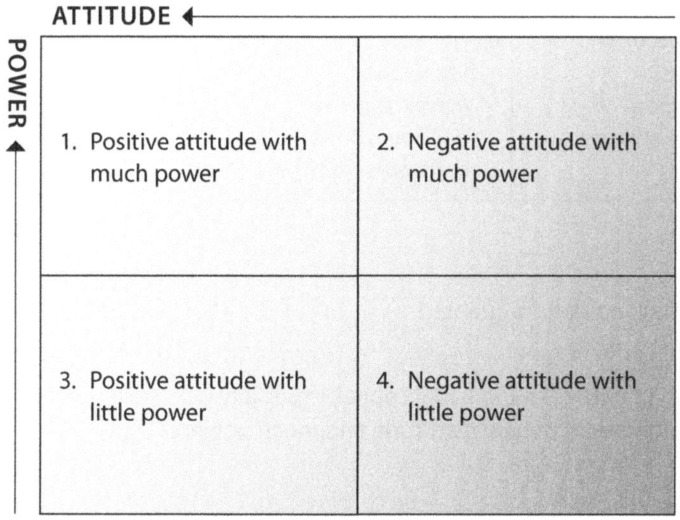

Worksheet 19: Power and Attitude Grid (page 139), is a blank grid that you can copy to use with your group. On this worksheet, include the stakeholders identified in your stakeholders analysis. List each one in the appropriate square, numbered 1 through 4, on the grid. Another option is to create a large flip chart, using the Power and Attitude Grid as a model. You may want to use one sheet for each numbered square.

Step 7. Decide how you will deal with each set of stakeholders

The Stakeholders Map and Power and Attitude Grid you created for Worksheets 18 and 19 give you a basis to engage each stakeholder in a purposeful, planned way. Draw from the ideas in Figure 12: Strategy Suggestions for Stakeholders (page 138), to plan your approach. Hand out copies of this figure or create a flip chart based on it. Discuss the strategies listed for each square and record any suggestions the group strongly favors.

Figure 12. Strategy Suggestions for Stakeholders

ATTITUDE ←

POWER ↑

1. Positive attitude with much power *(Nurture these)*	2. Negative attitude with much power *(Convince, communicate, confront)*
3. Positive attitude with little power *(Seed to empower them through linkages and information)*	4. Negative attitude with little power *(Keep them informed, don't burn any bridges, don't waste energy)*

Square 1

- Don't take these stakeholders for granted.
- Get them involved early on.
- Get them to use their networks and social capital, especially with stakeholders in Square 2 (stakeholders with negative attitude and much power).

Square 2

- Don't ignore these stakeholders in your planning.
- Manage conflict with these stakeholder in productive ways. See Tool 8: Managing Interpersonal Conflict (page 96).
- Remember that stakeholders who have negative attitudes about your current project may be potential allies on future projects.
- Consider changing the way that you frame the outcome of your project, using ideas from the tools listed in Part Two of this book. Be sure that the change in framing is something you can live with.
- Don't waste social capital unnecessarily.

Square 3

- Don't ignore these stakeholders.
- Keep them informed.
- Empower them by asking them to use their social capital and networks, especially with stakeholders in Square 2.

Square 4

- Keep these stakeholders informed.
- Don't waste social capital unnecessarily or make future enemies of these stakeholders.
- Don't waste resources here that could produce more results elsewhere.
- See whether changing the way that you frame the outcome of your project makes a difference in their response.

WORKSHEET 19 Power and Attitude Grid

List each stakeholder you identified in your stakeholders analysis in the appropriate square, numbered 1 through 4, on the grid.

ATTITUDE ←

POWER ↑

1. Positive attitude with much power	2. Negative attitude with much power
3. Positive attitude with little power	4. Negative attitude with little power

TOOL 12. Building Coalitions

This Tool at a Glance

Why Use It
Use this tool to form a broader, more sustainable base of support throughout your community than any single organization can.

When to Use It
This tool is intended to help you build coalitions that are intended to achieve specific goals based on a community analysis. Before building a coalition, strongly consider using the tools described in Part One of this book, including Tool 2: Analyzing Community Problems (page 34), Tool 5: Visioning (page 57), and Tool 6: Translating Vision into Action (page 68). Also complete Tool 11: Analyzing Stakeholders (page 132).

How to Use It
Steps in using this tool are

- Be sure that you need a coalition
- Decide who to recruit
- Recruit members
- Hold the first organizational meeting
- Follow up
- Keep the coalition going

Where to Learn More
Karen Ray. *The Nimble Collaboration: Fine-Tuning Your Collaboration for Lasting Success* (St. Paul, MN: Fieldstone Alliance, 2002).

Michael Winer and Karen Ray. *Collaboration Handbook: Creating, Sustaining and Enjoying the Journey* (St. Paul, MN: Fieldstone Alliance, 1994).

Work Group on Health Promotion and Community Development, University of Kansas. *Promoting Coordination, Cooperative Agreements, and Collaborative Agreements Among Agencies.* http://ctb.ku.edu/tools/en/sub_section_main_1229.htm.

The issues and opportunities that have the greatest effect on the health of your community are complex. To successfully address such issues, a critical mass of individuals and organizations with access to information, technical expertise, financial resources, and human resources must all work together. Unfortunately, many such efforts fail because they lack leadership and structure. Coalitions offer a solution—an effective way for leaders to provide structure for a collaborative effort.

Community Example: Creating a Coalition

The community's assessment and visioning processes lead to a goal: create a community technology center. This center, which was to be located in a struggling downtown shopping mall, would offer state-of-the-art technology and high-speed Internet access.

An action team formed to work on this goal. Members of the team included the owner of the only restaurant left open in the mall, a member of the city council, and a vice president of one of the local banks.

Team members knew that creating and sustaining something as complex as a community technology center would require the efforts and resources of more organizations than they represented. The city council member, who had been the director of a regional community development agency, suggested that they form a coalition to bring the needed resources together in a coordinated, focused way.

The first step in developing this coalition was to do a stakeholders analysis. Team members took the results of this analysis and used it to prioritize which stakeholders they would initially invite to join the coalition. Recognizing that not every stakeholder would make a good coalition partner, they ranked potential members according to three criteria, each expressed as a question:

- What self-interest of the stakeholder would be served if the technology center were successful?
- What would the stakeholder gain by joining the coalition rather than by working on the project independently?
- What resources does the stakeholder control or have access to, and how critical are those resources to starting the center, maintaining it, or both?

Eight stakeholders were chosen to form the coalition's nucleus. These included the local vocational-technical college, the community's largest manufacturing firm, and the Chamber of Commerce. Each organization brought a unique set of characteristics to the coalition. Members of the action team summarized this information in a list with these sample entries:

Vocational-technical college

- *Self-interest:* Their current technology center is outdated. Their students would have access to the center.
- *What they gain:* The college would not have to build their own new center. The new center would not be seen locally as another "school project." And the college would be more integrated into the life of the community.
- *Resources represented:* Technical expertise of their technology center staff, access to state funding, and a foundation interested in supporting technology training.

The community's largest manufacturing firm

- *Self-interest:* They need a technology training site for employees.
- *What they gain:* They would not have to create their own site. Having the vocational-technical college faculty in the same facility would allow the firm to develop a curriculum tailored to the company's needs.
- *Resources represented:* Financial capital, political influence, and power to shape public opinion through their communications staff.

Chamber of Commerce

- *Self-interest:* The technology center would help keep the downtown mall solvent.
- *What they gain:* The Chamber does not have the resources to independently create such a center. Joining the coalition identifies the Chamber with a high potential project and makes them a "player" in that project.

Resources represented: Strong links and high credibility with the local business community and expertise in organizing local initiatives.

Each of the selected stakeholders was invited to a meeting. The agenda was to clarify the coalition's goal, agree on indicators of success for the project, describe how the coalition would be structured to achieve the indicators of success, determine next steps, and schedule the next meeting.

By the end of the meeting, all agenda goals were met. In addition, stakeholders set up a steering committee, identified more participants, and set a time to develop an action plan.

The technology center became a reality. Use of the facility has been cyclical, but the coalition's support has sustained the center and kept it viable.

About this tool

This tool offers steps to help you, as a community leader, form an action-oriented coalition. A **coalition** is a group of individuals, organizations, or both that enters into a mutually beneficial relationship to achieve a common purpose. Coalitions can be long term or short term. Their purpose can range from sharing information to lobbying government officials or running programs.

Coalitions are particularly well suited for complex issues requiring more resources than any one group can access. Through coalitions, members gain an organized way to mobilize a critical mass of support for a community project. In addition, coalitions

- Increase the chance of initial success for a community project
- Increase the likelihood of continued success
- Help members develop a sense of ownership in the project

A basic tenet of any coalition is that members of the coalition can get more of what they want, or get it easier, through joint action than by working alone. In other words, a key factor in forming effective coalitions is self-interest. This can range from the desire for financial gain or accomplishing an organization's mission to a desire to serve the common good or do the "right thing." The self-interests served by a coalition are not necessarily "selfish."

Coalitions that work well have a common set of features:

- **The coalition has a clear purpose and stays focused on it.** Remember that the coalition is a means, not an end in itself. Coalitions fail when they get caught up in their own survival—when the primary purpose becomes maintaining the coalition at all costs. Coalitions also lose their effectiveness when they take on too many projects or fail to adequately focus the resources that they've mobilized.

- **The self-interest of each member is clearly stated.** Every coalition member knows why the other members joined and how each member benefits by joining.
- **Indicators of success are mutually agreed upon.** The various self-interests of members are reflected in a list of outcomes that indicate success. All members agree to work for those outcomes.
- **Roles and responsibilities are clearly defined and fair.** Coalition members understand *what* is expected of them and *when* it is due. The tasks assigned to members and the resources they are asked to bring are aligned with their available resources and the benefit they derive from the coalition.
- **The coalition starts small and expands over time.** Coalitions that start with a small group have an easier time building trust among members, managing the logistics of their meetings, and coordinating member efforts. The ideal group is small enough to manage but large enough to create early successes that attract additional members.

Step 1. Be sure that you need a coalition

To help determine if a coalition is the right tool for your community group, use Worksheet 20: Is a Coalition Necessary? Discuss this list of questions as a large group. If you do not have enough information to answer any of the questions, then determine how and when to get that information.

WORKSHEET 20 Is a Coalition Necessary?

Answer the questions below to determine if a coalition is needed to accomplish your community project.

1. Is the purpose or goal defined clearly enough so that potential coalition members can
   a. Identify their self-interest in it?
   b. Focus their efforts on it?

2. Is the issue or opportunity too complex for a single organization to fully address?

3. Is there enough social capital in the community, especially with potential coalition members, to make a joint effort possible?

4. Is there already an existing coalition or some other group that could bring the resources together without creating another group in the community?

Figure 13 shows sample responses to Worksheet 20.

Figure 13. Is a Coalition Necessary? (Example)

1. Is the purpose or goal defined clearly enough so that potential coalition members can Identify their self-interest in it?
   Focus their efforts on it?

   The Community Technology Center represents a clear goal, and each coalition member will benefit in a specific way from this project.

2. Is the issue or opportunity too complex for a single organization to fully address?

   The technology center requires technical expertise, financial resources, and a level of public support that is beyond what any organization acting alone could generate.

3. Is there enough social capital in the community, especially with potential coalition members, to make a joint effort possible?

   The Chamber of Commerce has a long history of working with both the vocational-technical college and the community's major employer. This social capital should suffice to get the coalition started.

4. Is there already an existing coalition or some other group that could bring the resources together without creating another group in the community?

   Although the Chamber of Commerce has brought groups together to work on projects, the technology center goes beyond their scope and resources. There is no other economic development agency in the community.

Step 2. Decide who to recruit

Remember that effective coalitions start small and expand. Also, an individual or group may be dedicated to dealing with a community issue or opportunity but *not* be committed to working with others on that issue. Start with members who easily recognize the value they gain by joining the coalition.

Using Worksheet 21: Potential Coalition Members (page 145), can help you determine who to recruit for your coalition. Three criteria make up the grid in this worksheet:

- The individual's or organization's apparent *self-interest* in the purpose or goal
- What the individual or organization *gains* by joining the coalition that they would not gain (or not gain easily) on their own
- The importance of the *resources* that the individual or organization controls or can access

You will find Worksheet 21 easier and more beneficial to use *after* you analyze the stakeholders who will be affected by your goal. Before completing this worksheet, also determine a maximum and minimum number of stakeholders that you want to invite.

If you use Worksheet 21 with a group, give each member a chance to fill it out individually. Then ask group members to share and discuss their responses. After this discussion, ask the group to agree on a preferred list of stakeholders. Invite all these individuals or groups, or set priorities for which stakeholders to invite now and which to invite later.

WORKSHEET 21 Potential Coalition Members

Stakeholder	Self-interest	What they gain	Resources represented

Figure 14 shows some sample responses to Worksheet 21.

Figure 14. Potential Coalition Members (Example)

Stakeholder	Self-interest	What they gain	Resources represented
Vo-tech college	*Their facility is outdated*	*Don't have to build their own*	*Technical expertise, access to funding*
Chamber of Commerce	*The tech center would help keep the downtown mall solvent*	*The Chamber does not have the resources to independently create such a center*	*Strong links and high credibility with the local business*
Potential member			
Potential member			

Step 3. Recruit members

Having decided what members the coalition needs, you can now recruit them. Start by contacting individuals who can speak for their organization. In addition, remember the following suggestions.

Use your social capital

If a group is doing the recruitment, group members should recruit the selected stakeholders with whom they have the best relationships. If an individual is doing the recruitment, he or she should use personal networks to help make connections with the selected stakeholders.

Use personal contact

A personal, face-to-face invitation provides an opportunity to clarify issues, answer questions, and affirm for the stakeholder how important their participation in the coalition is. The personal contact can be augmented with letters, brochures, and phone calls.

Use clear, consistent messages

Potential coalition members may be in touch with each other and compare notes on what they hear from you. Inconsistent messages create confusion and erode trust. Your messages should state the coalition's goal and why it matters. Be specific about what you want members to do at this time. Also ask each individual or group to attend a meeting with other potential members to help organize the coalition.

Step 4. Hold the first organizational meeting

The first meeting of a coalition is critical. If the attendees have a positive experience in terms of *product* (what gets accomplished) and *process* (how it gets accomplished), they will be back. If they have a negative experience, you may not get a second chance to bring them into the coalition.

In your agenda for the meeting, include the following items:

- **Make personal introductions.** You may know all the recruits, but they may not know each other.
- **Clarify purpose.** The goal of your coalition should be restated. Review the process you used to create this goal, such as the visioning process described in Tool 5 of this book (page 57). Also provide information that's relevant to the goal. In the example at the beginning of this tool, this could have included the square footage of available space in the mall and data about the community's current lack of available technology.
- **Declare interests.** Give people the opportunity to explain why they are interested in your goal and in the coalition. Encourage them to share how achieving the goal would benefit their organization's mission, values, or bottom line. If the attendees know each other well enough, this can be done in the personal introductions.
- **Develop indicators of success.** Identifying indicators of success makes the goal specific and tangible. During this conversation, attendees can link their self-interest to the goal, and gain motivation to achieve it. For more information on identifying indicators of success, refer to Tool 6: Translating Vision into Action (page 68).
- **Discuss strategy.** At this meeting it is too early to create a detailed action plan. However, a general discussion about how to achieve the goal in a way that meets the indicators of success lays the groundwork for future planning. It also gives attendees a sense of how practical and useful the coalition will be.
- **Choose next steps.** Clarify who will be responsible for certain tasks as the coalition gets started. These include handling logistics for the next meeting, such as time, location, and who will facilitate; contacting more potential coalition members; communicating with the public about the coalition; and creating an action plan.

At a future meeting, coalition members will need to create a long-term structure for the coalition—for example, whether to elect officers or set up a steering committee, and how to make decisions (by majority vote, consensus, unanimous vote).

Step 5. Follow up

After the first meeting, write up minutes or notes and send copies to each person who attended. Equally important is for each attendee to get a follow-up contact from whoever invited them. The purpose of this contact is to get attendees' reactions, respond to their concerns, and hear their suggestions.

Step 6. Keep the coalition going

No matter how noble its purpose may be, a coalition is like any other group: It can lose effectiveness over time or even fall apart. You can do several things to maintain your coalition:

- Recognize and manage conflict between coalition members before it escalates. See Tool 8: Managing Interpersonal Conflict (page 96).
- Conduct meetings that are effective in terms of both product and process.
- Communicate, communicate, and then communicate some more with members about what the coalition is doing and accomplishing. See Tool 7: Building Social Capital through Effective Communication (page 80).
- Recognize and acknowledge individual contributions to the coalition's success.
- Learn from your setbacks and failures without blaming anyone.
- Celebrate your successes all along the way.

TOOL 13. Building Effective Community Teams

This Tool at a Glance

Why Use It
Use this tool to build cohesive, goal-oriented teams that achieve their planned outcomes and increase social capital at the same time.

When to Use It
Learning about effective teams will help your community group at any point, whether you're organizing a new one or seeking to improve the performance of an existing group.

How to Use It
Steps in using this tool take place in the context of three stages.

Stage 1: Mission and Talent
- Clarify the elements of your team's mission
- Do a talent audit
- Define roles and responsibilities

Stage 2: Norms and Buy-in
- Develop norms for decision making
- Develop norms for communication
- Develop norms for meeting management
- Improve buy-in

Stage 3: Power and Morale
- Assess your team's power
- Assess your team's morale and results

Where to Learn More
Beth Gilbertsen and Vijit Ramchandani. *The Fieldstone Nonprofit Guide To Developing Effective Teams* (St. Paul, MN: Fieldstone Alliance, 1999).

Community Example: Hiring Committee

A longtime high school principal had announced his retirement. He was respected by his students, loved by his staff, and lionized by members of his community. The superintendent and members of the school board realized they had the responsibility for filling "some mighty big shoes." Hiring would be a politically sensitive job, both because of the principal's success and because the school itself was central to many community activities.

At the suggestion of the superintendent, the school board appointed a twenty-one-member task force to recommend a candidate for the principal's position. The superintendent and chairperson of the board were ex officio, nonvoting members. Before the task force met, the board and superintendent established some guidelines:

- The purpose of the task force was to recommend one person to become the high school principal. If they wished, task force members could suggest a second or third candidate. The board, in consultation with the superintendent, would make the final decision.
- During its first meeting, the task force was to select a chairperson and choose specific criteria for judging the qualifications of each candidate.
- The task force was encouraged to break into smaller groups, each with specific assignments, such as reading applications, visiting the home communities of finalists, and showing finalists and their families the school and community.
- The task force would be dissolved when it had completed its assignment.

Three months later, the task force presented its first and second choices. The top candidate was chosen for the principal's position, and she accepted it! During the follow-up celebration luncheon, the board, superintendent, task force members, and new principal discussed the process and lessons learned The consensus was that the process worked because task force members had a clear mission, understood their roles and assignments, and met on a regular basis to review their results and their effectiveness as a team, establishing clear agreements about how to make decisions and conduct meetings.

About this tool

We present the **Blandin Model of Community Team Building** visually as a three-stage rocket that delivers a payload of results. Figure 15, page 150, illustrates these stages.

Figure 15. The Blandin Model of Community Team Building

Stage 1: Mission and talent

The first stage of a rocket determines what kind of payload the rocket can carry and whether it will even get off the ground. Similarly, Stage 1 of the Blandin model is critical to team success.

Two things are needed for a strong first stage: mission and talent. By **mission,** we mean the team has a clear purpose, strategic objectives and benchmarks, and methods to track progress. In other words, the team knows what it wants and knows how to tell that it has accomplished its mission. **Talent** means that team members have clear roles and responsibilities, and that the team has the right number of people with the skills, experience, and connections it needs to succeed.

In short, a successful team's first stage includes a clear purpose, goals, benchmarks, and the talent to achieve those goals.

Stage 2: Norms and buy-in

The second stage of a rocket provides additional lift to boost the payload high into the atmosphere. In the Blandin model, Stage 2 has two components: norms and buy-in.

By **norms** we mean agreed-upon rules for decision making, communication, meetings, work handoffs, and debriefings. **Buy-in** means that the team builds commitment by having a compelling purpose and team members who are highly involved in setting goals and making decisions.

Stage 3: Power and morale

The third stage of the rocket provides the final boost to send the payload—results—soaring into orbit. In the Blandin model, Stage 3 includes power and morale. **Power** means that the team has enough money, equipment, time, and authority to accomplish its mission. **Morale** results when the team identifies potential areas of conflict and develops effective ways to deal with it.

The rest of this chapter will walk you through the critical steps of building a team and choosing what to do if the team is not making progress toward intended outcomes.

Stage 1: Mission and talent

Clarify the elements of your team's mission

The mission component of Stage 1 is about framing. It's well worth the time to clarify the elements of your team's mission—purpose, strategic priorities, goals, and indicators of success—*before* proceeding any further. Likewise, teams that are not doing well should review their mission to ensure that this component is in good shape before moving on.

With this in mind, use Worksheet 22: What Is Our Purpose? on page 152. Photocopy this page or download the worksheet from the publisher's web site (see page xxi for download instructions) and distribute it to team members. Even if the team is small, you may find it useful for each team member to fill out the worksheet individually and then share responses as a team. Another option is to have team members individually fill out the purpose section of the worksheet, share responses, reach agreement, and then move on to the goals and indicators.

Note: Being familiar with Tool 5: Visioning (page 57), and Tool 6: Translating Vision into Action (page 68), will help your team complete this worksheet.

WORKSHEET 22 What Is Our Purpose?

1. The purpose of this team is . . .

2. The goals we need to accomplish in order to achieve our purpose are . . .

3. Our indicators of success are:

   Product (What we get done)

   Process (How we get it done)

Do a talent audit

Your team's purpose and goals will determine what kind of talent the team needs to succeed. Use Worksheet 23: Talent Audit (page 153), to make this decision. Photocopy or download this worksheet for distribution. You may also wish to copy it onto a flip chart.

To use Worksheet 23:

1. Write down the team's purpose and goals.
2. Working as a team, fill in the Knowledge, Skills, and Attributes column of the chart. **Knowledge** includes understanding key elements of the issue or community. **Skills** include planning, project management, communication, leadership, financial, and group facilitation. **Attributes** usually include values, behaviors, attitudes, experiences, and connections that members need to get along with each other and achieve the team's goals.
3. List the names of current or potential team members. Check off the knowledge, skills, and attributes that each member brings to the team.
4. Now determine where your team still has gaps. Do you need to recruit people with additional skills or connections? Did you discover significant overlaps in knowledge, skills, and attributes? Could the team achieve its goals with fewer members?

WORKSHEET 23 Talent Audit

Team Purpose: ______________________________

Team Goals:

1.

2

3.

Knowledge, skills, and attributes the team needs	Team member names					
1.						
2.						
3.						
4.						
5.						
6.						
7.						
8.						

Define roles and responsibilities

To make the best use of a team's talents, clearly define the roles and responsibilities of each member. A talent audit usually makes this step easier because it identifies team members' skills and attributes.

To complete stage 1, ask your team to choose a goal and then create a simple action chart for achieving it. Create your action chart on a flip chart and fill it out as a team. Figure 16 illustrates a sample chart.

Figure 16. Action Chart

Task	By whom (role)	By when (responsibility)
1.		
2.		
3.		
etc.		

Stage 2: Norms and buy-in

Norms are the unwritten rules about how a team works. Some norms are about big issues: for example, what gets said at a meeting is not shared outside the meeting, and all decisions are made by consensus. Norms can also extend to smaller issues, such as the fact that some people always sit in the same place at the table during meetings.

There is nothing inherently right or wrong about team norms. What's important is that norms help the team achieve its indicators of success. Not all norms do this, such as a team that never starts its meetings on time. Another team might have a norm of avoiding conflict (which gets in the way of making good decisions), or a norm that those who speak a lot run the group (and quieter members feel left out).

Norms can be difficult to recognize and change because they seem to evolve without any conscious effort. Over time, team members settle on the "rules" for making decisions, and the impact of these rules is never discussed.

While teams develop many types of norms, this tool addresses three that are critical for effective teamwork: norms for decision making, communication, and meeting management.

Develop norms for decision making

Often the *process* for making team decisions is more of a problem than the decisions themselves. The following material reviews some common styles for decision making. None of these styles is better than any other; the most effective choice depends on your current situation.

However, your team should clearly decide which style to use most often and acknowledge when it makes exceptions to this norm. Choose a decision-making style that best draws on the resources of your members and produces decisions that they can "own" and commit to carry out.

Figure 17: Group Decision-Making Styles, presents a continuum of the typical norms for decisions. This continuum ranges from autocratic to consensus, with team input moving from low to high.

Figure 17. Group Decision-Making Styles

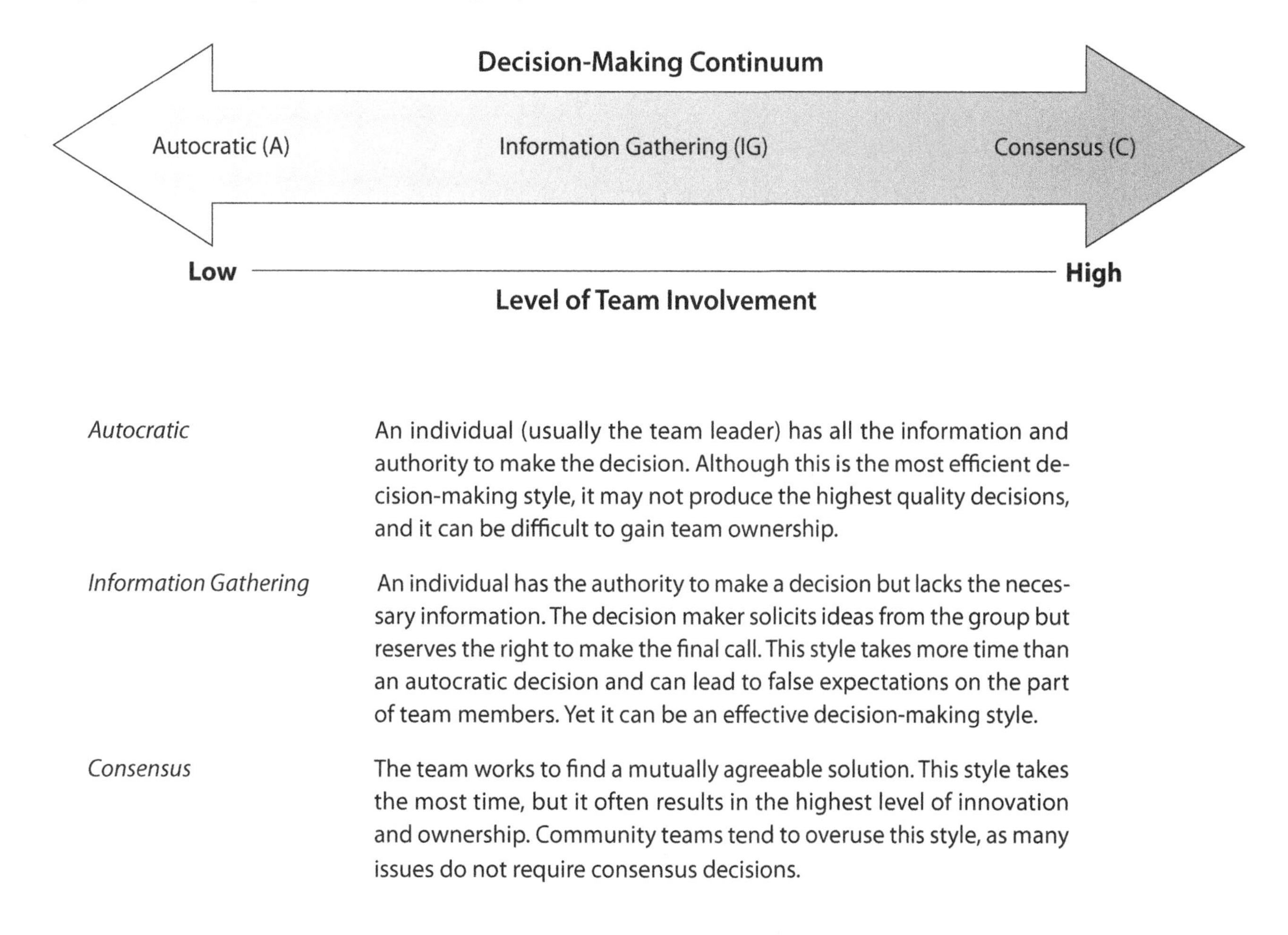

Autocratic — An individual (usually the team leader) has all the information and authority to make the decision. Although this is the most efficient decision-making style, it may not produce the highest quality decisions, and it can be difficult to gain team ownership.

Information Gathering — An individual has the authority to make a decision but lacks the necessary information. The decision maker solicits ideas from the group but reserves the right to make the final call. This style takes more time than an autocratic decision and can lead to false expectations on the part of team members. Yet it can be an effective decision-making style.

Consensus — The team works to find a mutually agreeable solution. This style takes the most time, but it often results in the highest level of innovation and ownership. Community teams tend to overuse this style, as many issues do not require consensus decisions.

To examine your team's decision-making style, complete Worksheet 24: Who Decides (page 156). You may find it helpful to create this worksheet on a flip chart so the team can work on it together. After your team completes this worksheet, discuss the norms for decision making that you will live by.

WORKSHEET 24 Who Decides

In the left-hand column, list the kinds of decisions that your team typically makes. In the center column, describe the way the team wants to make the decision (A = autocratic, IG = information gathering, C = consensus). In the right-hand column, name the person(s) responsible for the final decision.

What Topics?	**How Made?** (A, IG, or C)	**Final Decision Maker?**

Develop norms for communication

Setting and abiding by norms for communication creates a culture of openness and keeps your community appropriately informed. They can cover many areas, for example:

- What information stays in team meetings
- What information gets communicated back to the community
- When team members speak for the team and when they speak for themselves

The following exercise focuses on five positive aspects of team communication. You can add other aspects that you think are particularly important to your team. This exercise uses Worksheet 25: Communication Ground Rules (page 158). Worksheet 26: Team Communication Climate (page 159), is optional.

Note: If you are concerned about the communication norms in a team that is already formed, consider asking members to complete Worksheet 26 and discuss the results *before* doing this norm-setting exercise.

Here are the steps to follow:

1. Remind the team that the purpose of this exercise is to establish the norms (ground rules) for team communication.
2. Hand out Worksheet 25 and ask the team if any other aspects of team communication need to be added to it.
3. Ask team members to work individually, writing at least one ground rule that will foster each aspect of team communication listed in the worksheet.
4. Discuss each member's suggested ground rules. Agree on a list that you will commit to use.
5. Write up your ground rules and distribute them to the team. Give the ground rules to new members when they join.

WORKSHEET 25 Communication Ground Rules

Listed below are five positive aspects of communication that help teams be more effective. If there are other aspects that you think are particularly important for your team, please add them. For each aspect, write at least one ground rule that would support it and help make it happen in your team.

Aspect: Team members openly express their opinions during team meetings.

Ground rule: (*Example: On important topics, each individual is specifically asked to give an opinion and to state it the same way he or she would outside of the meeting.)*

Aspect: Team members listen to each other's perspectives.

Ground rule: *(Example: No side conversations when another team member is speaking.)*

Aspect: Team members can bring bad news to this team.

Ground rule: *(Example: Bad news about what the team is doing or not doing is shared during meetings, not in the parking lot.)*

Aspect: The team does not have group members who consistently dominate the discussions.

Ground rule: *(Example: Everyone is expected to speak at least twice during every meeting; no one can speak for more than five minutes at one time.)*

Aspect: Team members safeguard confidential information.

Ground rule: *(Example: What gets said in a team meeting stays in the meeting until the team agrees what gets shared outside the meeting and with whom.)*

Aspect:

Ground rule:

Aspect:

Ground rule:

Aspect:

Ground rule:

WORKSHEET 26 Team Communication Climate

Use the following scale to respond to the numbered items below.

1	2	3	4	5
Strongly Disagree	**Disagree**	**Neutral**	**Agree**	**Strongly Agree**

1. Team members openly express their opinions on this team. ________
2. Team members take the time to listen to others' perspectives. ________
3. Team members can bring bad news to this team. ________
4. This team does not have team members who dominate meetings. ________
5. Team members safeguard confidential information. ________

TOTAL SCORE ________

Add up your scores and circle the corresponding category below:

High = 20–25	My team has a supportive communication climate
Med. = 15–19	A solid score, but the team could create a more open communication climate
Low < 15	My team likely has a defensive climate

Scoring Guide

The communication climate of any team helps to determine its effectiveness. Teams with supportive environments encourage team member participation, free and open exchange of information, and constructive conflict resolution. Teams with defensive climates have team members who inappropriately share confidential information, make only guarded statements, and suffer from a lack of trust and reduced morale.

Develop norms for meeting management

Nothing can limit team performance more than poor meeting management. Yet the problem is easily solved. Team members often have different perspectives on how to run effective meetings. The sooner that your team can agree on norms for meeting management, the more effective the team will be. As a team, discuss and answer the following questions:

1. How frequently and when should the team get together?
2. How long should the meetings be?
3. Is meeting attendance mandatory?
4. Will an agenda be sent out prior to each meeting? (This is recommended.) If so, who is responsible for creating the agenda, and when will team members receive it?
5. Will the team stick to the agenda during meetings? If so, what are the rules for getting the meeting back on track or upholding time limits?
6. Will team members receive materials to review prior to the meeting? If so, are they expected to read it?
7. Are team members expected to show up on time and not leave early?
8. Who will document the team's decisions? How?
9. How will team members be informed of decisions?

Improve buy-in

Buy-in means commitment. Teams will not get very far if some team members are committed and others couldn't care less about team success. Two of the critical factors in buy-in are creating a compelling purpose and keeping team members involved.

Many people want to be a part of something bigger than themselves. They want to make a difference or an impact, and they realize that working on a team can be a good way to do that. People also want to feel a personal connection to what they do, and they're inspired by activities that align with their personal values. Joining a team with a compelling purpose can satisfy all these desires.

Perhaps the most effective way to build commitment is to keep members involved in creating the team's purpose, goals, and norms. This is easy when working with a new group. With existing groups, involvement can be renewed through continuing discussions about ways for members to contribute.

The following steps can help your team improve buy-in. Use them when forming a new team and framing its purpose, or when your team has been working together for a while and needs a "reenergizer."

1. Team members ask themselves, *Why is this team's purpose important to me?*
2. Members share their responses and remind each other about why they are part of the team.
3. Next, team members ask themselves, *Do all team members get adequate opportunities to be involved and contribute? What about this team helps or hinders members from being involved and contributing?*
4. Team members share their answers to the questions in step 3. You may find it helpful to record the answers on a flip chart using the following format.

Helps	Hinders

5. The team identifies ways to build on things listed in the Helps column and address the items in the Hinders column.

Stage 3: Power and morale

Power in this case means having the resources needed to achieve the team's purpose and goals. Needs for resources can come in many forms, but typically they involve time, money, equipment, connections, and latitude for making decisions.

Some teams may have enough time or equipment but lack money or decision-making latitude. For example, teams supporting operating levies to improve local schools may not have the funds needed to place ads in the weekly newspaper or do local mailings. Or a community task force may not have the decision-making authority to finalize the location of a playground.

Assess your team's power

Your team can run a quick assessment to measure its power. The talent audit (Worksheet 23, page 153) conducted in stage 1 of this tool gives a good baseline measurement of available resources. Review the audit as a team. Then create a simple checklist or flip chart that documents the resources the team has needed and how it obtained them. This practice can also help your team plan to seek other resources. The table on page 162 is an example.

Resource Needed	How Obtained
Information	
Money	
Authority	
Social Capital	
Facilities	
Other	

Assess your team's morale and results

Poor morale often indicates that things are not going well for a community team. Signs of poor morale include in-fighting, hidden agendas, and declining attendance.

Poor team morale is a symptom of an underlying problem. Perhaps team members are not getting along because

- The purpose or goals of the team are unclear
- The team has too many or too few people
- The norms governing team behavior are not appropriate
- Some team members are uncommitted
- The team does not have the resources it needs to succeed

Therefore, the first step in raising morale is to determine which aspects of the team are not working.

Results are the deliverables for the team—the rocket's payload. Like morale, results are produced by other components of the team. Results flow from having a compelling purpose, clear goals, the right talent, defined norms, a high level of commitment, adequate resources, and members who get along. If your team is coming up short on results, then examine these components.

Use Worksheet 27: Team Assessment Survey (page 164), for this purpose. Worksheet 28: Feedback Report for Team Assessment Survey (page 165), offers suggestions for strengthening the components ranked lowest by the members of your team in Worksheet 27. Note that Worksheet 28 includes an overview of the Blandin Model of Community Team Building.

Here is a brief process for using these two worksheets:

1. At a team meeting, give each team member a copy of Worksheet 27. Ask them to fill out the worksheet anonymously before your next meeting and to give their completed copies to a team member who will summarize the results. On the agenda for your next meeting, include time to discuss these results.

2. Contact the team member who agreed to create the summary. He or she can do this by tallying the individual scores on Worksheet 27 and entering them as instructed in Worksheet 28.

3. Distribute copies of this summary (the completed Worksheet 28) in preparation for your next meeting.

4. At that meeting, discuss Worksheet 28.Create flip-chart pages modeled on Figure 18: Assessment Results and Implications. Write down your team's strengths, areas of improvement, and surprises. Also list the implications of your results for the team's ability to drive change and get results. For the low scoring components in Worksheet 28, review the listed suggestions and select strategies to strengthen the team components that need attention.

Figure 18. Assessment Results and Implications

Assessment Results	Implications
Key strengths	
Areas of Improvement	
Surprises	

WORKSHEET 27 Team Assessment Survey

Depending on the team you are rating, you may find that some of the items do not apply. In that case, you should rate the item as a 3. In general, new teams are likely to receive lower ratings than more experienced teams. Use the following scale to respond to the items:

1	2	3	4	5
Strongly Disagree	**Disagree**	**Neutral**	**Agree**	**Strongly Agree**

Name and purpose of team:____

____

1. I have a clear understanding of our team's purpose. ________
2 I understand our team's goals. ________
3. I know the indicators of success for our team. ________
4. Our team has the right number of people. ________
5. Our team has the right mix of skills, experience, and connections. ________
6. Team members have clear roles and responsibilities. ________
7. Our team plans and manages meetings to make efficient use of time. ________
8. Our team spends enough time working on team goals versus dealing with more reactive issues. ________
9. Our team uses agreed-upon processes for making decisions. ________
10. Our team makes sound and timely decisions. ________
11. Team members communicate with each other openly and directly. ________
12. Team members are good at safeguarding confidential information. ________
13. Our team takes the time to learn from both successes and failures. ________
14. Team members are passionate about our team's purpose. ________
15. I believe my fellow team members to be trustworthy. ________
16. I believe our team has a high level of relevant knowledge, experience, and strong social connections. ________
17. Team members are actively involved with team goal setting and decision making. ________
18. Our team has the authority it needs to make important team decisions. ________
19. Our team has the resources necessary to achieve the team's goals. ________
20. Our team has enough time to achieve results. ________
21. Our team builds and executes plans to accomplish team goals. ________
22. People are proud to be a part of this team. ________
23. Our team works well together. ________
24. The people on our team trust each other. ________
25. Our team resolves conflict among team members in a timely manner. ________
26. Team members back up the decisions made by the team. ________
27. Our team adapts quickly to changing demands. ________
28. Our team produces high-quality work. ________
29. Our team stays on track and meets deadlines. ________
30. Our team gets results. ________

TOTAL ________

WORKSHEET 28 Feedback Report for Team Assessment Survey

An Overview of the Blandin Model of Community Team Building

The Blandin Community Leadership Program created its team building model to help community leaders understand the components a team needs to achieve the results desired. It is illustrated as a three-stage rocket delivering a payload of results.

The Blandin Model of Community Team Building

Stage 1
The first stage of a rocket determines what kind of payload the rocket can carry and whether it will even get off the ground. Similarly, the first stage of the Blandin Team Model is critical to team success.

Two components are necessary for a strong first stage: mission and talent. By *mission* we mean the team has a clear purpose, has set strategic objectives and benchmarks, and has developed methods to track progress. In other words, the team knows what it wants and has agreed on how it will know it when it has accomplished its mission. By *talent* we mean that the team members have clear roles and responsibilities, and that the team has the right number of people with the skills, experience, and connections it needs to succeed.

Stage 2
The second stage of a rocket provides additional lift to boost the payload high into the atmosphere. This stage includes two components: norms and buy-in. By *norms* we mean that the team sets agreed-upon rules for decision making, communication, meetings, work hand offs, and debriefings. By *buy-in* we mean that the team builds commitment through a compelling purpose and team members who are highly involved in goal setting and decision making.

In practice, Stage 2 includes setting the rules, or norms, for how team members will work together, and gaining the commitment of team members to the team's mission. To work effectively, team rules should cover decision making, communicating, and running meetings. Team members must also find ways to build commitment and buy-in to the team's mission.

Stage 3
The third stage of the rocket provides the final boost to send the payload (results) soaring into orbit. Stage 3 includes two components: power and morale. By *power* we mean that the team has enough money, equipment, time, and authority to accomplish its mission. By *morale* we mean that the team has identified potential areas of conflict and developed effective ways to deal with it.

About this report
Each member of the team has completed a survey of the team's performance. The results are compiled here for group discussion. The group scores are listed based on the three-stage model above. Your team goal is to find ways to improve *mission, talent, norms, buy-in, power,* and *morale* so that the team can improve its *results.* Following is an analysis of results for each of these components.

Worksheet 28 continued

Stage 1: MISSION

Team Assessment Survey Items 1–3

1.	I have a clear understanding of our team's purpose.	________
2.	I understand our team's goals.	________
3.	I know the indicators of success for our team.	________
	TOTAL	________
	Number of team members who responded	________

Score: Add up the total rankings for items 1–3 and divide by the number of team members who responded. This will give an average response for the group. Fill in this number as the team's MISSION score.

Team MISSION score ____________

High = 12–15	The team has a clear sense of direction and there are good clear indicators for tracking progress toward team goals.
Med. = 11–9	A solid score, but there may be some confusion about the purpose, goals, or indicators of success.
Low < 9	The team may lack clarity about its purpose, goals, and indicators of success.

Suggestions for Improvement

- Develop a clear purpose for the team
- Identify the priorities and create goals as a team
- Develop and/or ensure that all team members understand the indicators of success for the team's product and process
- Create a system for tracking progress against team goals
- Make clear the links between team accomplishments and the community change initiative

Notes:

Worksheet 28 continued

Stage 1: TALENT

Team Assessment Survey Items 4–6

4.	Our team has the right number of people.	______
5.	Our team has the right mix of skills, experience, and connections.	______
6.	Team members have clear roles and responsibilities.	______
	TOTAL	______
	Number of team members who responded	______

Score: Add up the total rankings for items 4–6 and divide by the number of team members who responded. This will give an average response for the group. Fill in this number as the team's talent score.

Team TALENT score: ______________

High = 12–15	The team has the right number of people with the right skills, experience, and connections to accomplish the team's goals.
Med. = 9–11	A solid score, but the team may not have the right number of people, has ill-defined roles, or lacks some critical skills, experience, or connections.
Low < 9	The team may lack the talent it needs to accomplish its goals. There may be too few people to adequately handle the workload or too many people involved in work or decision-making processes. Team members may lack clear roles.

Suggestions for Improvement

- Determine the skills and experience the team needs to accomplish its goals.
- Conduct a talent audit to determine whether the team has the required skills.
- Analyze workload to determine whether there are too few or too many team members. If workload is high, it may be that team members lack needed skills or experience or they lack the resources needed to get the work done.
- Ensure that individual team members have clear roles and responsibilities.

Notes:

Worksheet 28 continued

Stage 2: NORMS

Team Assessment Survey Items 7–13	
7. Our team plans and manages meetings to make efficient use of time.	_________
8. Our team spends enough time working on team goals versus dealing with more reactive issues.	_________
9. Our team uses agreed-upon processes for making decisions.	_________
10. Our team makes sound and timely decisions.	_________
11. Team members communicate with each other openly and directly.	_________
12. Team members are good at safeguarding confidential information.	_________
13. Our team takes the time to learn from both successes and failures.	_________
TOTAL	_________
Number of team members who responded	_________

Score: Add up the total rankings for items 7–13 and divide by the number of team members who responded. This will give an average response for the group. Fill in this number as the team's norms score.

Team NORMS score: _____________

High = 28–35 The team has developed good processes for getting work done, looks for ways to work better, uses its time wisely, makes good decisions, and spends needed time on proactive issues.

Med. = 21–27 A solid score, but the team may be too reactive, may not use its time as wisely as it could, could make better decisions, or may be using inefficient work processes.

Low < 21 This team is not using efficient meeting management, has poor decision-making processes, is too reactive, and/or is not using time wisely. These lower scores may also be associated with newer teams.

Suggestions for Improvement

- Develop agreed-upon processes for making team decisions
- Improve meeting management techniques
- Spend time in meetings addressing both proactive and reactive issues
- Set rules for confidentiality and team communication processes
- Use debriefings to identify root causes of problems and mistakes

Notes:

Worksheet 28 continued

Stage 2: BUY-IN

Team Assessment Survey Items 14–17.

14. Team members are passionate about our team's purpose.	______
15. I believe my fellow team members to be trustworthy.	______
16. I believe our team has a high level of relevant knowledge, experience, and strong social connections.	______
17. Team members are actively involved with team goal setting and decision making.	______
TOTAL	______
Number of team members who responded	______

Score: Add up the total rankings for items 14–17 and divide by the number of team members who responded. This will give an average response for the group. Fill in this number as the team's buy-in score.

Team BUY-IN score: ______________

High = 16–20	There is a high level of buy-in to team goals and roles
Med. = 12–15	A solid score, but the level of buy-in to team goals and roles could be better
Low < 12	A low level of buy-in to team goals and roles

Suggestions for Improvement

- Team members should work together to build a compelling team purpose.
- Ensure that all team members agree with the team's purpose and goals. Have a team meeting to review and possibly modify the team's purpose and goals.
- Ensure that all team members are comfortable with their individual roles and responsibilities.
- The team may have to be more intentional about making sure all members have adequate opportunity to be involved and to contribute.
- Ensure that all team members understand how team accomplishments contribute to the community change initiative.

Notes:

Worksheet 28 continued

Stage 3: POWER

Team Assessment Survey Items 18–21.

18.	Our team has the authority it needs to make important team decisions.	______
19.	Our team has the resources necessary to achieve the team's goals.	______
20.	Our team has enough time to achieve results.	______
21.	Our team builds and executes plans in order to accomplish team goals.	______
	TOTAL	______
	Number of team members who responded	______

Score: Add up the total rankings for items 18–21 and divide by the number of team members who responded. This will give an average response for the group. Fill this in as the team's POWER score.

Team POWER score: ____________

High = 16–20	The team has the necessary resources, money, and decision-making latitude and builds and executes action plans to accomplish its goals.
Med. = 12–15	A solid score, but the team may not have everything it needs or does not know how to create and carry out action plans.
Low < 12	The team does not have the resources it needs to accomplish its goals. It may not be doing any planning or acting in accordance with its plans.

Suggestions for Improvement

- Do a stakeholders analysis (Tool 11) to find ways to increase decision-making latitude
- Devise ways to help the team get the resources it needs to accomplish its goals
- Revise timelines if the team needs more time to acquire the resources, money, time, or talent it needs to be successful
- Create team action plans (see Tool 6, page 68); hold team members accountable for their action plan deliverables

Notes:

Worksheet 28 continued

Stage 3: MORALE

Team Assessment Survey Items 22–26.

22.	People are proud to be a part of this team.	________
23.	Our team works well together.	________
24.	The people on our team trust each other.	________
25.	Our team resolves conflict among team members in a timely manner.	________
26.	Team members back up the decisions made by the team.	________
	TOTAL	________
	Number of team members who responded	________

Score: Add up the total rankings for items 22–26 and divide by the number of team members who responded. This will give an average response for the group. Fill in this number as the team's MORALE score.

Team MORALE score: ____________

High = 20–25	The team has a high level of morale and uses effective methods for resolving internal conflict.
Med. = 15–19	A solid score, but team morale and conflict management could be better.
Low < 14	Team morale may be suffering. These lower scores could be due to poor internal communication, the use of poor conflict resolution techniques, or problems with one or more of the other team components.

Suggestions for Improvement

- Make sure everyone is encouraged to voice ideas in team meetings
- Ensure team members practice good listening skills (Tool 7, page 80) during team meetings
- Bring up, discuss, and resolve intrateam conflict as it occurs
- Confront problem behavior immediately and directly
- Ensure team members agree with and will back up team decisions
- Gather information about the other five team components to determine areas of dissatisfaction (poor morale is usually an indicator or result of trouble in other aspects of teamwork)
- Discuss areas of team dissatisfaction and develop and implement action plans to resolve these issues

Notes:

Worksheet 28 continued

Payload: RESULTS

Team Assessment Survey Items 27–30.

27. Our team adapts quickly to changing demands. ________
28. Our team produces high-quality work ________
29. Our team says on track and meets deadlines. ________
30. Our team gets results. ________

TOTAL ________

Number of team members who responded ________

Score: Add up the total rankings for items 27–30 and divide by the number of team members who responded. This will give an average response for the group. Fill in this number as the team's RESULTS score.

Team RESULTS score: ____________

High = 16–20	This is a high performing team that accomplishes a great deal.
Med. = 12–15	A solid performing team, but it could have even more impact.
Low < 12	Team impact needs to be improved. These results could be because the team is new or may have problems in one or more components of the Blandin Team Model.

Suggestions for Improvement

- Determine whether a team is really necessary to accomplish your purpose and goals.
- Determine whether goals and objectives could be done more effectively by another team.
- Review the results of the Team Assessment Survey and identify low-scoring components. Devise plans for improving low scores.

Notes:

TOOL 14. Recruiting and Sustaining Volunteers

This Tool at a Glance

Why Use It
Use this tool to help your community group attract volunteers and keep them involved.

When to Use It
This tool was written for community leaders who are working with volunteers in specific community initiatives. It is not intended for directors of institutional programs that work with volunteers on a long-term basis to provide a service or carry out a program.

How to Use It
Steps in using this tool are

- Create a volunteer job description
- Find and recruit volunteers
- Keep volunteers on the job

Where to Learn More
Gary Stern. *Marketing Workbook Volume II: Mobilize People for Marketing Success* (St. Paul, MN: Fieldstone Alliance, 1997).

Work Group on Health Promotion and Community Development, University of Kansas. *Community Tool Box: Chapter 11. Recruiting and Training Volunteers.* http://ctb.ku.edu/tools/en/chapter_1011.htm.

In community life, little gets done without volunteers. They are the people who make the phone calls, attend the meetings, raise the funds, and clean up after the party is over. Volunteers' time is a nonrenewable resource, and effective community leaders treat it that way.

Community Example: Citizen of the Year

The proclamation naming Tina as the community's Citizen of the Year included these words:

> The first year we thought it was a successful event because it was new. The second year we thought it was because the organizers were lucky. Now that the event is in its fifth year and is bigger than ever, we recognize that this is due in large part to Tina's leadership.

The proclamation referred to Children's Night Out, which in its fifth year involved 150 volunteers and served over 2,000 people. It started as a simple idea to provide an affordable, fun night for young children and their parents. The first event featured games, prizes, cookies, and hot chocolate. Now the event includes open skating, live entertainment, workshops on parenting, and a fireworks display. Except for a small grant from the local community foundation, all costs were covered by donations, and all the work was done by volunteers.

Tina's contribution to the event, which won her recognition as Citizen of the Year, was that since the beginning she recruited and coordinated the volunteers. Many of these people gave their time to this effort on a year-round basis. In spite of the number of hours the volunteers put in and the complexity of some of the tasks they were asked to do, the word in the community was clear: "If you are going to volunteer for only one thing this year, go to Tina and sign up for the Children's Night Out. She makes it worthwhile."

During her interview with the Citizen of the Year committee, Tina was asked how she managed to get and keep so many people involved when numerous other worthwhile community efforts were struggling to get volunteers. Her response was:

"When I recruit volunteers, I don't try to convince people to do something they don't really want to do. Instead, I try to show them that this is an opportunity to do something they already want to do. I make sure every volunteer has a clear job description. If it entails something they haven't done before, I have someone show them how to do it.

"I also make sure that people get acknowledged and thanked for what they accomplish. Volunteers give us one of their most scarce resources—their time. It's my job to see that we don't waste it and that they have a good time giving it."

About this tool

An effective community leader knows that volunteers are people who have chosen to participate in a project, and that they can *at any time* choose other options. In other words, a volunteer is someone who could just as easily be somewhere else doing something else. And they probably will be if their experience in your community initiative is not a positive one.

Why people volunteer

As you get ready to recruit volunteers for your community initiative, ask yourself why people volunteer. What motivates others in your community to give of their time, energy, and expertise? And how do the tasks you give them match up with what motivates them?

Keep in mind that people may volunteer for more than one reason. Following are some typical reasons and their implications for you as a community leader.

To make a difference. Many people volunteer because they want to make things better, to fix a problem, to produce something for others in the community. Wanting to make a difference means wanting to see results. As a community leader, ask, *What specific results will volunteers in this community initiative see as the result of their involvement?*

To be with people. Volunteering can help new people in the community to meet others. It can be a way to develop networks that help people professionally. And it can provide an opportunity for family members to be together by volunteering together. In short, volunteering can be a way to feel like a part of a group. As a community leader, ask, *Who will volunteers be working with in this community initiative? What benefit would a volunteer gain from those relationships?*

To gain experience. Volunteering for a project can help people learn more about important community issues or opportunities. This activity assists people to develop skills that transfer to the work world and provide experience that looks good on a résumé. As a community leader, ask, *What will volunteers learn or what new skills might they develop by being involved in this community initiative? How might that be helpful to them?*

To respond to a sense of duty. Sometimes people volunteer because, for them, it is simply the "right thing to do." Their effort may come from a desire to give something back to the community. It may be based on religious convictions or other values. Many community volunteers come from families with a tradition of volunteering and assume that it is a normal part of life. As a community leader, ask, *What basic values or traditions does this community initiative appeal to that would make it the right thing to do?*

To have fun. Volunteering is work. But work does not have to be oppressive. Remember, volunteers are not doing this for a paycheck. If their experience is unpleasant, they can always do something else. As a community leader, ask, *Given what we want volunteers to do, how do we want them to do it? Who do we want them to work with, and how can they have some fun while getting the work done?*

To do something different. For some people, one of the rewards in volunteering is the chance to escape a routine. It may be a chance to get out of the house. It may be an opportunity to use skills that are underused at work. Volunteering can be a time to step off the treadmill for a while. As a community leader, ask, *How will this community initiative tap volunteers' strengths and expertise and still give them a chance to do something different if they choose?*

Types of volunteers

As you develop your strategies for recruiting and sustaining volunteers, identify the type of volunteers who are most likely to become involved in the different phases and activities of your project. Generally, volunteers can be categorized based on whether they want to make a long-term or a short-term commitment. One type of volunteer is not better than another. However, their interests and motivations are somewhat different, leading to different levels and kinds of involvement. The same individual can be a short-term volunteer with one project and a long-term volunteer with another. Both are important to the success of community initiatives.

Long-term volunteers tend to be dedicated to the cause or the organization. These volunteers are in it for the "long haul" because the purpose of the group is very important to them. That purpose may tap a deeply held value of theirs, such as gender and racial equity. Or the purpose might relate to a significant experience in a volunteer's life, such as losing a child in a car accident with a drunken driver. As a community leader, ask, *Does this initiative have a purpose that connects with people at that level?*

Long-term volunteers are often willing to do whatever needs to be done. Because they are so committed to the purpose and the group, these volunteers will take on almost any assignment. While this dedication can be a great source of strength for a community initiative, it can also become a problem in at least three ways:

- Volunteers may take on assignments that they are ill-suited for
- Even the most dedicated volunteer can become exhausted or start to feel used if they are continually asked to be "all things to all people"
- Because they will "do it all," long-term volunteers can become exclusive and not bring others into the project, the assumption being that "it's easier to do it yourself than to take the time to find someone else to do it"

As a community leader, ask, *What can our initiative do to minimize these potential problems?*

Long-term volunteers are usually motivated by both achievement *and* affiliation. Because of their belief in the purpose of the group or project, these volunteers expect their efforts to produce results related to that purpose. They often share values or life experience with other volunteers. Long-term volunteers can become friends and being together is an important part of their volunteer experience. As a community leader, ask yourself, *How will this project meet the achievement and affiliation needs of long-term volunteers?*

Some long-term volunteers are "recruited" when they step forward and initiate contact with the group or project as they learn about it. Other long-term volunteers are recruited by existing project volunteers who have similar values or lives. This type of recruitment is often how long-term volunteers replace themselves. As a community leader, ask, *How will potential long-term volunteers find out about this project, especially during its initial phases? How will we help our long-term volunteers recruit other long-term volunteers?*

Short-term volunteers tend to be interested in but not dedicated to the cause or organization. They support the cause or purpose, but it is not a passion for them. It can be a temptation for those staff and volunteers who are passionate about a group's purpose to either try to "convert" a volunteer who is not as interested, or to simply dismiss them. This usually results in the loss of potential volunteers. So, as a community leader, ask, *How will our initiative communicate its purpose in such a way that people with differing levels of interest will consider volunteering?*

Short-term volunteers usually look for a well-defined assignment that will be completed within a specific, limited amount of time. They want to know what the expected result of their effort is, how that result is going to get accomplished, and when the job will be done. Their commitment centers on getting the task done, not on doing whatever it takes to keep the project going. As a community leader, ask, *Will our project have well-defined, time-limited activities that volunteers can get involved in?*

Short-term volunteers are often motivated by achievement on a specific project. While short-term volunteers may enjoy the company of the other volunteers, their satisfaction comes primarily from getting the job done. At times, short-term volunteers who are very focused on the task can seem brusque or controlling to those for whom relationships with other volunteers are important. If you are going to need short-term volunteers, ask, *How will our project help them meet their achievement needs and still meet the affiliation needs of other volunteers?*

Short-term volunteers are recruited through attraction to the project or personal connection. Some will sign up for a particular job because they like to do what is entailed in that task (for example, set up the booths for the silent auction). As with long-term volunteers, one of the best sources of short-term volunteers are people who are already involved in the project who are willing to recruit others. In this case, however, new people are recruited not in terms of making a long-lasting commitment to the group or project, but in terms of helping out with a very specific task. As a community leader, ask, *Will our project have clearly defined tasks and job descriptions that attract short-term volunteers? How will we help those already volunteering for the project recruit short-term volunteers?*

Sources of volunteers

There are many sources of volunteers. Significant numbers can be found by contacting employers, by networking with organizations that serve retirees, by contacting professional groups willing to provide pro bono services, and by contacting organizations that serve people training for new positions (postsecondary schools, job training sites, trade associations, and so forth).

Workplace volunteers. For many places of employment, part of being a good corporate citizen involves letting employees use work time for preapproved volunteer activities. And in some cases, employers will assign an employee to a specific volunteer activity for a limited period of time. As a community leader, find out the policies regarding employee volunteer activities of the businesses, institutions, and agencies in your community. *Instead of asking local businesses for direct financial contributions to your project, consider asking for their employees' time.*

Retirees. Not only does our society have an increasing number of retirees, but these retirees represent a highly educated generation with a wide range of skills and experience. As a community leader, ask, *What is the best way to connect with retirees in the community—churches, the golf club, the health spa? What networks do you have access to that could help you recruit retirees as volunteers?*

Professional volunteers. Some professionals will offer their services to the project without charging for them. For example, a lawyer may help set up contracts, an accountant may set up a bookkeeping system or do an audit, a realtor may help find a site, or a graphic designer may create a brochure. As a community leader, ask, *What professional* *services will our initiative need? Are there professional associations or individual professionals that can help get those services on a volunteer basis?*

Transitional volunteers. Many people are available and open to volunteering because they are in a time of transition. A transitional volunteer may be a college senior or recent college graduate who wants to make contacts and add experience to their résumé. It may be someone who is in a job transition and sees volunteering as a way to explore career options, or it may be someone who has lost their life partner and needs something productive to fill their time. As a community leader, ask, *How would we identify these people in our community? How will transitional volunteers be able to identify our project as an opportunity?*

Step 1. Create a volunteer job description

No matter what type of volunteer you seek or what volunteer source you're tapping, remember that getting and keeping volunteers requires that you and they are clear about what they're expected to do and why it's important. The best way to achieve this is through developing job descriptions for your volunteers.

A volunteer job description can help you specify the skills and qualities that volunteers need for your initiative. The description can also motivate people to volunteer for roles that meet their interests and talents. In addition, you can use a job description to guide and reward a volunteer's work on a project.

Having a written job description for each individual volunteer in your project would be ideal, but it may not be necessary. However, having a written job description for each type of volunteer *activity* in your initiative is necessary.

Structure the position to motivate volunteers

The first step in preparing volunteer job descriptions is to develop a checklist of all the tasks that need to be done in your initiative. These tasks may range from chairing subcommittees to answering the telephone for the project's information hotline.

The next step is to list, for each task, the required knowledge, skills, abilities, and attitudes. You may find it helpful to ask yourself, *What kind of person could really do this job well and would enjoy doing the job?*

With the above checklists in hand, frame the volunteer positions in such a way that they move people to say, *Yes, I will spend time on your project.* Volunteer positions that motivate people to say yes and *keep* saying yes are structured so that

- **Volunteers gain a sense of ownership.** Given the level of involvement and responsibility in the job description, volunteers feel that their contribution is important and they are part of the team.
- **Volunteers have some discretion about how the job is done.** Sometimes there are very specific ways to complete a task—for example, when everyone on the phone bank

uses the same script for soliciting donations. Even in these situations, volunteers need to know that they have some leeway to deal with unexpected situations as they arise.

- **The outcomes or indicators of success are clearly defined.** Most volunteers are glad to accept responsibility, but they need to know what they are responsible for. Moreover, they need to have a clear picture of what indicates success so that they know how their performance will be judged.
- **Clear boundaries are established.** The time commitment for the position is explicitly stated both in terms of how much time the volunteer is expected to spend (say, four hours a week) and for how long (until March 1). If any activities or behaviors are excluded, those should also be made clear. For example: *When delivering meals to the elderly you may not offer them transportation in your vehicle.* You can also set boundaries regarding what the volunteer is not responsible for: *Volunteers are not responsible for closing the facility after evening activities; that is the job of paid staff.*

Write the job description

Once volunteer jobs are structured, your next step is to write a job description. There are many available formats. Most of them contain the elements included in Figure 19: What to Include in a Volunteer Job Description.

Figure 19. What to Include in a Volunteer Job Description

Element	Answers This Question	Example
Job title	What will we call this job?	Fundraising Committee Chair
Reports to . . .	Who is this position accountable to—where does the volunteer go if he or she has a problem?	This position reports to the steering committee
Purpose	What is the job meant to accomplish—what are the results expected and what contribution does the job make to the project?	To develop a diverse, sustainable base of financial support
Activities	What kinds of things do we expect the volunteer to do to achieve the purpose?	Organize a fundraising committee; develop a database of donors
Indicators of success	What will tell you and the volunteer that the purpose is being accomplished?	The basic activities of the project are adequately funded; donors give at least the same amount each year
Qualifications	What skills, knowledge, and attitudes are needed to successfully do the job?	Good communication skills; prior relationships or contacts with potential major funders
Time commitment	How much time is the volunteer expected to put in and for how long?	Eight hours per month for twelve months

You can use Worksheet 29: Volunteer Job Description (page 180), as a checklist for writing job descriptions.

WORKSHEET 29 Volunteer Job Description

Job title:

Reports to:

Purpose:

Activities:

Indicators of success:

Qualifications:

Time commitment

Length of commitment:

Hours committed:

Other Notes:

Step 2. Find and recruit volunteers

You now have determined what you want volunteers to do. Next, identify who you will ask to fill those roles. To help you make this decision, apply the following questions to your job descriptions:

- Who would want this job?
- Given the factors that motivate people to volunteer, what would motivate someone to take this position?
- Who could do this job?
- Who has (or could develop) the qualifications for this job?
- How specialized are the knowledge and skills needed for this position?
- How does the job fit with the characteristics of
  - Long-term volunteers?
  - Short-term volunteers?
  - Workplace volunteers?
  - Retirees?
  - Professional volunteers?
  - Transitional volunteers?

Use strategies to reach potential volunteers

A variety of strategies can be used separately or in combination to reach potential volunteers. Some strategies may be better suited to some activities or phases of development of your project than others. Following are some strategies for reaching potential volunteers.

A general or community-wide appeal. In this approach, try to get the word out to as many people as possible and in as many ways as possible. Media coverage, public service announcements, mass mailings, and appeals to service clubs and community groups are all part of the general appeal. This strategy works best when the volunteer positions do not require many specialized skills, and when a community initiative is just being launched and you want the public's attention.

A targeted or directed appeal. This approach focuses your recruitment effort on specific individuals or groups you think would be particularly qualified for and motivated by your project and volunteer jobs. The targeted approach is particularly suited to situations where specialized skills are required or where you need volunteers highly dedicated to your projects.

Three questions can help you decide who to target:

- Who would want this job?
- Who could do it?
- How does the job fit with the characteristics of the different types of volunteers?

"Go to those you know" appeals. This strategy is based on the assumption that the best way to reach potential volunteers is through people already involved in your initiative. Current volunteers use their networks and contact individuals who are suitable for the roles they are being asked to fill.

This approach is often used as a way to replace volunteers. Its key strength is use of personal contacts in recruitment. Over the years, research has consistently shown that at least 50 percent of those people who volunteer got involved because someone they know asked them to do so.

Use key messages in recruiting. Regardless of the strategy you use to reach potential volunteers, be sure to communicate some key messages. These should tie directly to the volunteer job descriptions for which you are recruiting.

Why the job is important. What is it about this project and this job that merits the potential volunteer's time and attention? Link the job to meeting some critical need or issue in the community. If this project or initiative comes out of a community visioning process, then make that connection clear.

This key message is really about the "meaning" of the job. In the example at the beginning of this chapter, the meaning of the job of setting up display tables at the annual Children's Night Out is summed up in one of that project's recruitment messages: "Children are our future. Help build that future."

What the job actually is. Use the job description as the basis for this message. Show what specific contribution the job makes to meet the community need or opportunity that you identified.

Fears or concerns potential volunteers might have. Potential volunteers are often more afraid of the unknown than they are of risks that have been acknowledged. Specific concerns you may want to address are how volunteers will be trained for the job; legal, physical, or emotional risks that the job may entail; who volunteers will be working with; and how much time the job will take.

What the benefits are. Point out what the volunteer will get out of this. (Review Why people volunteer on page 174 as you prepare this message.) Reinforce the importance of the job by pointing out how the community will benefit from the volunteer's time and effort.

Step 3. Keep volunteers on the job

A volunteer's experience with your group or project should add to the community's pool of volunteers, not drain it. Several factors contribute to keeping volunteers once you've recruited them, such as providing good orientation, adequate training, support, and recognition. The amount of training and orientation that a volunteer requires will depend on the nature of the job. Volunteers with institutional programs (for example, a women's and children's shelter) may require extensive training; other community projects may require less.

Even if the volunteer job is as simple as painting the benches in the park on cleanup day, make sure your new volunteers know

- Their job description
- How the activities related to their job description are to be carried out
- Who they "report" to
- What resources are and are not available to them
- What the grievance procedure is
- What to do in an emergency

As a community leader, you are involved because you want to get something done and this community initiative is a way to do that. However, this takes so much energy that you may find it hard to support your volunteers. Yet without these volunteers, you won't accomplish what you want to get done.

Four key things can help you get the best return on the time and effort you put into supporting volunteers: stay in touch, ask for and give feedback, create a recognition plan, and understand the "life cycle" of volunteers.

Stay in touch

Make sure all volunteers get the same information about your project and its progress in a timely way. Check in with volunteers regularly to see if they have what they need to do their jobs. If they lack a resource, reach an agreement with them on how and when it will get to them.

Be prepared to meet privately with volunteers who are having a problem or find that their position is not a good fit for them. Work with these volunteers to find a mutually acceptable solution.

Ask for and give feedback

Show respect for your volunteers by taking them seriously. Ask them for feedback about their project and its progress. Ask them for feedback about their job description now that they are engaged in carrying it out. Be open to their comments about your role in the project.

Use job descriptions to give volunteers feedback on their performance. If they are underperforming, be honest about it. Then help them improve or take on a role that is better suited to their motivation, skills, and available time.

Create a recognition plan

The surest way to lose volunteers is to take them for granted. Be intentional about recognizing what volunteers accomplish. Plan to recognize volunteers in formal ways, such as a plaque given at an annual banquet. Also use informal recognition, such as an e-mail saying "job well done" to a particular individual or committee.

Use the following guidelines to develop your recognition plan:

- **Be honest.** Give recognition or say thank you only if you mean it and think it is deserved. Being insincere promotes cynicism on your part and on the part of volunteers.
- **Be timely.** Recognize contributions on an ongoing basis. Do not wait until the end of the year or until the project is completed. Give the recognition close to the time of accomplishment .
- **Recognize the volunteer, not the task.** For example, "The fundraising task force composed of Bill, Ahmed, Cleo, and Ly did a great job of exceeding our annual goal." This is more effective than, "We exceeded our annual fundraising goal."
- **Match the amount of praise to the size of the accomplishment.** If volunteers get elaborate praise for everything they do, the impact of the recognition is weakened. The volunteer who stuffed envelopes should be recognized and thanked. However, the volunteer who put in fifty hours researching and writing a grant that provided three years of funding deserves more elaborate recognition. Remember to give similar recognition for similar accomplishments achieved by different volunteers.
- **Match the recognition to the volunteer.** Different people like to be recognized in different ways. Some people would appreciate having their name in a public thank you that was published in the local newspaper. Others would be embarrassed if that happened. You need to know your volunteers well enough to be able to judge how they will experience and respond to the way in which you recognize and reward them.
- **Focus recognition on what you want to develop.** Recognizing volunteers and their accomplishments reinforces positive behaviors *and* creates a positive role model for other volunteers.

Understand the volunteer "life cycle"

No matter what you do to recruit and sustain volunteers, you'll find that they sometimes have to say no or reduce their level of involvement. When volunteers turn down an invitation to work or choose to step back, make sure that your organization maintains a positive relationship with them. Later, when circumstances change, these people may be willing to join your effort or increase their involvement. It's always wise to keep in mind an old saying: "Our ability to work together tomorrow depends to a large degree on how we treat each other today."

Appendixes

Appendix 1: Getting the Most from Your Meetings— A Primer for Facilitating Community Groups

Many of the tools in this book involve working with others in a group. These tools require someone—perhaps you—to take the role of group facilitator. Following are some commonsense ideas for helping you fulfill that role. For related ideas, see Tool 13: Building Effective Community Teams (page 148).

Define your role

To begin, consider two words that could describe what you do after calling a meeting to order. Some members of your group might refer to you as a group **leader.** According to the *Encarta® World English Dictionary*, a leader is someone who "guides or directs others by showing them the way or telling them how to behave."

At first glance, that word might seem just fine. Yet this definition of leader implies that

- There is only one way for a group to accomplish its task
- The leader knows that way
- Because of the leader's special knowledge, he or she should tell everyone what to do

In reality, there are often many ways for a group to accomplish any given result, and part of the group's work is to choose among the various options. Also, effective groups depend on contributions from all their members—not just dictates from one person who stands at the front of the room and issues directions like a traffic cop.

As an alternative, think of yourself as a group **facilitator.** This is a bulkier word. But its definition from the same dictionary quoted above suggests some good reasons to use it: A facilitator is someone who "aids or assists in a process, especially by encouraging people to find their own solutions to problems or tasks."

There are some valuable notions here. First, a facilitator is a kind of public servant—someone who aids, assists, and encourages people. Also, a facilitator helps a group tap into its collective wisdom and discover its own solutions.

A facilitator's job description

The job description for a group facilitator is potentially a long one, with tasks that include

- Setting a positive tone for meetings
- Clarifying the meeting agenda
- Keeping discussions focused on the agenda
- Monitoring the time
- Asking questions that probe for details
- Ensuring that everyone in the group has the chance to be heard

There are a variety of ways to fill this job. You can take on the role of facilitator, share the responsibility, or recruit someone else to handle it. If you choose the third option, then select carefully. A facilitator who is well known in your community group or organization can bring credibility to the task and an insider's knowledge. However, someone from outside your group might be seen as more objective and open to a variety of viewpoints. Experiment with both options and see what works.

Some community groups hire a professional facilitator to guide their meetings or ask a skilled volunteer to take that role. If you choose this option, use the suggestions in this appendix as a checklist for defining the facilitator's job and evaluating that person's effectiveness.

Some basics: The mechanics of meetings

While group communication is complex, the day-to-day business of facilitating groups revolves around three basic tasks: preparing for meetings, conducting them, and following up.

Preparing for meetings

- Gather contact information for all group members
- Distribute a written agenda well in advance of the next meeting
- If group members need to complete any tasks before the meeting, include a reminder along with the agenda

Conducting meetings

- Start meetings on time
- Take notes during the meeting, or delegate the task to another group member
- Clarify the meeting agenda
- Ask for agreement on how much time to spend on each agenda item
- If one or two group members dominate the discussion, ask them to hold further comments until other people have been heard
- Ask quieter members of the group to contribute their ideas
- Restate each decision reached during the meeting, checking in with group members for accuracy
- Clarify next steps—what needs to get done before the next meeting—and who is responsible for each task
- Ask for agreement on a time, place, and agenda for the next meeting.
- End meetings promptly

Following up

- Publish meeting minutes, or a simple summary of key points, decisions, and next steps
- Distribute the minutes to each group member
- Carry through with the steps that you agreed to complete before the next meeting

Beyond the basics: Remembering product *and* process

Communities form groups to take a certain kind of action—efforts that go beyond what any individual can accomplish alone. This action produces results, and group members can work together in a variety of ways to achieve those results.

Stated in another way, group meetings are about

- Product, or *what* gets done
- Process, or *how* it gets done

Effective groups make efficient use of time to create a *product*—a set of results that serves the larger community. In addition, these groups use a *process* that encourages community members to work together on additional projects in the future. As explained in the introduction to this book, community health depends on leaders who devote sufficient time and effort to both areas.

The distinction between product and process might seem technical, but it's worth remembering. It reminds everyone in the community that there's more to an effective group than producing results.

Of course, results are important. But on the way to delivering its product, a group might use a process that strains personal relationships or makes it hard to get things done. In contrast, strong community groups deliver a product by using a process that promotes long-term relationships.

Some people in your group might feel tempted to rush into action and start creating results right away. Encourage them to step back for a little while, lift their eyes to the horizon, and operate from a bigger picture of group process. Remind group members that *how* they work together is just as important as *what* they produce.

To help your group succeed at both product and process, add the following questions to your group's next meeting agenda.

What is our purpose?

To produce a result, your group needs a clear sense of purpose. For example, the purpose of your group might be to

- Promote the development of new businesses in your community
- Create safer neighborhoods
- Build a new playground for your local elementary school

As a facilitator, use your statement of purpose to help the group set an agenda for each meeting—and then stick to it. Ask: *How will today's session move us closer to accomplishing our group purpose?* This question has a variety of answers. Some general possibilities are to share information, discuss preliminary ideas, make decisions—or all of the above.

You can get even more specific. Create a meeting agenda by asking your group to choose a specific outcome for each meeting. Do this by completing the following sentence: *We will be successful by the end of this meeting if we . . .* For instance:

- We will be successful by the end of this meeting if we decide whether to apply for a grant that will fund a training program for local entrepreneurs.
- We will be successful by the end of this meeting if we have the information needed to convene neighborhood watch groups.
- We will be successful by the end of this meeting if we have an action plan for building a school playground.

Help your group set aside enough time for each agenda item needed to achieve the outcome. Also set benchmarks for tracking the group's progress. For example, *By 8:15 we will hear from every small business owner who wants to speak to the group.*

Remember that an effective meeting agenda does *not*

- Become overloaded, stocked with too many items to accomplish in one meeting
- Reflect only one person's point of view
- Come as a surprise to any of the group members

Who should be here?

A second element of your group's product relates to who you invite to meetings.

If you read the literature about effective teams, you'll find a variety of suggestions for the ideal size of a small group—anywhere from three to twelve members. The danger of following such suggestions is that your group might focus on meeting quotas more than fulfilling its purpose.

Effective group size is not about getting the "right" number of members; it's about achieving a workable balance. Start by making your group *large* enough to ensure that the necessary knowledge, viewpoints, and stakeholders are involved. In other words, you want group members who

- Know what they're talking about
- Bring a diverse set of opinions to the table
- Represent the people who will eventually be affected by the group's decisions

If your group is too large, however, members might walk away from a meeting saying things such as, "It was a waste of time—they really didn't need me." "There were so many people that I just couldn't participate." "It took us three times longer to organize the meeting than to actually conduct it."

To avoid such comments, keep your group *small* enough to

- Draw on the resources that each member brings to the table
- Encourage high participation from all members; also encourage a sense of ownership in the group's work
- Ensure that the group remains manageable

What are the rules?

Some facilitators just assume that people come to meetings with a clear sense of the "ground rules," or how to work together effectively during meetings. Often that assumption is not justified.

Psychologists refer to a group's ground rules as its **norms**—a set of expectations for how people will behave during meetings. Norms are an important part of your group's process. Take the time to define them as your group begins.

Each group has the freedom to create its own norms. Ask members of your group to think about groups they've joined in the past and reflect on the factors that created their success or failure.

Norms vary from group to group. However, you could start by stating that members are expected to

- Start meetings on time

- Follow the agreed-upon agenda
- Share their disagreements with each other
- Listen to each other, even when they disagree
- Continue to participate even if they don't like what is going on, and to make suggestions for improvement

Also ask members *not* to

- Let one person dominate the discussion
- Use group time for issues that fall outside the group's agenda
- Discredit or interrupt each other
- Come to meetings with a hidden agenda

Whatever your ground rules, put them in writing and distribute them to group members. Share the list with new members. And at least once each year, schedule some meeting time to review the list of ground rules and revise it as needed.

How do we make decisions?

One set of norms is so important to group process that it deserves a separate discussion. These are the ground rules that relate to decision making. In particular, effective groups make decisions with input from all members. Group members also have a clear sense of when they actually *arrive* at a decision.

Your group can create these norms by answering several questions:

- What steps will we take to make a decision?
- Whose input will we seek in making a decision?
- Who will be affected by our decisions?
- Who has the power to make final decisions?

There are a variety of ways to make decisions, and your group can experiment with several. One option is to make all decisions as a complete group. Another is to let some decisions be made by a smaller group—one that includes some but not all of your members. And for decisions that require specialized knowledge, you can ask an outside expert to suggest a decision and then discuss it as a group.

Most group decisions are reached by consensus or democratic methods. **Consensus** involves reaching a general agreement that everyone in the group will support. Members of the group offer this support even when they have different individual opinions about this agreement. Those opinions can range from *It's a great decision and I'll work to achieve it* to *I don't fully agree with this decision, but I won't block it.*

Reaching a consensus means asking all group members to share information and ideas. Encourage members who disagree with others to openly state their views. You have built consensus when each group member can say yes to the following questions:

- Have you made your best case?
- Do you think you were heard?
- Do you think you were understood?
- Will you support the decision?

Making decisions by consensus can spark creativity, build trust, and create commitment. Yet this method takes time and relies on group members who are skilled at speaking and listening. When time or energy are in short supply, your group might choose democratic decision making instead.

Democratic decisions are based on discussion followed by a vote. The decision that wins the most votes becomes final. This method offers the benefit of simplicity and efficiency. Yet it can divide your group into "winners" and "losers"—people who believe they got what they wanted, and those who did not.

Gaining skill at decision making takes time. As a group facilitator, you can shorten the learning curve by

- Asking questions, which often moves a group further and faster toward a decision than making statements
- Setting time limits on how much "air time" group members get
- Calling on the quiet group members
- Letting the group know when a discussion has moved off the agenda
- Assisting group members to clarify or elaborate ideas as needed
- Making sure that people who are interrupted get a chance to finish their comments
- Holding yourself and group members accountable for following the group's other ground rules
- Helping the group recognize any and all progress it makes in the areas of product, process, or both

How can we make our meetings more effective?

To take your group process to higher levels, make it an agenda item for one of your next meetings. Pose two questions: *What has our group done well? What can we do to improve?* Brainstorm a list of answers to each question, then set priorities. Agree on two or three things that your group will do differently in the future to improve its process. At a later meeting, renew this discussion and choose a new set of changes to make.

Talking about group process takes time, and members may be tempted to postpone this discussion in favor of producing more immediate results. As a facilitator, one of your tasks is to respectfully resist this tendency. Remind members that good results depend on good processes. Clarifying purpose, membership, ground rules, and norms for decision making allows you to become an effective steward of community resources for today—and to create reserves of goodwill for the future.

Taking the next steps

The above suggestions can get you started at facilitation. And there are plenty of ways to learn more. Many publications—both in print and online—are devoted to this topic. For suggestions, see Appendix 2: Additional Resources (page 193).

You might also have access to a personal coach who can help you and other group members develop facilitation skills. Check with state government agencies, local nonprofit organizations, county extension programs, and colleges for this type of service.

Appendix 2: Additional Resources

Publications

Angelica, Emil. *Fieldstone Nonprofit Guide to Crafting Effective Mission and Vision Statements.* St. Paul, MN: Fieldstone Alliance, 2001.

Angelica, Marion Peters. *Resolving Conflict in Nonprofit Organizations: The Leader's Guide to Finding Constructive Solutions.* St. Paul, MN: Fieldstone Alliance, 1999.

Barry, Bryan. *Strategic Planning Workbook for Nonprofit Organizations.* St. Paul, MN: Fieldstone Alliance, 2001.

Bobo, Kim, Jackie Kendall, and Steve Max. *Organizing for Social Change.* St. Paul, MN: Fieldstone Alliance, 2001.

Gale Research Company. *Encyclopedia of Associations.* Farmington Hills, MI: Thomson Gale, 2005.

Blumenstock, Doni. *Community Organizing for Prevention: The First Steps.* Boston: Massachusetts Department of Public Health, 1994.

Gilbertsen, Beth, and Vijit Ramchandani. *The Fieldstone Nonprofit Guide To Developing Effective Teams.* St. Paul, MN: Fieldstone Alliance, 1999.

Hickman, James, Doni Blumenstock, S.W. Reponen, G. Raley, and L.W. Stern. *The Community Collaboration Manual.* Washington, DC: National Assembly of National Voluntary Health and Social Welfare Organizations, 1991.

Hoskins, Linda, and Emil Angelica. *The Fieldstone Nonprofit Guide to Forming Alliances.* St. Paul, MN: Fieldstone Alliance, 2005.

Kretzmann, John, and John McKnight. *Building Communities from the Inside Out.* Chicago: ACTA Publications, 1993.

Mattessich, Paul, and Barbara Monsey. *Community Building: What Makes It Work.* St. Paul, MN: Fieldstone Alliance, 1997.

Ray, Karen. *The Nimble Collaboration: Fine-Tuning Your Collaboration for Lasting Success.* St. Paul, MN: Fieldstone Alliance, 2002.

Stern, Gary. *Marketing Workbook Volume II: Mobilize People for Marketing Success.* St. Paul, MN: Fieldstone Alliance, 1997.

Temali, Mihailo (Mike). *Community Economic Development Handbook: Strategies and Tools to Revitalize Your Neighborhood.* St. Paul, MN: Fieldstone Alliance, 2002.

Winer, Michael, and Karen Ray. *Collaboration Handbook: Creating, Sustaining and Enjoying the Journey.* St. Paul, MN: Fieldstone Alliance, 1994.

Organizations

Academy for Education Development
1825 Connecticut Avenue NW
Washington, DC 20009-5721
202-884-8000
http://www.aed.org

The academy works globally to solve critical social problems. Its major areas of focus include health, education, youth development, the environment, and leadership development. The web site offers access to its publications, annual reports, and discussion notes; information about its centers, institutions, departments, and projects; and links to other resources.

Annie E. Casey Foundation
701 St. Paul Street
Baltimore, MD 21202
410-547-6600
http://www.aecf.org

The foundation works with neighborhoods and state and local governments. It provides grants to public and nonprofit organizations to strengthen the support services, social networks, physical infrastructure, employment, self-determination, and the economic vitality of distressed communities. This web site provides data and analysis on critical issues affecting struggling families and at-risk kids, as well as information on the foundation's programs.

Appreciative Inquiry Commons
Case Western Reserve University
10900 Euclid Avenue
Cleveland, OH 44106-7166
216-368-2215
http://appreciativeinquiry.cwru.edu/

A worldwide portal devoted to the fullest sharing of academic resources and practical tools on Appreciative Inquiry and the rapidly growing *discipline of positive change.*

The Aspen Institute
One Dupont Circle NW
Suite 700
Washington, DC 20036-1133
202-736-5800
http://www.aspeninst.org

Using the rigorous discipline of informed dialogue and inquiry, the institute's seminar and policy programs enhance the participants' ability to think clearly about the issues presented, mindful of the importance of moral perspectives and differing viewpoints. The web site includes a calendar, book store, information about seminars, giving opportunities, and policy programs, as well as access to useful reports and resources.

Center for Community Change
1536 U Street NW
Washington, DC 20009
877-777-1536
http://www.communitychange.org

The center provides on-site assistance to grassroots groups, to connect people to resources, and to increase the capacity of community-based organizations. The web site gives information about the center and focuses its resources on jobs, economic development, housing, and community development.

Community Leadership Association
J.W. Fanning Institute for Leadership
1240 S. Lumpkin Street
Athens, GA 30602
706-542-0301
http://www.communityleadership.org

Through training seminars, annual leadership conferences, collaborations, partnerships, and educational publications, the association seeks to inspire and encourage community leadership programs across the country and to help them address issues of vital importance to their respective communities. The web site includes a discussion forum, a directory, access to publications, information concerning professional development, list of awards given, conferences, and memberships.

Institute for New Americans
1730 Clifton Place, Suite 100
Minneapolis, MN 55403-2342
612-871-6350
e-mail: institute@pdeducation.org

The institute focuses on creating an environment of enrichment within a world of diversity, providing education and advocacy for refugees and immigrants in Minnesota.

Jossey-Bass Publishers
111 River Street
Hoboken, NJ 07030-5774
201-748-6000
http://www.josseybass.com

This organization's mission is to publish books, training materials, periodicals, and other media for people interested in developing themselves, their communities, and their organizations.

Julian Samora Research Institute—Rural Latino Resources
Michigan State University
301 Nisbet Building
1407 S. Harrison
East Lansing, MI 48823-5286
517-432-1317
http://www.jsri.msu.edu/

The Rural Latino Resources Guide is a carefully compiled list of researchers, scientists, educators, and organizations throughout North America who have become willing partners in the documentation, research, and support of rural Latino issues. It lists individuals and organizations, providing specific contact information for each. This guide, the first of its kind published by JSRI, also lists publications and other work produced by the guide's participants. A downloadable version of this guide is provided on the web site.

Ewing Marion Kauffman Foundation
4801 Rockhill Road
Kansas City, MO 64110
816-932-1000
http://www.emkf.org

The Kauffman Foundation is a private foundation that works toward the vision of self-sufficient people in healthy communities. Its work focuses on two areas: youth development and entrepreneurial leadership. The web site offers information on programs, partnerships, research, reports, and press releases.

Kellogg Collection of Rural Community Development Resources
University of Nebraska–Lincoln
Lincoln, NE 68588
402-472-7211
http://www.unl.edu/kellogg

This web site provides access to an online collection that contains rural community development materials—guidebooks, manuals, workshop materials, reports, books, and videos.

Leader to Leader Institute
320 Park Avenue, 3rd Floor
New York, NY 10022
http://www.pfdf.org

The institute provides conferences, leadership and management resources, awards, and fellowships. Its web site offers resources, notes about the institute's work, and access to the Drucker Foundation Self-Assessment Tool, which leads nonprofit organizations to clarify mission, define results, set goals, and develop a focused plan.

Lutheran Immigration and Refugee Service
700 Light Street
Baltimore MD 21230
410-230-2700
http://www.lirs.org/index.htm

This program teaches immigrant leaders to work as a team within political structures. In addition, immigrant leaders learn how to maintain their cultural values while establishing a new life in the United States.

Manpower Demonstration Research Corporation (MDRC)
19th Floor
16 East 34th Street
New York, NY 10016-4326
212-532-3200
http://www.mdrc.org

MDRC focuses on three areas: welfare and income security, education, and employment and community initiatives. The web site offers information about organizations, as well as MDRC programs, publications, and contact information.

National Youth Leadership Council (NYLC)
1667 Snelling Avenue North
Suite D300
St. Paul, Minnesota 55108
651-631-3672
http://www.nylc.org

As one of America's most prominent advocates of service-learning, the NYLC is at the forefront of efforts to reform education and guide youth-oriented public policy. The web site provides access to publications, videos, online resources, program information, professional development, and access to the national service-learning exchange.

Pew Partnership for Civic Change
5 Boar's Head Lane
Suite 100
Charlottesville, VA 22903
434-971-2073
http://www.pew-partnership.org

The partnership's research explores how innovative partnerships, citizen participation, and accessible technology catalyze civic solutions in these areas. The web site has links to its publications and other resources. It also provides information on topics such as thriving neighborhoods, living-wage jobs, viable economics, healthy families and children, and collaborative leadership.

Rural Development Leadership Network (RDLN)
PO Box 98, Prince Street Station
New York, NY 10012
212-777-9137
http://www.ruraldevelopment.org

The RDLN, a national multicultural social change organization founded in 1983, supports community-based development in poor rural areas through hands-on projects, education and skills building, leadership development, and networking. The web site gives information about earning a degree while working in rural development, as well as other educational programs.

Work Group on Health Promotion and Community Development
4082 Dole Human Development Center
University of Kansas
1000 Sunnyside Ave.
Lawrence, KS 66045-7555
785-864-0533
http://ctb.ku.edu/index.jsp

This organization offers consulting services, publications, and the Community Tool Box, an online resource that includes over 6,000 pages of practical information on ways for citizens to promote community health.

Community Data Resources

American Factfinder
http://factfinder.census.gov

American Factfinder's *Factsheets* give detailed community profiles with data from the 2000 census. Included in the profile are basic population statistics, economic statistics on labor force income and occupations, and housing characteristics.

Bureau of Labor Statistics
http://www.bls.gov

The U.S. Department of Labor provides a wealth of information, including wages by area and occupation, earnings by industry, occupational employment and wages, employment projections, employment by occupation, state and local employment and unemployment rates, state and county employment and wages, and geographic profiles of employment and unemployment.

Career InfoNet
http://www.acinet.org/acinet

This site provides information from a variety of sources, including the Bureau of Labor Statistics, Department of Labor, Department of Education, Bureau of Economic Analysis, Department of Commerce, Census Bureau, and other federal, state, and private institutions. Using this site, you can find wages and employment trends, occupational requirements, state labor market conditions, job market trends for various education levels, and wage and occupational trends. Some of the more popular rankings available include fastest growing occupations, occupations with the most openings, and highest paying occupations.

Centers for Disease Control and Prevention (CDC)
http://www.cdc.gov

Frequently updated reports from the CDC can give you national information on the rates of many diseases, such as AIDS. Also look for general health information and strategies for promoting public health.

County & City Data Book
http://www.census.gov/statab/www/ccdb.html

This web site provides tables with data from all sorts of government agencies. You'll find vital and health statistics; information about crime, agriculture, business, and government finances; and more. Geographies covered include U.S. counties; cities with 25,000 or more inhabitants; and towns with 2,500 or more inhabitants. To compare conditions in your community with those in other states, look for links to the *Statistical Abstract of the United States* and the *State and Metropolitan Area Data Book.*

County Business Patterns

http://www.census.gov/epcd/cbp/view/cbpview.html

This web site is useful for studying the economic activity of small areas and analyzing economic changes over time. You can use this database to learn the number of companies within counties or ZIP codes, with companies classified by industries and size. Data from 1994 to 2001 are available online, with newer data using NAICS (North American Industrial Classification System) codes and older data using SIC (Standard Industrial Classification) codes.

Economic Census

http://www.census.gov/epcd/www/econ97.html

The Economic Census is conducted every five years, and the data are available online. This differs from County Business Patterns in that the data gathered by the Economic Census are much more detailed—total sales or value of shipments, production and operating costs, minority business data, and more. This site also provides links to additional and more recent business data from various federal government programs. Similar to County Business Patterns, data can be broken down by state, county, metropolitan area, city, or ZIP code.

Joint Center for Poverty Research

http://www.jcpr.org/index.html

This site includes a number of different sections, all dealing with aspects of poverty. For statistical data, the Poverty Info section provides easy-to-use statistics on populations in poverty, measures of poverty, and related issues. The Links section lists dozens of web sites including policy and research centers, publications, and poverty research projects. The Joint Center for Poverty Research, housed at Northwestern University and the University of Chicago, is funded primarily by the U.S. Department of Health and Human Services.

State & County QuickFacts

http://quickfacts.census.gov/qfd/

Look here for the most commonly requested demographic data on states and counties, including ethnicity, population growth, education, housing, and business. Data can be downloaded into spreadsheet format.

U.S. Census Bureau

http://www.census.gov

This web site allows you to access census data directly from the source. Look for links to information about your state.

U.S. Census Bureau Poverty Site
http://www.census.gov/hhes/www/poverty.html

Here you will find links to data from the current population survey, the survey of income and program participation, the small area income, and poverty estimates survey and census income data.

USDA Office of Community Development
http://ocdweb.sc.egov.usda.gov

The Office of Community Development (OCD) is a part of the U.S. Department of Agriculture's Rural Development activities. This agency operates community development programs and initiatives throughout rural America. This web site includes a lot of free resources, such as information on best practices and benchmarks, sample bylaws for community development groups, administrative handbooks, tax incentive information, and more.

Index

c indicates chart
f indicates figure
t indicates table
w indicates worksheet

S

T

V

W

More results-oriented books from Fieldstone Alliance

Community Building

Community Building: What Makes It Work
by Wilder Research Center
Reveals twenty-eight keys to help you build community more effectively. Includes detailed descriptions of each factor, case examples of how they play out, and practical questions to assess your work.
112 pages, softcover *Item # 069121*

Community Economic Development Handbook
by Mihailo Temali
A concrete, practical handbook to turning any neighborhood around. It explains how to start a community economic development organization, and then lays out the steps of four proven and powerful strategies for revitalizing inner-city neighborhoods.
288 pages, softcover *Item # 069369*

The Community Leadership Handbook
by Jim Krile
Based on the best of Blandin Foundation's 20-year experience in developing community leaders, this book gives community members 14 tools to bring people together to make change.
240 pages, softcover *Item # 069547*

The Fieldstone Nonprofit Guide to
Conducting Community Forums
by Carol Lukas and Linda Hoskins
Provides step-by-step instruction to plan and carry out exciting, successful community forums that will educate the public, build consensus, focus action, or influence policy.
128 pages, softcover *Item # 069318*

The Creative Community Builder's Handbook
How to Transform Communities Using Local Assets, Art, and Culture
by Thomas Borrup
Creative community building is about bringing community development, arts and culture, planning and design, and citizen participation together to create sustainable communities. This book provides examples and tools to help community builders utilize human cultures and the creativity in everyone.
272 pages, softcover *Item # 069474*

Collaboration

Collaboration Handbook
Creating, Sustaining, and Enjoying the Journey
by Michael Winer and Karen Ray
Shows you how to get a collaboration going, set goals, determine everyone's roles, create an action plan, and evaluate the results. Includes a case study of one collaboration from start to finish, helpful tips on how to avoid pitfalls, and worksheets to keep everyone on track.
192 pages, softcover *Item # 069032*

Collaboration: What Makes It Work, 2nd Ed.
by Paul Mattessich, PhD, Marta Murray-Close, BA, and Barbara Monsey, MPH
An in-depth review of current collaboration research. Major findings are summarized, critical conclusions are drawn, and twenty key factors influencing successful collaborations are identified. Includes The Wilder Collaboration Factors Inventory, which groups can use to assess their collaboration.
104 pages, softcover *Item # 069326*

A Fieldstone Nonprofit Guide to
Forming Alliances
by Linda Hoskins and Emil Angelica
Helps you understand the wide range of ways that they can work with others—focusing on alliances that work at a lower level of intensity. It shows how to plan and start an alliance that fits a nonprofit's circumstances and needs.
112 pages, softcover *Item # 069466*

The Nimble Collaboration
Fine-Tuning Your Collaboration for Lasting Success
by Karen Ray
Shows you ways to make your existing collaboration more responsive, flexible, and productive. Provides three key strategies to help your collaboration respond quickly to changing environments and participants.
136 pages, softcover *Item # 069288*

Lobbying & Advocacy

The Lobbying and Advocacy Handbook for Nonprofit Organizations
Shaping Public Policy at the State and Local Level
by Marcia Avner
The Lobbying and Advocacy Handbook is a planning guide and resource for nonprofit organizations that want to influence issues that matter to them. This book will help you decide whether to lobby and then put plans in place to make it work.
240 pages, softcover *Item # 069261*

The Nonprofit Board Member's Guide to Lobbying and Advocacy
by Marcia Avner
Written specifically for board members, this guide helps organizations increase their impact on policy decisions. It reveals how board members can be involved in planning for and implementing successful lobbying efforts.
96 pages, softcover *Item # 069393*

For current prices or to order, visit us online at www.FieldstoneAlliance.org

The Nonprofit Mergers Workbook Part II

Unifying the Organization after a Merger

by La Piana Associates

Once the merger agreement is signed, the question becomes: How do we make this merger work? *Part II* helps you create a comprehensive plan to achieve *integration*—bringing together people, programs, processes, and systems from two (or more) organizations into a single, unified whole.

248 pages, includes CD-ROM *Item # 069415*

Nonprofit Stewardship

A Better Way to Lead Your Mission-Based Organization

by Peter C. Brinckerhoff

You may lead a not-for-profit organization, but it's not your organization. It belongs to the community it serves. You are the steward—the manager of resources that belong to someone else. The stewardship model of leadership can help your organization improve its mission capability by forcing you to keep your organization's mission foremost. It helps you make decisions that are best for the people your organization serves. In other words, stewardship helps you do more good for more people.

272 pages, softcover *Item # 069423*

Resolving Conflict in Nonprofit Organizations

The Leader's Guide to Finding Constructive Solutions

by Marion Peters Angelica

Helps you identify conflict, decide whether to intervene, uncover and deal with the true issues, and design and conduct a conflict resolution process. Includes exercises to learn and practice conflict resolution skills, guidance on handling unique conflicts such as harassment and discrimination, and when (and where) to seek outside help with litigation, arbitration, and mediation.

192 pages, softcover *Item # 069164*

Strategic Planning Workbook for Nonprofit Organizations, Revised and Updated

by Bryan Barry

Chart a wise course for your nonprofit's future. This time-tested workbook gives you practical step-by-step guidance, real-life examples, one nonprofit's complete strategic plan, and easy-to-use worksheets.

144 pages, softcover *Item # 069075*

Marketing

The Fieldstone Nonprofit Guide to
Conducting Successful Focus Groups

by Judith Sharken Simon

Shows how to collect valuable information without a lot of money or special expertise. Using this proven technique, you'll get essential opinions and feedback to help you check out your assumptions, do better strategic planning, improve services or products, and more.

80 pages, softcover *Item # 069199*

Marketing Workbook for Nonprofit Organizations Volume I: Develop the Plan

by Gary J. Stern

Don't just wish for results—get them! Here's how to create a straightforward, usable marketing plan. Includes the six Ps of Marketing, how to use them effectively, a sample marketing plan, tips on using the Internet, and worksheets.

208 pages, softcover *Item # 069253*

Marketing Workbook for Nonprofit Organizations Volume II: Mobilize People for Marketing Success

by Gary J. Stern

Put together a successful promotional campaign based on the most persuasive tool of all: personal contact. Learn how to mobilize your entire organization, its staff, volunteers, and supporters in a focused, one-to-one marketing campaign. Comes with *Pocket Guide for Marketing Representatives*. In it, your marketing representatives can record key campaign messages and find motivational reminders.

192 pages, softcover *Item # 069105*

Board Tools

The Best of the Board Café

Hands-on Solutions for Nonprofit Boards

by Jan Masaoka, CompassPoint Nonprofit Services

Gathers the most requested articles from the e-newsletter, *Board Café*. You'll find a lively menu of ideas, information, opinions, news, and resources to help board members give and get the most out of their board service.

232 pages, softcover *Item # 069407*

The Nonprofit Board Member's Guide to Lobbying and Advocacy

by Marcia Avner

96 pages, softcover *Item # 069393*

Keeping the Peace

by Marion Angelica

Written especially for board members and chief executives, this book is a step-by-step guide to ensure that everyone is treated fairly and a feasible solution is reached.

48 pages, softcover *Item # 860127*

Funder's Guides

Community Visions, Community Solutions

Grantmaking for Comprehensive Impact

by Joseph A. Connor and Stephanie Kadel-Taras

Helps foundations, community funds, government agencies, and other grantmakers uncover a community's highest aspiration for itself, and support and sustain strategic efforts to get to workable solutions.

128 pages, softcover *Item # 06930X*

A Funder's Guide to Evaluation: Leveraging Evaluation to Improve Nonprofit Effectiveness
by Peter York

More and more funders and nonprofit leaders are shifting away from proving something to someone else, and toward *im*-proving what they do so they can achieve their mission and share how they succeeded with others. This book includes strategies and tools to help grantmakers support and use evaluation as a nonprofit organizational capacity-building tool.

160 pages, softcover *Item # 069482*

A Funder's Guide to Organizational Assessment
Tools, Processes, and Their Use in Building Capacity
by GEO

In this book, funders, grantees, and consultants will understand how organizational assessment can be used to build the capacity of nonprofits, enhance grantmaking, impact organizational systems, and measure foundation effectiveness.

216 pages, includes CD-ROM *Item # 069539*

Strengthening Nonprofit Performance
A Funder's Guide to Capacity Building
by Paul Connolly and Carol Lukas

This practical guide synthesizes the most recent capacity-building practice and research into a collection of strategies, steps, and examples that you can use to get started on or improve funding to strengthen nonprofit organizations.

176 pages, softcover *Item # 069377*

Violence Prevention & Intervention

The Little Book of Peace
24 pages (minimum order 10 copies) *Item # 069083*
Also available in ***Spanish*** *and* ***Hmong*** *language editions.*

Journey Beyond Abuse: A Step-by-Step Guide to Facilitating Women's Domestic Abuse Groups
208 pages, softcover *Item # 069148*

Moving Beyond Abuse: Stories and Questions for Women Who Have Lived with Abuse
(Companion guided journal to *Journey Beyond Abuse*)
88 pages, softcover *Item # 069156*

Foundations for Violence-Free Living:
A Step-by-Step Guide to Facilitating Men's Domestic Abuse Groups
240 pages, softcover *Item # 069059*

On the Level
(Participant's workbook to *Foundations for Violence-Free Living*)
160 pages, softcover *Item # 069067*

What Works in Preventing Rural Violence
94 pages, softcover *Item # 069040*

ORDERING INFORMATION

Order online, or by phone or fax

Online: www.FieldstoneAlliance.org
E-mail: books@fieldstonealliance.org

Call toll-free: 800-274-6024
Internationally: 651-556-4509

Fax: 651-556-4517

Mail: Fieldstone Alliance
Publishing Center
60 Plato BLVD E, STE 150
St. Paul, MN 55107

Our NO-RISK guarantee

If you aren't completely satisfied with any book for any reason, simply send it back within 30 days for a full refund.

Pricing and discounts

For current prices and discounts, please visit our web site at www.FieldstoneAlliance.org or call toll free at 800-274-6024.

Quality assurance

We strive to make sure that all the books we publish are helpful and easy to use. Our major workbooks are tested and critiqued by experts before being published. Their comments help shape the final book and—we trust—make it more useful to you.

Visit us online

You'll find information about Fieldstone Alliance and more details on our books, such as table of contents, pricing, discounts, endorsements, and more, at www.FieldstoneAlliance.org.

Do you have a book idea?

Fieldstone Alliance seeks manuscripts and proposals for books in the fields of nonprofit management and community development. To get a copy of our author guidelines, please call us at 800-274-6024. You can also download them from our web site at www.FieldstoneAlliance.org.

CPSIA information can be obtained at www.ICGtesting.com
Printed in the USA
LVOW021950240513

335454LV00001B/1/P